Journeys beyond the Pale

Journeys beyond the Pale

Yiddish Travel Writing in the Modern World

Leah Garrett

THE UNIVERSITY OF WISCONSIN PRESS

The University of Wisconsin Press
1930 Monroe Street
Madison, Wisconsin 53711

www.wisc.edu/wisconsinpress/

3 Henrietta Street
London WC2E 8LU, England

1   3   5   4   2

Printed in the United States of America

Library of Congress Cataloging-in-Publication Data
Garrett, Leah V.
Journeys beyond the pale: Yiddish travel writing
in the modern world /Leah Garrett.
pp.   cm.
Includes bibliographical references.
ISBN 0-299-18440-4 (cloth)
ISBN 0-299-18444-7 (paper)
1. Yiddish literature—History and criticism.   2. Travel in literature.
3. Roads in literature.   4. Railroads in literature.
5. Ships in literature.   I. Title.
PJ5120.7.T73 G38   2003
839'.109355—dc21   2002010219

The quotation from *Angles in America, Part 1: Millennium Approaches,* by Tony Kushner,
© 1992, 1993 by Tony Kushner, published by Theatre Communications Group, is used
by permission of Theatre Communications Group.

The quotation from "Jewish Travel," by Yehuda Amichai, originally published in
Open Closed Open, by Harcourt, Inc., is used by permission of Harcourt, Inc.

Chapter 3, "The Train," appeared in a different form as "Trains and Train Travel
in Modern Yiddish Literature," *Jewish Social Studies: History, Culture and Society* 7,
no. 2 (Winter 2001).

for Adrian and for Arwynn:

”פֿון יענער זײַט ליד קענען ווונדער געשען.“
— *Rohkl Korn, "Fun yener zayt lid"*

RABBI ISIDOR CHEMELWITZ: *[He looks at the coffin.]* This woman. I did not know this woman. I cannot accurately describe her attributes, nor do justice to her dimensions. . . . So I do not know her and yet I know her. She was . . . not a person but a whole kind of person, the ones who crossed the ocean, who brought with us to America the villages of Russia and Lithuania. . . . You do not live in America. No such place exists. Your clay is the clay of some Litvak shtetl, your air the air of the steppes—because she carried the old world on her back across the ocean, in a boat, and she put it down on Grand Concourse Avenue, or in Flatbush, and she worked that earth into your bones, and you pass it to your children, this ancient, ancient culture and home.

You can never make this crossing that she made, for such Great Voyages in this world do not any more exist.

—Tony Kushner, *Angels in America*

Contents

Acknowledgments

This book developed out of graduate work at the Jewish Theological Seminary and was made possible in a large part by fellowships from the Charles H. Revson Foundation, the Memorial Foundation for Jewish Culture, and YIVO. I wrote much of the first draft while I was a Fulbright Fellow at Tel Aviv University, where I had great support, both intellectual and otherwise, from professors Dan Laor, Avraham Novershtern, and Hana Wirth-Nesher.

In New York, Dan Miron was a source of great inspiration for me, and being his student was key to my intellectual development and approach to Yiddish literature. At the Jewish Theological Seminary I wish to give particular thanks to the dean, Stephen Garfinkel, for being a great advocate and sounding board for me over the years.

My dissertation committee was central in my reworking of the original text, and I wish to thank David Roskies, David Fishman, Anne Hoffman, Anne Lerner, and Nili Gold for reading and commenting on that draft with such sophistication and care.

At the University of Denver, where I rewrote the book, my friends and colleagues supported and inspired me. In particular I wish to thank Nancy Reichman for being such a tireless advocate and a smart, warm, and witty colleague.

To Mikhail Krutikov, Allison Schachter, and Jeremy Dauber— thank you for carefully reading part or all of the work and giving me invaluable suggestions for changes that vastly improved the book. Needless to say, I am completely responsible for any problems that remain.

To my friends and family on both sides of the Atlantic, I am grateful for your belief in me and help over the years, and my deepest thanks go to my mother, Susan Vladeck, and grandparents Irene and Abraham Klein for awakening in me a love of Yiddish culture.

From an early age I was inspired to learn Yiddish in order to read the works of my great grandfather Baruch Vladeck and his brother Shmuel Niger.

Thank you to the staff at the University of Wisconsin Press for their wonderful work on the book.

My most profound thanks go to my teacher and mentor, David Roskies, who has worked with me patiently, inspired me, and guided me over the years.

And to Adrian, thank you not only for your endless faith in me but for keeping me laughing through the journey of this book.

Journeys beyond the Pale

1

Introduction

Of course, it's one hell of a way to get from Petersburg to Stockholm; but then for a man of my occupation the notion of a straight line being the shortest distance between two points has lost its attraction a long time ago. So it pleases me to find out that geography in its own turn is also capable of poetic justice.
—Joseph Brodsky, Nobel Prize acceptance speech, Stockholm, December 1987

The journey in this book will traverse roads and forests on the trail of Jewish princesses and kings, cross-dressers and dreamers, soothsayers and fragmenting quest seekers. It will include trips on exilic wagons, comedic trains, and steam- and sail-powered crossings of the ocean by restless souls seeking to find their selves and places on a new shore.

The Jews of eastern Europe were a displaced people who made minor appearances in Polish and Russian literature of the nineteenth century: a cameo in Dostoyevsky, a small part in Chekhov's tales. But the Jews themselves saw their presence everywhere and as central to the landscape. The British built the Raj railway to transport soldiers throughout their empire, yet in the works of Kipling this great imperial railroad was transformed into an Indian space full of Hindus, Muslims, merchants, and holy men. Similarly, the Jewish writers reinvented their geographical surroundings and filled the great tsarist railway with

Yiddish-speaking tinkers and travelers, rabbis and revolutionaries. The imperial Prussian and Russian roads became the byways for Jewish salesmen, storytellers, and even latter-day knights errant. The writers transformed the great, gleaming, transcontinental ship into a dream vessel symbolizing the difficult journey of the Jewish immigrant from the Old World for the new one across the sea.

Yiddish literature of travel during the period of this analysis (the 1870s to the 1930s) often reconceived the world as a *Jewish* space. The literary transformation of eastern Europe into a Jewish land enabled writers to indirectly represent individual Jews who were confronting the vast changes brought by the rise of modernization and urbanization. What we see in Yiddish literature of travel is a profound reluctance—expressed in a Judaized space—to confront directly the changes wrought by modernization. Instead of a direct confrontation, the writers would frequently level their attacks on the forces that they deemed to be destructive of Jewish life; to do so they would use the tools that Yiddish writers have employed for much of their greatest work: irony, metaphor, symbolism.

What these writers seemed to desire was to be able to have, like any other people, a literature for telling stories of travel in public spaces and the adventures encountered therein, without always having to focus on how being in public spaces was risky for the characters because they were Jews. The means for the writers to circumvent the real road was to transplant genres, such as the quest, into ahistorical mythic landscapes. The manipulation of genres and the use of mythic, patently fictional, literary locales is a trend of modernist writing, particularly Russian modernism, that greatly influenced Yiddish authors.[1] However, because Russian culture often positioned Jews in public spaces as minorities and outsiders, the Jewish author's use of patently "unrealistic" locales had the added effect of creating literary spaces in which the Jews were central. Much of the literature, then, reflects the general modernist trend of the manipulation of genres. However, at the same time the Yiddish authors used literature as a means to redraw the borders of "center" and "margin."

When Jewish writers chose as their setting the land beyond the shtetl, one would have expected that they would describe it in a "realistic" way. The road would be the place that represented the relationship between Jews and the broader world, and it would be the arena for portraying individuals who confronted outside sociopolitical forces. Instead, Yiddish writers often used the same set of tools to construct the image of the road that they had used to build the image of the shtetl. Dan Miron's description of the shtetl in Yiddish literature as a "Judaized" space applies as well to the fictional construct of the road.[2] Jewish writers often made the space of the road into an ahistorical, apolitical realm beyond real space and time, instead of the place for delving into issues about the relationship between Jews and non-Jews.

While the road, like the shtetl, was frequently a Judaized space in Yiddish literature, it was different from the shtetl in a number of ways. Although male writers constructed the shtetl as domestic, they saw the road as the terrain of the "male." This we see most emblematically in Sholem Aleichem's *Menakhem-Mendl;* the husband's letters are from a series of towns and cities beyond the shtetl, and the wife's letters are rooted in the static yet safe domestic shtetl. Moreover, the shtetl reflects a communal narrative, whereas tales of travel, with the exception of the train stories, are of individuals or pairs out on their own. Thus the tale of travel by road or ship is frequently the story of an individual, whereas stories set in the shtetl are communal.

Taken as a whole, modern Yiddish travel literature serves as a forceful counterstory to the mainstream narratives of European prose. It tells of the world from the perspective of a people who were often considered by others to be outsiders yet who found ways to envision themselves as insiders within an imagined Jewish world. The diachronic development of travel tropes in Yiddish literature, from the road to the train and the ship, matches the processes of modernization. And with modernization and the increased bureaucratization of public spaces, envisioning closed, Judaized public spaces became more difficult. As the travel changed, descriptions of it had to reckon more frequently with the way that modernization was causing the breakdown of traditional Jewish life.

Jewish writers, however, were not composing in a vacuum but were greatly influenced by Russian literary trends. The notion of "homelessness," a key concept in this book, was, for instance, played out throughout Russian literature. In Russian literature images of homelessness evolve from eighteenth-century conceptions, in which *homeless* connotes the Russian gentry without deep roots in their own country or in European culture, to the nineteenth century's more positive idea of homelessness as "the hero's search for a more meaningful domesticity in the future and/or the rejection of existing models of home in the present (for example, Gogol's Chichikov, Lermontov's Pechorin Turgenev's Bazarov)."[3] The nineteenth-century Russian literary conception of homelessness was, however, complicated: Its personification was the homeless intellectual who should be a creator and critic of culture but instead finds himself disconnected from the Russian masses.[4] This trend is matched in Yiddish literature, in the development of the *talush,* or dangling intellectual, who finds himself disconnected from the "real" life of the people and caught in a self-obsessive overintellectualization of the world.[5] However, what differentiates the Jewish from the Russian model of homelessness is that the Jewish vision adds a religious construct to the equation in the larger idea of the Galut, or Jewish exile.[6] And to further complicate matters, in addition to the religious dimension is the historical reality, that Jewish disenfranchisement makes Jews, in a sense, homeless in Russia. The Jewish religious and historical aspects of homelessness are not elements of the homelessness that Russian intellectuals were writing about.

The religious Jewish notion of homelessness meant that before the establishment of the State of Israel in 1948, much of the Jewish community often perceived life as conducted on dual terrain: the real space where one lived in the present and the mythical locale of Eretz Yisrael (the Land of Israel, or Zion). The Bible generated the notion of dual locations; exile was one of the curses on the people of Israel for not following God's commandments: "The Lord will scatter you among all the people from one end of the earth to the other, and there you shall serve other gods, wood and stone, whom neither you nor your ancestors have experienced. Yet even among those nations you shall find no peace, nor shall your foot find a place to rest. The LORD will give you there an anguished heart and eyes that pine and a despondent spirit. The life you face shall be precarious; you shall be in terror, night and day, with no assurance of survival" (Deut. 28:64).[7] Exile would arise repeatedly as the enforced state of being of a disenfranchised people and would become a central communal vision of Jewish selfhood.[8] Diaspora Jews would often use the motif of exile and punishment, with its implied redemption and "return," as a way to find meaning in exile. As W. D. Davies states, "In spatial terms, they did not stand in chaos if they knew which way to look."[9]

This dual positioning meant that Jews often constructed notions of home, away, the road, public, and private differently than non-Jews did. This raises several questions, including, What constituted home and where was it located? Was it one's present home in the shtetl or the mythical place of return to Eretz Yisrael? And how did this bispatial perspective alter or influence a specifically Jewish notion of travel in literature? Where does the model of Galut consciousness intersect with travel? Is exile the larger framework of travel? If this is the background model, how does it contrast with Christian models?

In literature geography is a construct. While "London" is a real physical space in the world, "London" in a literary work will be mapped out according to the author's consciousness, as will the roads leading in or out of it. Henry Fielding's London and Virginia Woolf's London are different not only because they describe a London of different eras but because the personal viewpoint of these authors affects the way that they envision the city. Although the word *London* will suggest the same area and will likely connote for the reader a series of similar impressions, Fielding and Woolf are nevertheless giving us varied, mediated views of the city because both are taking part in the act of "topography," or the "writing of a place."[10]

In order to interpret Jewish images of travel in literature, I first must sketch the imagined terrain that served as the base for tales of movement, with the European map replaced by a Jewish one that calls both exile and Eretz Yisrael home. An example of a European literary mapping is Franco Moretti's *Atlas of the European Novel,* which seeks to trace imagined geographies in European novels and to map out the connection between geography and literature.[11] Taking as a given the obvious notion that all geography in literature is filtered through the consciousness of the author, and thus is fictional to greater or lesser degrees, Moretti seeks to show the geography of literature. However, throughout his groundbreaking work, filled with fascinating maps such as the locales of Jane Austen's novels, as well as maps of where villains in nineteenth-century novels were based (for the most part in France), he does not really question the use of a two-dimensional map as a starting point for literary geographical renderings. In Moretti's construction of European literary spatial consciousness, home is simply where one's house or family is. In contrast to Moretti, Wai Chee Dimock suggests that in conceptualizing literary geography, we must move beyond conflating the literary with the territorial and instead consider how literature "unsettles" national boundaries by offering to readers "dimensions of space and time so far-flung and so deeply recessional that they can never be made to coincide with the synchronic plane of the geopolitical map."[12] Literature, according to Dimock, offers "a continuum" where St. Petersburg can be juxtaposed with Berlin.

For Jewish literature of travel a two-dimensional map is inadequate to make "the connection between geography and literature explicit" because home was not always simply where one's house or family was. Home was often both the here and now and the "not yet home" with a sideward glance toward Eretz Yisrael. For some this notion of "not yet home" continues to this day, as in Simon Schama's *Landscape and Memory* (1995), in which he says, "I remembered someone in a Cambridge common room pestering the self-designated 'non-Jewish Jew' and Marxist historian Isaac Deutscher, himself a native of this country [Lithuania], about his roots. 'Trees have roots,' he shot back, scornfully, 'Jews have legs.' And I thought, as yet another metaphor collapsed into ironic literalism, Well, some Jews have both and branches

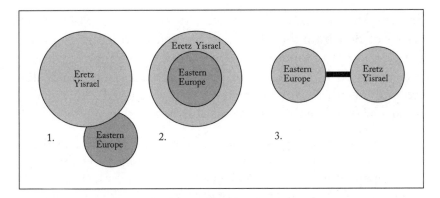

Figure 1.1. Three pre-modern Jewish world views.

and stems too." Yet after a painful visit to the destroyed Jewish cemetery of the Lithuanian town of his family's origins, Schama changes his notion of Jews as having "branches," stating, "Perhaps Deutscher was right, I thought. Trees have roots; Jews have legs."[13]

This is a vision of rootlessness and either no home (as for Schama) or a dual home. However, at the same time Schama expresses a real desire for a groundedness that the marginalized Jews do not have. A map of Jewish literary consciousness up to 1948 should therefore include a rendering of Galut geography, where *away* means, on the micro level, being away from one's house or family and, on the macro level, away from Eretz Yisrael. See figure 1.1 for some examples of this mapping. In the first map, Eretz Yisrael is a large shadow over daily life in eastern Europe. In the second, life in eastern Europe and life in Eretz Yisrael run in concentric circles but the latter is on a much larger scale. And in the third, the two spheres of Eretz Yisrael and eastern Europe exist at the same time but in different locales.

In spatial terms, in a "diasporic consciousness," linear time is reordered into a synchronic past, present, future, here, and there.[14] It is a dual perspective, where parts of the day-to-day reality are in a constant mode of mythic signification. This is not a world of univocal signifiers but a world in which aspects of the here and now also evoke the otherworld of mythic Israel. For instance, in

Sholem Abramovitsh's *Kitser masoes Binyomin hashlishi* (The brief travels of Benjamin the Third), we see a clear presentation of the Jewish concept of landscape: The diaspora is a temporary home overshadowed by the Land of Israel. Here Abramovitsh is describing how the Jews of Benjamin's town, Tuneyadevka, react to the arrival of a date from the Land of Israel:

> Alpi mikre hot eyner a mol in dem shtetl grod gebrakht a teytl, hot ir badarft zen, vi azoy men iz dos gelofn onkukn oyf khidushim, men hot oyfgemisht a khumesh un gevizn, der teytl shteyt in khumesh! S'taytsh der teytl, ot der teytl vakst dokh fun Eretz-Yisrael!. . . Kukndik oyfn teytl hot zikh oysgedakht, Eretz-Yisrael iz far di oygn, ot geyt men iber dem Yardn, ot iz di meyres-hamakhpeyle. Der muter Rokhl's keyver, dos koyslmayrovi; ot bodt men zikh in khamey-tverye, men krikht aroyf oyfn har-hazeysim, men est zikh on mit boksern, mit teytln un men leygt on fule keshenes mit Eretz-Yisrael erd. Akh, hot men gekrekhtset, un in di oygn hobn itlekhn zikh geshtelt trern. Yene tsayt, azoy zogt Binyomin, iz gantz Tuneyadevke, vi groys zi iz, geven in Eretz-Yisrael.

> (Once, it so happened, someone arrived in Tuneyadevka with a date. You should have seen the town come running to look at it. A Bible was brought to prove that the very same little fruit grew in the Holy Land. The harder the Tuneyadevkans stared at it, the more clearly they saw before their eyes the River Jordan, the Cave of the Patriarchs, the tomb of Mother Rachel, the Wailing Wall. They bathed in the hot springs of Tiberias, climbed the Mount of Olives, ate dates and carobs, and stuffed their pockets with holy soil to bring back to Tuneyadevka. There was many a heartfelt exclamation and damp eye on that day.
>
> "For a moment," Benjamin has recalled of that occasion, "the whole of Tuneyadevka was in the Land of Israel.")[15]

In the story the fruit arrives while the Jews are suffering increased persecution. The date offers them a means to retreat into a fantasy world where they all live safely in the Land of Israel. The passage also clearly expresses how the landscape of Eretz Yisrael has become such a part of the day-to-day landscape of eastern Europe that it is as "real" as the "real" world of eastern Europe.

As James Clifford has shown, diaspora populations, such as the Jews in Russia, destabilize nationalist identities and nation-states, because their history of continual displacement can make them less responsive to nationalistic rhetoric.[16] When the people considered to be "permanent strangers" resist marginalization and refuse to be located anywhere but the center of cultural discourse, the resulting "diasporic consciousness" decenters the European map by giving groups from the "margins" status equal to that of European nationals. Diasporic consciousness can therefore be a challenge to the nation-state by its resistance to a territorial, nationalistic perspective. Stories of travel generated by a people with this geographical consciousness offer alternative models to literary reckonings by writers comfortably located in nation-states. The Jewish population of eastern Europe, particularly during the advent of the modern era and rise of nationalistic longings, can thus be seen as an antinationalist community because of its marginalization from "the nation" (although many Jewish individuals embraced nationalistic rhetoric).

The authors of European travel fiction often defined characters as figures representative of either the "native" or the "alien," and in some texts the character is both. For example, at the beginning of Robert Louis Stevenson's *Kidnapped,* the protagonist, David Balfour, is happily domesticated and a native at home in his lowland Scotland. He speaks the language, his world is peaceful, he takes for granted the landscape around him because he knows it so well. However, once he is kidnapped and escapes by making his way to an island and then the mainland, he shifts into a figure of the alien, even though the terrain that he is traversing is still Scotland. Now it is highland Scotland, and the language is no longer familiar (it is Gaelic rather than English), the terrain is new (at first he gets brutally sick by eating raw shellfish on the island where he takes refuge), and everything is so foreign that he does not realize his refuge is separated from the mainland by a shallow channel that he can walk over at low tide. He is thrust into the role of an alien within his own country, a condition intensified by his being on the run. Everything is strange, new, and scary because his perspective has changed from that of a native to an alien. (Yet the nebulous relationship of Scotland to England in the mid-eighteenth century breaks down strict differences between "native" and "alien." For instance, Alan Breck Stewart is a Scottish protonationalist [or native] who is made an alien within his own country.)

Nevertheless, regardless of the series of hardships that David Balfour must face in *Kidnapped,* he believes that things will eventually be sorted out once he returns "home" because Scotland is a nation with a fixed safe order. The police or government officials will eventually make things right for him because he is a member of this nation. While he may now be on alien terrain, the nation is his, and he is a part of it. In European literature the dangers in travel tended to run the gamut from war *(Vanity Fair)* to abusive adults *(David Copperfield),* yet the protagonist remained for the most part a member of the nation rather than an Other to the nation, even when the protagonist was an outsider such as Becky Sharp or David Copperfield. For the Jews of eastern Europe this equation often shifts. These works offer little of the sense of security that David feels in *Kidnapped;* he assumes that all will be made right in the end. For the Jewish traveler, the police and the officials are frequently representative of danger.

The writers of Yiddish travel literature could get around this by creating Jewish geographies and Judaizing the place where they lived. It seems to me that while critics such as Daniel Boyarin and Jonathan Boyarin are on the right track in terms of attempting to create a positive universal model from the diaspora experience, they have largely overlooked how the Jews conceptualized these experiences. For instance, the Boyarins write that in the diaspora, Jews learned that they should respect difference for, "as the radical slogan goes, 'no one is free until all are free.'"[17] They are suggesting that diasporic consciousness (in contrast to Zionism) taught many Jews a belief in pluralism. Yet as Dan Miron has shown, throughout both shtetl literature and travel literature, Jewish writers constructed space for the most part *not* as multicultural or pluralistic but as Jewish, with Christians completely missing or, when they appeared, as drunk, stupid, or anti-Semitic.[18] There are, of course, many notable exceptions to this, but in general Christians appear more as "types" than as individual, rounded characters.

Although Clifford is correct when he writes that diasporic peoples can serve as a challenge to nationalism, this challenge is often in how they are perceived by others. How they saw themselves in Yiddish literature, particularly of the premodern and classical era, frequently was as a people with a single identity. When Christians show up in the literature, they are often drawn as temporary obstacles (to one's safety, money, practice of Judaism) to be overcome, rather than as members of the broader world to be invited in. While the Jewish experience can offer lessons about what it means to live in a multicultural environment, Jews themselves did not necessarily become multiculturalists.[19] Yiddish literature, as shown most prominently in road tales, often offers a rebuttal to a pluralistic or multicultural philosophy. Rather, this literature re-envisions the world as, ideally, Jewish.

Both modernism and postmodernism often have used the figure of the exiled Jew as a metaphor to exemplify dislocation from rigidly oppressive and fixed nationalistic political and historical discourse. *Exile* becomes a positive term of a decentered consciousness that is able to see the whole and to subvert it. Many high modernist writers sought "to recreate the effect of statelessness — whether or not the writer [was] literally, in exile."[20] When writers such as Gertrude Stein and Ezra Pound moved to Paris to integrate an expatriate consciousness into their literary vision and thus conflate modernism with exile, they perpetuated the notion of "aesthetic gain through exile."[21] In the alternate modernist and postmodernist representation, the Jews became emblematic of "lethal" modernism, sacrificial victims of the forces of modernization that culminated in the Holocaust.[22]

In postmodern discourse, postmodern fragmentation becomes analogous to the position of the marginalized minority that is decentered from the main locations of power.[23] Exile represents a resistance to rigidly patriarchal constructs and is appropriated as a means of resisting binary oppositions in order to achieve a more fluid, inclusive consciousness. In this "nomadic" ideology the mobile migrant is a hybrid that breaks down the dominant Western narratives and becomes an emblem of the postmodern condition.[24] Typical of this viewpoint is this statement by Susan Suleiman in her introduction for a symposium focusing on exile: "To the degree that exile is a matter not only of physical displacement but of interior experience, we may all, independently of our actual religion, nationality, or place of birth, be (as the walls of the Sorbonne proclaimed in 1968) 'German Jews.'"[25] Or consider Julia Kristeva's universalizing, dehistoricizing statement about "foreigners": "The foreigner lives within us: he is the hidden face of our identity, the space that wrecks our abode, the time in which understanding and affinity founder."[26]

Susan E. Shapiro shows in her essay "Écriture judaïque: Where Are the Jews in Western Discourse?" how postmodern critics, in particular Jean-François Lyotard, have continued this tradition to the present day by "erasing" real Jews and instead using them only as tropal figures. Making the Jews into tropal figures such as the "Wandering Jew" means that they no longer have a history of real suffering.[27] Shapiro proposes that, to help rectify this situation, "Western discourses must be ruptured by voices of those who have been made invisible through their/our erasure and objectification. Jews must speak for them/ourselves — and be heard — in/outside of Western discourses."[28]

Ironically, Edward Said is the central critic writing against the "instrumental use" of exile in modern culture (of which the Wandering Jew is but one example) by constantly reiterating that while exile is a compelling idea, living it is terrible.[29] According to both Susan Shapiro and Said, to adopt exile as a subversive humanistic force is to deflate the real suffering that real exile causes.[30] A number of recent theorists have thus begun to challenge appropriations of the exilic experience by seeking to "put the 'place' back into 'displacement'" and to work against theories that use exile as an aesthetic notion that depoliticizes the real, very painful, experiences of exile.[31] Critics such as Mary Pratt, Caren Kaplan, James Clifford, bell hooks, and others have sought not only to resist the appropriation of exile as an aesthetic trope but to challenge the gamut of terms that reflects the motions of peoples. In particular, they have shown how commonplace has been the trend to view "travel" in literature only through the lens of white European males.[32] According to Dennis Porter, that perspective seeks to colonize public domains and organize the world with one's self as the center and with those whose lands one visits as the Others. Traditional travel analysis, according to James Duncan and David Leys, is thus frequently a means to structure the world according to the perspective of a white male European elitist.[33]

Moreover, recent works on Jewish literature have also specifically challenged the depoliticization of the Jewish exilic reality. For instance, Michael Gluzman's essay "Modernism and Exile: A View from the Margins" shows that while European modernists may have appropriated exile for "aesthetic gain" and made the "double conflation of modernism and exile, of exile and Jewishness," Hebrew modernism offered a "negation of exile."[34] And Daniel Boyarin and Jonathan Boyarin, in "Diaspora: Generation and the Ground of Jewish Identify," show how Western theorists have used the term *exile* to turn Jews into tropal rather than real figures and, by so doing, "effaced" real Jews from the "discourse(s) of Western identity," as Susan Shapiro puts it.[35] Moreover, Chana Kronfeld's *On the Margins of Modernism: Decentering Literary Dynamics* plots out a new way to understand modernism, taking into account how Yiddish is "landless," as she terms it; thus exile is normative in the literature, not an aesthetic choice.[36]

In European literature, the Jewish traveler has also often been fixed in the "Christian" image of the Wandering Jew.[37] The Wandering Jew was a Jerusalem shoemaker, Ahasuerus, who was cursed by Jesus and as result became a repentant Christian, forced to wander the Earth until the Second Coming. As Hyam Maccoby points out, the Wandering Jew is a "dignified figure" but this is a double-edged sword: The Wandering Jew's debasement can become dignity only through Christianity.[38] The Wandering Jew is similar to the "mammy" figure of the wise, gentle, female slave of the American South or the "noble savage" of eighteenth-century European literature. All are figures that mark out the total disenfranchisement of a people and the need of the disenfranchisers to re-create what they have done into a positive image.

One objective here is to move beyond the Wandering Jew and to have the Yiddish writers speak for themselves. This book is therefore not concerned with how Christians constructed the figure of the Jew in literature but instead asks how Jews understood their position in the modern world. My intent is to build an alternative model to the commonplace notion of the Wandering Jew as constructed from without, to examine instead how the Jews themselves conceived of wandering, travel, and their relationship to the modern world.

This notion, or the "politics of location," as Carole Boyce Davies describes it, considers how "positionality" is structured in society in a whole series of ways (by class, race, sexual orientation, gender), with one's mobility, or lack thereof, influenced by where one is positioned in the broader society.[39] The "politics of location" thus understands travel and public spaces as imbued with real sociopolitical forces that affect the movement of people. For Yiddish literature, to consider the politics of location means to see and note the very real way that power structures affected the movement of Jews, not to assume that public spaces are free, unrestricted areas. Instead, the politics of location means to be aware of the unique problems that Jewish travelers had to face and how this influenced the stories that they told and how we should read them. bell hooks writes of being a black woman traveling alone through white America: "To travel, I must always move through fear, confront terror."[40] While many Jewish and non-Jewish travelers faced dangers, such as robbers, traditional Jewish travelers (which is to say, Jews who dressed traditionally) moving alone through eastern Europe in the late nineteenth and early twentieth centuries must also have felt themselves to "move through fear, confront terror."[41] And they must have had a host of additional concerns as well, such as reaching home before the Sabbath or trying to keep kosher while on the road. These basic realities of Jewish travel must be acknowledged in order to understand how and why Yiddish writers chose to describe public spaces.

In European literature, travel was frequently what James Clifford calls "Good travel": "heroic, educational, scientific, adventurous, ennobling." It did not include people who were servants. The servants were excluded not only because they were of a lower class than "proper" travelers but also because many were people of color, whose experiences were disregarded as not matching the image of the traveler as hero, aesthete, or scientific authority.[42] The general trend of European literature had been to assume that most people could partake of bourgeois travel (or, it was only interested in describing the class, gender, and race of people who could) and therefore excluded all other types of travel from consideration. In reality, travel and public locations vary according to who is doing the moving.

Jews were often excluded from "good" forms of travel ("heroic, educational, scientific, adventurous, ennobling"); rather, Jewish travel tended to be more a matter of necessity than of free, positive choice. Instead of the sentimental tour of the eighteenth century, in Jewish literature we have traveling merchants on the move for economic gain. In place of tourism, adventure, and science we have Jewish travel by necessity: forced migration or the search for better economic opportunities. In Yiddish travel literature, the displaced family or the traveling salesman often replaces the tourist.

Jewish culture did have constructs of "good travel" that broaden Clifford's topology. In the premodern era, Jewish merchants moved between the Holy Roman Empire and the Ottoman empire, and there were occasionally great Jewish traveling chroniclers, such as Benjamin of Tudela in the twelfth century.[43] Throughout Jewish history, a recurring theme is the trip to the Holy Land, whether to visit, emigrate, or die and, from the eighteenth century, the journey to one's revered Hasidic Rebbe. These trips were teleological: The trip itself was less important than the goal of reaching Eretz Israel or the Rebbe. In Abramovitsh's *Kitser masoes Binyomin hashlishi* (The brief travels of Benjamin the Third," 1878), and Der Nister's "Tsum barg" (To the mountain, 1914), the authors conflate teleological travel with the romantic journey (travel for its own sake) to create a hybrid of Jewish and non-Jewish "good travel." In the late nineteenth and early twentieth centuries, Jews in eastern Europe, unlike their predecessors, were forced to be fairly sedentary because of numerous curtailments of Jewish travel. (This is the reverse of how travel tended to work for Christians, with the premodern era generally quite sedentary and the modern era bringing the possibility of more movement.)

While Yiddish writers would often appropriate the framework of non-Jewish "good travel," for example, the adventure tale, at times they would manipulate the generic framework to Judaize the space of travel rather than express any realistic form of Jewish movement. The writer would thus use genres such as the adventure tale but downplay the specific dangers that a Jew would face (because a Jewish adventurer who did not have to face hostility on the roads of Poland, Russia, and the Ukraine was so implausible as to border on fiction). Some, such as Der Nister—like Dante, Joyce, and Nabokov—did it because they were "more at home, for whatever reasons, in the conjured spaces of their works than in their actual homelands."[44] The Jewish writers learned from their European brethren, some of whom were equally uncomfortable in their homelands, how to use travel stories to transport readers away from the "real world."

This book considers the trope of travel as it compares with both internal models of Jewish discourse (the shtetl) and external ones (non-Jewish travel literature) and examines the differences between the literary constructs of the road, the train, and the ship. For example, the space of the road, where Jews were physically moving through an often hostile territory, inevitably raised a different set of questions than the ship, where the ship was located on the pseudo-international terrain of the ocean. In ship literature questions of the "national" were embedded in the characters with whom the Jewish protagonist would interact, not the actual terrain. Furthermore, where Jewish stories of the road tended to be about individuals or pairs, train stories tended to be about the movement of communities of Jews. In the stories of ship travel, particularly Jacob Glatstein's 1934 *Ven Yash iz geforn* (When Yash went forth), the setting is no longer a "Jewish" space but an international one in which the Jewish individual must face the broader non-Jewish world.

It was much easier for Yiddish writers to Judaize the road than trains or ships because the latter required operators. The Jew who traveled by rail or ship inevitably confronted Christian

officials—conductors, ticket collectors, or the other myriad workers involved in rail and ship travel. (While on the road, Jews
would generally have to deal with Christian officials at boarder
crossings.) Where "different modes of travel produce their own
chronotopes," road travel for Yiddish writers was most conducive
to constructing Judaized spaces, because road travel did not ne-
cessitate the constant intrusion of officials.[45] The machinery of
rail and ship travel altered the landscape and meant that to reap-
propriate public spaces writers would have to rely on a new range
of narrative means, from turning the train car into a premodern
wagon of sorts, as in Abramovitsh's "Shem un Yefes in a vogn"
(Shem and Jefes in a wagon, 1890), to making the ship a symbol of
a romantic journey of selfhood in Lamed Shapiro's *Oyfn yam* (On
the ocean, 1910). On the train, Jewish passengers tended to travel
in carriages with other Jews (or at least that is how the writers described it); on the ship the Jewish immigrants often mixed throughout the journey with other immigrants who were not Jewish.

For the writers of train and ship stories, the train car or ship
deck was conducive to storytelling, and the tale often focused on
the storytelling that took place during the journey. The train and
the ship became a new setting for storytelling at a time when
shtetl stories were on the wane as literary settings. In the train
and ship stories, the narrator (including Abramovitsh's usually
rambunctious Mendele) remains strikingly silent and lets other
passengers tell their stories.[46] On the train, which remains for
the most part a "Jewish space," the passengers telling their stories
are Jews, whereas aboard ship the stories are imparted by non-
Jews as well as Jews. In both cases the narrator's role is not to
speak but to *listen*. This is in marked contrast to the shtetl setting, where the give and take of questioning and debate often
would fill the storytelling. On a train or boat, severed from the
shtetl and representative of a "modern" space (versus the "premodern" shtetl), storytelling makes a significant shift from communal dialogue to monologic act. On a train or ship that was
moving through an alien, non-Jewish terrain, the Jewish passengers did not always act as a community; instead, each voice became a carrier of the community. The train stories considered the

vast negative changes that the Jewish community was undergoing at the turn of the century, whereas aboard ship the stories were often expressions of individuals who were seeking to find their place in the modern world. Because the stories were told on transports associated with the modern era, the setting became not only a plot locale but a mirror of the stories told by passengers about how modernization and urbanization were forever changing Jewish life.

Looking within the corpus of travel accounts, one sees how Yiddish writers used the tools (modernist prose) and motifs of modernism (the train) to write out and lament the changes that modernization was causing. According to the critic Dean Mac-Cannell, this perspective is typical of modernism, with its nostalgic longing for the past and "purer, simpler lifestyles" that reflect the modernist search for authenticity.[47] This is to say that basic to modernization is the process of lamentation. The nostalgic backward glance to the shtetl is part and parcel of the modern gaze and began in Yiddish literature with the Jewish modernizers, or *maskilim*.[48] To be alienated, to be modern, is to feel the shadow of the idealized premodern reality. To be modern is to define one's self in opposition to the static premodern shtetl. The nostalgic look backward to the lost shtetl is an act of appropriation, a reconstitution of the past under the rubric of the modern consciousness. For many modern Yiddish writers travel is a trope for the processes of disruption and change wrought on the cohesive, unified shtetl of their nostalgic imagination. Travel is the place and expression of the modern in opposition to the static premodern shtetl. To be modern is to move—physically, semantically, and spiritually—from the shtetl while looking back at it with a longing gaze.

Development of Travel Literature

The modernists did not pioneer the use of travel narratives as a means to create a Jewish world. Rather, the travel narrative grew from a tradition that began with the *Bovo d'Antona* (1541) and the

Mayse-bukh (1602), in which, in the latter, Jewish heroes have adventures in Judaized terrains.[49] Jewish writers saw Jews as being forced into a marginal position in eastern Europe, and their literature often became a political means of resisting that status by creating a literary world where they were in control of their destiny. These writers were asserting that the Jews had a literature of their own and that it was not relational but central. The use of a Judaized terrain was not new but part of the Yiddish literary tradition. What did change was the intention of the authors who used such an approach.

The periods of modern Yiddish literature are generally divided into the following eras: the maskilic, or the era of the Jewish Enlightenment, and the Hasidic (1720s–1880s); the classical era (1880–1905); and the modern, or second-generation, era (post-1905).[50]

The Maskilic Era, or the Era the Jewish Enlightenment

Yoysef Vitlin's popular retelling of Robinson Crusoe, *Robinzon di geshikhte fun Alter Leb* (Robinson, the history of Alter Leb, 1820) re-creates Robinson Crusoe as the Jew Alter Leb.[51] Typical of the writing of the Jewish Enlightenment, or Haskalah, the story is meant to both entertain and educate the Jewish reader. For instance, in the opening chapters, before Alter Leb is shipwrecked on the island, he discovers that all people are more alike than different, even if they pray to separate gods (15). Alter Leb, the only child of a Hamburg couple, is so parochial that he thinks London is merely a few miles away. Yet he learns in his travels that the broader world is an exciting and interesting place. There, Christians go out of their way to help Jews, and all Jews can educate themselves, master the world, and become heroes. Typical of the maskilic approach, the main character is a pious Jew (like the imagined readership) who ultimately becomes a man of broad learning by entering the greater world.

Yisroel Aksenfeld's *Dos shterntikhl* (The headband, 1861) further establishes the maskilic construct of travel as beneficial and educational, in contrast to Jewish isolationism. In *Dos shterntikhl* the character Mikhel, like Alter Leb in *Robinzon,* develops morally and intellectually by leaving the town and heading out into the great world. Where Alter Leb ends up in a rural island space, Mikhel goes to the city of Breslau, which he finds to be antithetical to the corrupt Jewish town of Nosuchville, where most of the story takes place. Like Alter Leb, he eventually returns to his town to introduce his new modern outlook to other Jews. *Dos Shterntikhl* thus manifests the maskilic notion of town-to-city movement as positive for both the Jewish individual and community.

Both Alter Leb from *Robinzon* and Mikhel from *Dos shterntikhl* introduce to their coreligionists the lessons from their travels and by so doing seek to move the Jews away from their marginalization and toward Enlightenment Europe.

Hasidic Era

In the central collection of Hasidic stories of the eighteenth century, *Shivhei haBesht* (In praise of Ba'al Shem Tov), the Besht often takes on the guise of a wandering healer or magician, hiding his true self while performing miracles.[52] The people he encounters are mostly Jewish (although a few Christians are mentioned), and the terrain for the most part is Judaized. In Nahman of Bratslav's *Seyfer sippurey mayses* (The tales, 1806–10), the terrain through which the characters move has few Christians.[53] A Jewish landscape enables the narrative to shift from a focus on the relationship between Jews and the broader non-Jewish world to a setting in which Nahman's Hasidic cosmology resonates. In the Hasidic tale, travel becomes a connotative act that transports the reader to a deeper faith. Where travel takes on mythic overtones in *Seyfer sippurey mayses*, in *Shivhei haBesht* travel presents a panorama of seventeenth-century shtetl life. By giving meaning to the text, the reader of *Seyfer sippurey mayses* enacts self-restoration. In *Shivhei haBesht* the Besht is able to enact miracles for the "children of Israel" in the here and now of eastern Europe. Eastern Europe thus becomes a sanctified terrain, like Israel, where miraculous events can and do occur.

The Classical Era Writings of Sholem Abramovitsh,
Sholem Aleichem, and I. L. Peretz

In the classical era, fictional accounts of travel were frequently a means to represent the communal changes brought on by the massive dislocations in Jewish life in the late nineteenth and early twentieth centuries. Narratives of travel often connoted communal change and marked a trajectory into the broader world (as in the maskilic narratives), while travel showed the changes that were transforming the traditional Jewish world, as occurred with the establishment of a rail network in Russia. Travel and change could be positive or negative, and narratives of travel were a tool to show the Jewish community in flux.

Mendele the book peddler became a means for the author Sholem Abramovitsh to extend the frame of his story into the terrain beyond the shtetl and to present the individual (although his voice was always part of an imagined dialogue) rather than the shtetl community. Mendele, moreover, Judaized the space beyond the shtetl by consistently using a system heavily embedded with Jewish iconography to describe it. Mendele was most comfortable in the broader world and in natural settings. Yet the broader world, as it was described in the tales, was a Judaized rendering, with Christians few and far between.

The Sholem Aleichem persona, who was also always traveling, gives us a "comically mysterious being with fantastic mobility, who is everywhere and nowhere in particular, going to and from in the earth and walking up and down in it."[54] As a literary tool, the mobility of Sholem Aleichem, like that of Mendele, was a means for situating the tale within a "real" voice of the people, traversing literary borders, and making the story part of a dialogue. Although Sholem Aleichem was "lighter" and less of a character than Mendele, both extended the framework of the narrative into the spaces beyond the shtetl.[55] The world constructed in these tales is one in which the principle of mobility (as exemplified by both Mendele and Sholem Aleichem) extends the Jewish individual into the land beyond the shtetl.

Modernism

In modern Yiddish literature travel narratives were often a means to express the search of Jewish individuals for their place in the modern world when many of the traditional locales of meaning (religion, community) had broken down. In the modernist narratives of travel we have a nostalgic glance back at the shtetl, a community that helped individuals to know their place in the world. In the maskilic and classical genres travel was a counterpoint to the shtetl for better or worse, whereas the modernists often regarded the shtetl as the locale of a unified, meaningful existence that the individual had left behind and now was seeking to integrate, through memories, into her or his current self. The movement back to the shtetl was thus an individual act of self-integration rather than a physical return.

Although we typically understand the second generation of Yiddish writers (1905–1940) as being more receptive to modernism, more urbane, and more interested in creating new literary models than were their predecessors of the classical generation, the works of four great modern Yiddish writers—Der Nister, Lamed Shapiro, David Bergelson, and Jacob Glatstein—show a profound reluctance regarding modernization.[56] These writers present the changes wrought by modernization as leading, in part, to the atomization of Jewish life and the resultant loss of meaning of the individual in the modern world. However, none of these writers tackles this head-on but uses the metaphor of travel and change to connote what has occurred. The ambivalence of these writers toward modernity reflects their simultaneous attraction to and fear of the forces causing such change.

For the second-generation writers the prose could also become a locale of the modern. In Der Nister's "A mayse mit a lets" (A tale of an imp, 1929), for instance, the world and the word are fractured. Travel becomes both the physical motion of the characters through the terrain and linguistic motion: The narrative is intrareferential, and all the symbols bounce off each other within a cryptic symbolic code system. Movement and travel, then, are not only in the plot but in the stylistics of a fragmented narrative composed of self-referential narrative loops that endlessly signify but are lacking cohesion.

In David Bergelson's *Arum vokzal* (At the depot, 1909), motion is also embedded in discourse, in the stylistics of his prose. Here, the main character, Benish, and the setting, the depot, are symbols of inertia, whereas the trains are symbols of movement. In the claustrophobic reality of the depot, the locale of movement is in the heavy-handed impressionistic prose that, like the depot, overrides plot development (plot *movement*). The prose stilts plot development and focuses instead on descriptions. The narrative voice is like a moving camera, endlessly shifting around the same still landscape. In both Der Nister and Bergelson, motion means discursive motion as often as it means physical motion.

With the second generation of Yiddish writers we do not have figures like Mendele and Sholem Aleichem as literary embodiments of narrative mobility. In the second-generation narratives political realities are insistent impediments, and the means of depoliticizing the terrain generally is either a stock literary genre, such as patently fictional romance (Lamed Shapiro), or a reconstruction of the political reality as the multivalent, unreadable symbol that suggests yet resists a singular political interpretation (Der Nister, Bergelson). Jacob Glatstein's 1934 novel, *Ven Yash iz geforn* (When Yash went forth), is the exception to this, and in his work the main character moves through a politicized landscape and must constantly reckon with being Jewish in Europe during the rise of Nazism.

Conclusion

In all eras Jewish travel narratives expressed their writers' changing perspective of the world around them and their place in it. What is clear is that the writers were not defining themselves in relation or in opposition to a broader non-Jewish world but were defining the broader world on their own terms, with their Jewish experience in the center. By creating the world in their literature, these writers normalized their place in it and made themselves less marginal, instead of writing prose that was a mere reflection of life from an outsider's perspective.

This book seeks to find the nexus of the Jewish notion of the Galut, the political reality of exile, and literary portraits of travel in order to discern how Yiddish writers imagined the world during the modern era. My goal is not to examine how the world positioned Jews but to understand how Yiddish writers placed themselves in the world, one of real, harsh, and oppressive political constraints that suppressed Jews' freedom of movement and their political rights. I will show how Yiddish literature of travel spoke of and to itself about Jews and public spaces and how it engaged European literature in dialogue. My intention is to put the "place back into displacement" by examining how Jewish writers themselves conceptualized travel and their locales.

2

The Road

In the Middle of the Road

Ikh hob zikh yorn gevalgert in der fremd,
Itst for ikh zikh valgern in der heym.
Mit eyn por shikh, eyn hemd oyfn layb,
In der hant dem shtekn. Vi ken ikh zayn on dem?

(For years I wallowed about in the world,
Now I'm going home to wallow there.
With a pair of shoes and the shirt on my back,
And the stick in my hand that goes with me every-
    where.)
                    —Itsik Manger, "Ikh hob zikh yorn gevalgert"

For Jewish travelers "the road" could connote two distinct notions. The first was the "territorial" road, the physical path that
snaked over the land where the Jews lived. The second was the
"extraterritorial" road of the Galut, or Jewish exile, a road that
symbolized how wandering mythopoetically marked the path of
the Jews, like the path of the road.[1] For many Jews the mythic
road of exile intersected with the territorial, physical road, making
the traveler move through both historical and mythopoetic time
and space.

Thus Jewish road stories often synchronically juxtapose extraterritorial and territorial notions of the road, whereas the road

itself is a premodern dirt path that one travels on foot or by horse and carriage. It is different from the train or ship, which are considered modern mechanized arenas. Although the road is a premodern setting, the wandering of the character over paths that branch out in many ways means that the road can also be a space on which to symbolize the individual's seeking of her own true path in the choice-filled reality of the modern world. Where the train can be seen as a trope for considerations of community and dissolution, and the ship as a trope for immigration and arrival, the road is a space that can symbolize the external or internal quest of the individual. Yet the road, like all travel forms, can also be used allegorically to problematize historical and political realities.

An exemplary writer of the Yiddish road story was Sholem Yankev Abramovitsh (1835-1917). The literary figure of Mendele the Bookseller, the paradigmatic road traveler of Yiddish literature, is the narrator of Abramovitsh's tales. Mendele is not truly at home in the domestic realm or in the shtetl but only on the road. The road offers him a relief from the claustrophobic, overly intimate shtetl and allows him to have direct contact with nature. Abramovitsh uses Mendele to extend the frame of his story into the terrain beyond and between the shtetl. Mendele's discourse of the road also serves to create a state of flux around the story itself.[2] The stories are thus rooted in a landscape that comes to life through Mendele's physical movement through the fictional world's time and space.

Mendele is the archetypal outsider and nature man, marking out an individual who exists beyond the shtetl's constricting societal borders. Furthermore, Mendele levels the hierarchical framing of humans in the natural kingdom by consistently pointing out the rich interconnectedness of all things—words, animals, nature, society, history. He often speaks of circular flows rather than static, hierarchical constructs. Although Mendele frames the narratives, the stories themselves are frequently about a male protagonist impelled to hit the road for a number of years. The emblematic example is *Fishke der krumer* (Fishke the Lame, 1869), which tells of a lame man who is manipulated into a marriage and then forced to go on the road with a pack of poor scam-artist beggars.[3] As the story unfolds, Abramovitsh interweaves Fishke's wandering and Mendele's travels with another bookseller, Alter.

In both *Fiske der krumer* and the later novella *Kitser masoes Binyomin hashlishi* (The brief travels of Benjamin the Third, 1878), the protagonists are wandering beggars (although in *Kitser masoes* they have the pretension of being adventurers), and the Jews of the towns that they visit generally help them in some way. In this way the individual shtetl becomes a Jewish world shtetl where the characters occasionally encounter Christians (usually in a comic way) but where roads generally lead into and out of a predominantly Jewish space and where the greatest dangers are from corrupt Jews.

While they are wandering, the "Jewish gypsies" of *Fishke der krumer* break free of the worlds of Jews and Europeans alike: "Zey zaynen fraye mentshn, poter fun ale zakhn, fun nesines, takses ukhdoyme, oykh poter funem davnen un funem gantsn yidishkayt. Nishto keyn oyberhar" (81). (They are free folk in every way, neither owing allegiance nor paying tribute to any king or country. [Free from having to pray, free of all things Jewish, free of even God himself.])[4] Although they are completely dependent on Jews for room and board, they are not part of the community. Abramovitsh is suggesting that actively being Jewish is tied to place and that wandering breaks free of place and thus of Judaism, as we see in the liberated road traveler Mendele. This directly refutes the Galut image of wandering as a Jewish act of eventual redemption. Instead, Jewishness here is located in place, while wandering is a zone in which to re-create one's self without pressure from the Jewish community. Intentionally or not, Abramovitsh is mimicking the Western literary idea of the adventurer as found in *Robinson Crusoe,* for instance, where the protagonist learns to re-create himself in the absence of the bonds of the settled society. This travel-as-liberation notion contrasts with the Galut idea of wandering as an inherently Jewish act.

Yet the story also has a great deal of ambivalence about the gypsy lifestyle, shown in the ironic critique of these Jewish travelers who rely on other Jews to take care of them. In both *Fishke der krumer* and *Kitser masoes Binyomin hashlishi*, the wandering lifestyle, while liberating for the individual, is nevertheless a burden for the Jewish community, because it enables people to shirk familial and societal responsibilities while requiring the care of settled Jews. The lifestyle is simultaneously attractive and problematic for Sholem Abramovitsh.

In this chapter, I examine the road tale in Yiddish literature, briefly considering Nahman of Bratslav's tales, then Abramovitsh's *Kitser masoes Binyomin hashlishi;* I. L. Peretz's 1901 "Dray khupes: Tsvey royte-eyne a shvartse" (Three wedding canopies, two red and one black); and Der Nister's 1914 "Tsum barg" (To the mountain) and "A mayse mit a lets, mit a moyz un mit dem Nister aleyn" (A tale of an imp, of a mouse, and of Der Nister himself, 1929).

An unusual aspect of Yiddish literature of the road is that while the paradigmatic writer of the road story, Abramovitsh, sets his characters on a semirealistic road, the other writers I discuss transform the road into an ever more ahistorical, ageographical setting that is more typical of the enchanted realm of fairy tales than the roads of the European novel from *Tom Jones* to *David Copperfield*. These Yiddish writers tended to use genres associated with the premodern era (e.g., the medieval romance), although they used the genres in modernist ways, manipulating them to suggest real world issues. For instance, Anita Norich and Dan Miron have astutely interpreted *Kitser masoes Binyomin hashlishi* as a political allegory of imperialist movement versus Jewish stasis.[5] Peretz's "Dray khupes," while cloaked as a wondertale, is a dark critique of urbanization.[6] And Der Nister uses the quest setting to portray a breakdown of meaning in the modern world.

Quest refers both to a broad enterprise analogous to a *search* and a specific genre of writing. According to the *Oxford English Dictionary,* the broad definition is a "search or pursuit, made in order to find or obtain something." The genre definition is specific to romances: "In medieval romance: An expedition or adventure undertaken by a knight to procure some thing or achieve some exploit; the knights engaged in such an enterprise." In the latter definition the road is the setting for the quest, whereas in the broad definition a quest can use any mode of travel and can include a range of works from the *Odyssey* to *Ulysses*. But in both definitions, to be on a quest means that the bulk, if not all, of the narrative unfolds in the framework of travel.

In the broad definition, the protagonist seeks something that must be reckoned with in order to enable her to return home to the domestic world from which she has banished herself or been banished. In a medieval quest the quest matrix is bound up with Christian concepts, and the object of desire (generally the Grail) is an embodiment of Christianity.[7] In other words, the protagonist has done something to evoke God's wrath, which leads to banishment and the need to undertake a quest. Once the quest is completed, the protagonist restores order and can return to being a good Christian.

As Tzvetan Todorov writes, "There are two types of episodes in a narrative: those that describe a state (of equilibrium or of disequilibrium) and those that describe the transition from one state to the other."[8] In the quest framework the bulk of the narrative unfolds in the transition state between equilibrium (the opening section where everything is in order) and disequilibrium (the obstacles presented on the quest as well as the general state of a search). In this narrative, transition, and a sense of being "between states," dominates. In Yiddish literature of travel the journey is an expression of the transitive state; in contrast, in the shtetl novel interactions between characters, not just physical movement, express a transitive state. In the quest the transitive state is the norm for the characters, who ultimately seek a return to a quiet and settled reality and an end to the flux of the journey.

The quest narrative often "signals its own fictionality" by being part of a genre with a set series of rules about plot and characters and is structured to be read not strictly as truth but as a fictional construct mediating a fictional world (in contrast to the travelogue or pseudo-ethnographic accounts such as Peretz's *Bilder fun a provints-rayze* [Impressions of a journey]).[9] The patently fictional generic structure may have appealed to the Yiddish writers because they could readily use it to critique the Jewish proclivity to avoid the real and retreat into communal fantasies of utopian otherworlds. In other words, the writers may have turned to this genre as a means to implode it and present a commentary on the dangers of living in fantasy instead of confronting the real world. For instance, the Der Nister quest subverts structural expectations of the quest and breaks down the category as a whole.

Nahman of Bratslav's *Seyfer sippurey mayses* (The tales, 1845) shares the religious matrix (mystical Judaism) of the medieval quest, while the stories of Peretz and Der Nister are secular and fall under the broad definition of an individual or pair on the road to search for something that will enable them to return home again. In *Kitser masoes Binyomin hashlishi* Abramovitsh appropriates the utopian quest, which in European literature was generally for Atlantis or El Dorado and in Jewish lore was for the land of the Ten Lost Tribes. Benjamin the "Third" is meant to be third in a line of "real" travelers, as is typical of the utopian quest genre; therefore, in this work questions of truthfulness repeatedly arise, whereas the other stories take place in invented realms that are nevertheless suggestive of the extraliterary world.[10]

Each writer uses a distinct set of interpretive codes. In attempting to understand the larger meanings that lie within these stories, it is helpful to consider them in light of the specific intentions of the writers and their varied philosophies, be it the cabalistic vision of Reb Nahman, the classical outlook of Abramovitsh, the folkloristic imperative of Peretz, or the modernist focus of Der Nister. If quest stories of the road in Yiddish literature suggest anything unilaterally, it is, as David Roskies writes, that "context is nine-tenths of the meaning in storytelling."[11] However, all the works share the setting of road travel, and, except for Der Nister's "A mayse mit a lets," which subverts the genre, the narratives unfold along the tensions of a forward-looking, forward-moving perspective. Along the way the protagonists encounter characters that will either help them along or temporarily hinder the completion of their quest.

Yet the way each story ends problematizes the quest. In none of the stories do the characters simply return home after learning a lesson on the road. Instead, the endings are either open or very dark. In *Kitser masoes Binyomin hashlishi* the final scene is extremely open and impossible to interpret in singular way. In "Dray khupes" the story closes with the suggestion that things are on a downward spiral, although how things will ultimately resolve themselves is not clear. In "Tsum barg" the protagonist is on an endless spiral—once he arrives home, he must immediately begin yet another quest. (The "nonarrival" aspect of all the stories may have been influenced by the writings of Nikolai Gogol, because failure to arrive is "paradigmatic of Gogol's oeuvre.")[12]

Kitser masoes Binyomin hashlishi and "Dray khupes" are, in part, critiques of what the writers saw as the Jewish proclivity to believe fantasy and a call for a return to a real and realistic reading of the world. Abramovitsh and Peretz impart this critique by putting their characters in a setting in which they must reckon with their location within a specific framing genre. In *Kitser masoes Binyomin hashlishi* the main characters—the Jewish Don Quixote, Benjamin, and his Sancho Panza, Senderl—move through a landscape in which all Jews share their inability to differentiate fact from fiction (whereas the original Don Quixote has this disorder, but the characters he encounters do not).[13] Benjamin's quest to find the Lost Tribes is, in the end, successful. Fiction becomes reality, in contrast to the end of *Don Quixote*, when Don Quixote gains his sanity and returns to reality.

By making the fantastic adventure real in the framing device of Mendele's voice, Abramovitsh has his narrative fluctuate between the fictional and the nonfictional, between "art" and "daily life."[14] Yet because the story is told with such humor, the nonfictional aspects serve as a critique of the Jewish proclivity for self-delusion and a refusal to "move into" the modern world. In his work Abramovitsh imparts this critique by using a narrative that extends its boundaries into the real world while critiquing this extension. These characters from Cervantes' tale become real, and their deluded world becomes the real world.

Similarly, Peretz takes characters that are clearly part of a genre, the fairy-tale quest, and transplants them into the locale of the real, the city. This forces his characters from an idealized, utopian space to face the brutal modern urban world. Within this confrontation he also presents an indictment of the Jewish communal habit of escaping into fantastic communal fantasies. In both *Kitser masoes Binyomin hashlishi* and "Dray khupes" naive characters from a premodern, closed shtetl confront the modern city and find it a wholly negative experience. In "Dray khupes" the characters are extremely naive about the broader world, and their naïvêté is a manifestation of their being characters from a genre of fictionality (to use Wolfgang Iser's word) who arrive in a genre of the real—the urban tale. Thus the city expresses the current period, whereas the rural is the place of the utopian past.

Kitser masoes Binyomin hashlishi is a satire that levels a critique against Jewish premodern "backwardness" and political isolation, as well as against modernization and urbanization.[15] While the main characters do encounter some Christians, wealthy Jews cause the protagonists the greatest troubles. Although the final scene of the work is open to interpretation, clearly the story is mainly internally directed. "Dray khupes," in contrast, is largely a consideration of the effect of urbanization on the shtetl. *Kitser masoes Binyomin hashlishi,* which is typical of maskilic satire, shows the shtetl as a negative, self-obsessed, and backward environment. However, Abramovitsh draws the large town and small city as equally stagnant, suggesting that the hope of urbanization offered by the *maskilim* may be an illusion. In Peretz's work the modernist's nostalgic glance back to the ideal shtetl has begun. And by the time that Der Nister wrote his quest stories, the real world has been completely obliterated, and all that exists are characters caught in endlessly recycling stories. Here the story is the thing, and the world outside and beyond it is spied from a distance, as in "Tsum barg," but is inaccessible to the main character. This story has no nostalgic shtetl but instead retreats into fantasy, while the real world exists outside the borders of narrative. Where we can see that Abramovitsh uses Mendele as a framing device to break down static hierarchies while focusing on the interconnectedness of the natural world, the world of Der Nister's

"A mayse mit a lets" is comprised of grotesque connections and self-imploding narratives, not the positive connections drawn by Mendele. Der Nister's road is a manifestation of a profoundly pessimistic, isolated, grotesquely overconnected world.

The Nahman Quest

A central literary model for the quest stories of both Peretz and Der Nister is the allegorical folktale of Rabbi Nahman of Bratslav (1772–1810).[16] In Nahman's tales, which he recounted to his disciples orally and later transcribed, the interpretive code is the cabala.[17] According to his scribe, Nathan of Nemirow, who wrote the introduction to the collection, popular folktales influenced some stories, but Nahman modified and "repaired" them and, most important, put them in their proper order and presented them as cohesive, eloquent tales.[18] Although his stories may have a loose tie to the German *Kunstmärchen,* Nahman transmutes them into tales to express his theology.[19]

Nahman's stories invert the relationship of reader and text: Instead of asking the reader to interact with the text and supply it with a cohesive meaning, the text supplies the reader with a cohesive meaning. In other words, the Nahman tales seek to act upon readers by having the story's symbols move beyond the textual borders to establish a relationship with readers that brings them into the paradigm of the mystical. Nahman's role is to transform the processes of mysticism into literary geographies and characters, and the reader's role is to transform the literary geographies and characters into the processes of mysticism.

The act of reading is thus an act of appropriation and metamorphosis wherein readers restore the text to the realm of the mystical and by so doing restore their own soul while enacting universal restoration, or *tikkun.* As Roskies writes, "The more difficult the tale—in its details, its plotting, its bizarre symbolism—the more redemptive weight it carried."[20] In a Nahman tale the literary act of "making strange" (to use Victor Shlovsky's terminology) is redemptive because it impels the reader into the mystical process of transforming text to meaning, and the more difficult the process, the deeper the spiritual resonance.[21]

Nahman's tales all include quest elements, with the central character at some point setting out on the road in order to work through something that will lead to his restoration. The obstacles within the text work in the same way—the reader is restored by facing the difficult literary hurdles throughout the story. If in the cabalistic vision God and the Jews are in a sense in exile and the act of restoration means putting together the scattered pieces, then what better literary means of exemplifying this than quest tales with archetypal characters that move around, restoring the scattered reality?[22]

The tales take place for the most part in ahistorical, archetypal folktale settings, using the stock enemies of the fairy tale.[23] Where in a romantic quest the story is of the moments on the road, here the moments on the road can pass in a word, whereas the narrative instead focuses primarily on the fateful moments.[24] Nahman's narratives are less concerned with expressing a realistic unfolding of sequential time and more interested in the moments of integration (rather than motifs of successive action that so pre-dominate in Der Nister's quest).

Nahman's stories not only appropriate the fairy tale but suggest the medieval quest matrix as found in the Arthurian romance. In the Arthurian romance the quest is for the grail or chalice that Jesus used at the Last Supper. This does not mean that Nahman read the Arthurian romances. However, the way in which Nah-man uses allegory and constructs the quest very much resonates with the Arthurian legend. As Kathryn Karczewska writes in *Prophecy and the Quest for the Holy Grail,* in the Arthurian quest the line to heaven is not straight but through allegorically significant, detour-filled movements.[25] This is also true of Christian quests, such as the sixteenth-century *Dark Night of the Soul* by the mystic St. John of the Cross, and John Bunyan's *The Pilgrim's Progress* (1678), in which the protagonists must undertake an allegorical quest with many detours and in the end find the gates of heaven.

Nahman's tales also feature the notion that a circuitous, alle-gorical route leads one to a sacred realm that cannot be accessed directly. This conflation of allegory and sacredness is not found in the fairy tale, which is tied to pagan myths.[26] Where in the medieval romance the allegorical road leads to God, in the fairy tale the allegorical road often leads to a restoration of a holistic pagan sympathy with the extended natural world.[27] Yet Nahman's tales extend the religious quest. Not only is the quest itself an enactment, through allegory, of a return to God but the reader partakes of the return. Nahman brings the act of reading (or, more exactly, the act of listening, because these were originally oral tales) into the quest paradigm, positioning reading or listening as questlike moves toward God through the interpretation of allegories.

In Nahman's literary model, although the plot and characters often suggest the stock fairy tale, its meaning matrix comes from a religious quest in which "geography and faith" merge.[28] However, his stories are based on real geography. He mentions three central European locales as destinations: Leipzig, Breslau, and Warsaw.[29] The Nahman tales are archetypal settings situated broadly within a definite east European map. They are archetypal locales within or just beyond real geography. The plots and characters, as Roskies writes, "are devoid of the standard heroes, settings, and props of Jewish storytelling."[30] These are the archetypal characters of the Bible, the fairy tale, and the Arthurian quest. Nahman appropriates the archetypal, psychology-free characters as blank slates, or as one-sided beings, on which to overlay religious notions.

The road in Nahman's tales is often a symbol of two things: spiritual growth and faith. Where the path to God is vertical, the path of life is horizontal. Within Nahman's mystical framework, simultaneous with each forward or backward moment is an upward or downward movement toward or away from the holy realm. The path is thus a nexus of physical and spiritual movement. Each soul is seeking its own way, both forward and upward, as in this passage from "The Master of Prayer": "Elijah ascended to the heavens on a certain path, and the name of that path was written there. And Moses, our teacher, ascended to the heavens on another path, and that path, too, was written there.

And Enoch, too, ascended to the heavens on another path and that, too, was written there."[31]

Like the Christian quest, the search is not strictly an individual search but is an allegory for communal religious growth. However, in the case of Nahman, the communal growth is specifically Hasidic and represents *tikkun* restoration.

The road is a place to move both forward and upward while cycling back, because this is, after all, a quest in which the ultimate goal, in the traditional generic framework, is to return home. Moreover, the road suggests the notion that some paths are right and some are wrong. As many characters go astray on the "wrong path," they negotiate their way back to the correct road. This idea is very different from the trope of the train or the ship, where the path is linear in terms of track layout, but where an individual could take the wrong train or become waylaid. On the road and free of scheduled, mechanized routes, one has more freedom to choose one's path.

The road as a path of faith also connotes the notion of the leader and the follower. If one follows the proper guide, one's quest can bring one closer to the primal order. The wrong guides move the quester away from God. For instance, in the story called "The Rabbi's Son," the rabbi does not grasp that the journeys with the most obstacles are those that bring him closest to God. Rather, he states, erroneously, "This is how I shall test. If the journey proceeds without mishap, it is from heaven. And if not, it is not from heaven and we shall return."[32] In the logic of Nahman's narrative framework, if one approaches God through detours, a journey with mishaps is sent from heaven. Nahman's eloquent use of an allegorical presentation of road travel subtly and overtly influenced later Yiddish writers of the quests, particularly Der Nister.

The Brief Travels of Benjamin the Third

Briefly, the plot of *Kitser masoes Binyomin hashlishi* (The brief travels of Benjamin the third) is as follows: Benjamin, the Jewish

Don Quixote from the small eastern European town of Tuneya-devka, convinces his friend Senderl, the Jewish Sancho Panza, to join him on a search for the ten Lost Tribes. Deserting their wives and families, they set out on foot. After a comic interlude with a calf in a tavern, they make their way to the large town of Tete-revke, which Benjamin describes as a big bedroom where people sleep through life. In the town the local men debate the two trav-elers and their mission, and Benjamin and Senderl collect goods from the locals for their trip. When Senderl's wife spots them there, they flee to Glupsk, which Benjamin describes as mired in sewer. They cross the filthy Fetidnelevka River, and upon setting foot into the big, broad world, they are tricked into military ser-vice. They are taken to a "bathhouse" where they have their *payes* shaved off and come out as "new men," or soldiers. However, they are ridiculously inept soldiers and try to escape from the military camp. They are caught, and after lecturing the military tribunal (which laughs at them), they are released from service. The pro-logue "written" by Mendele asserts that they do eventually make it to Eretz Yisrael and receive great acclaim as adventurers.

Kitser masoes Binyomin hashlishi interweaves different genres overlain on a seemingly straightforward, humorous tale of two Jewish travelers. The narrative threads include the utopian quest (two characters on a mythic search for the lost Jewish tribes), the travelogue (first-person, pseudo-ethnographic accounts of towns visited), and the adventure tale. The rich mixture of the three travel narratives is made even more complex by the relationship between *Kitser masoes Binyomin hashlishi* and *Don Quixote,* which Abramovitsh appropriates and re-creates as nineteenth-century Poland.[33] Further complicating matters is that Benjamin is the third in a line of Spanish Jewish explorers, so his adventures are connected not only to European literature in the form of *Don Quixote* but to Jewish history. This relationship between fact and fiction, between Jewish history and European literature, adds rich layers to the plot line. *Kitser masoes Binyomin hashlishi* pushes themes from *Don Quixote* to satiric extremes. For example, in *Kitser masoes Binyomin hashlishi* nearly everyone is as crazy as the Jewish Don Quixote, Benjamin, and the relationship between him and Sancho Panza (Senderl) is more like a marriage than a friendship. The similarities and differences between *Don Quixote* and *Kitser masoes Binyomin hashlishi* give the novella much of its comic power and satiric leverage.

Abramovitsh's decision to use *Don Quixote* as a model to satirize Jewish immobility may have happened for the following reasons:

1. *Don Quixote* presents a character so captivated by medieval literature that he has lost touch with the real material world.[34] The shtetl Jews whom Abramovitsh wished to parody were also enthralled by literature and storytelling and used them to escape the real world. The shtetl Jews were fascinated by both Bible stories and Jewish adventures, as popularized in Yiddish chapbooks (*mayse-bikhlekh*).[35]

2. Before he published *Kitser masoes Binyomin hashlishi*, Abramovitsh had used the "posited author" device found in *Don Quixote*. In fact, the figure of Mendele as a narrative tool resembles Cide Hamete Benengeli, the purported author of the Arabic version of *Don Quixote*.[36] Abramovitsh's desire to mimic *Don Quixote* may have been influenced by Cervantes' use of a narrative model at which Abramovitsh himself was adept.

3. Abramovitsh could use *Don Quixote* to show the intrinsic differences between Jewish and non-Jewish forms of delusion. Unlike Don Quixote, whose madness is an individual idiosyncrasy that he could outgrow, Benjamin's madness is generated by history and would not change until the plight of the Jews improved. Where Don Quixote can thus mature and become more rooted in the real world, Benjamin cannot because the real world excluded Jews. His stasis, like that of Jewish culture, is total, unchangeable, and historically generated. *Don Quixote* is thus an exemplary model for conveying the historical roots of Jewish cultural stagnation.

4. *Don Quixote* is set in a premodern rural locale. Abramovitsh needed a premodern setting to show how backward the Jews were and that even in the midnineteenth century their condition was equivalent to that of seventeenth-century rural Spain.[37]

5. *Don Quixote* tells the story of a madman. Making a madman the protagonist may have appealed to Abramovitsh because it matched his feeling at the time that his heroes should be extraordinary characters.[38]

Although *Kitser masoes Binyomin hashlishi* is clearly a rewriting of *Don Quixote,* much of its brilliance lies in the deviations. Foremost are the radically different settings of the two works. Unlike *Don Quixote,* in which the road is a generally safe terrain (except for occasional robbers) on which a feudal lord can re-create himself, for the Jewish traveler in nineteenth-century Poland the road is a place where he may be exposed to anti-Semitic locals. (In the end it turns out that Benjamin has more to fear from other Jews than from the local peasants.)

Like Don Quixote, Benjamin is a passive man seeking to activate his stagnant life by becoming a heroic character. Although chivalric stories may be the catalyst for Don Quixote's quest, he is the real author of his plot. Within the book other characters enact his chivalric imaginings by playing the parts of knights, damsels in distress, and the like. While the other characters inhabit the "surface La Mancha," they at times pretend to be characters of Don Quixote's imagined La Mancha. There thus exists in *Don Quixote* a bipolar reality of two La Manchas, the one that Don Quixote inhabits and that of the other characters.[39] Only Don Quixote lacks the ability to enter and exit the mad realm at will and instead is the sole inhabitant of the mirage La Mancha.

In *Kitser masoes Binyomin hashlishi* Benjamin's imaginings are inspired by *mayse-bikhlekh* (chapbooks) and legends of Jewish explorers rather than Don Quixote's tales of knights.[40] Moreover, the bipolar reality of *Don Quixote* is singular, with no stark division between Benjamin's madness and the rest of the world's sanity. In fact, *all* the male Jewish characters in Benjamin's world are deluded. Day after day they sit around talking and weaving elaborate fantasies while relegating all work to their wives. Unlike Don Quixote, whose quest is generated by his unique inability to differentiate fact from fiction, in Benjamin's culture no men are able to do this. The only difference between Benjamin and the other men is that while all shtetl Jews believe the communal fantasies, only Benjamin and Senderl seek to act them out.

Benjamin and Senderl's journey marks a movement from the poor, static, decaying Jewish life in late nineteenth-century Volhynia (often referred to as Russian Poland) to the fantasy world of

Eretz Yisrael that the shtetl Jews spend so much time discussing. Where Don Quixote's travels thus bring a shift within him from insanity to sanity, and an acknowledgment that he is not a knight but a petty feudal lord, Benjamin's journey marks a move from the real world of small town shtetl life to the mythic landscape of Eretz Yisrael. Yet in both works the towns that the main characters visit are nearly interchangeable in terms of the collective social vision that they present. In Abramovitsh's work, most of the characters are manifestations of Jewish stasis.

Moreover, the contrast in the endings of the two stories is stark. Don Quixote's death at the end of *Don Quixote* marks the close of an "epoch of useless dreaming, of social stagnation" in Spanish society, according to Michael Nerlich. He asks, "What remains when the dream is finally over, after Don Quijote has died, except the illusion-free affirmation of the real world, of active life?"[41] In contrast, *Kitser masoes Binyomin hashlishi* ends with Benjamin and Senderl marching on to Eretz Yisrael. Where Don Quixote's death symbolizes in a large part a return to the "real world," the Jewish characters do not make a symbolic return. Instead, Benjamin continues his adventures and actualizes them.

The discrepancy between the two endings points out that Benjamin's adventures are also teleological. His journey is an example of Jewish return to the Holy Land of Eretz Yisrael. Like numerous Jewish emigrants to Eretz Yisrael, Benjamin is following a religious mandate of return. While he may undergo a series of adventures on the way, the goal, the Holy Land, is a central focus. *Kitser masoes Binyomin hashlishi* thus varies from *Don Quixote* because it points to the specific Jewish journey to the Holy Land, where the end point, the teleological focus on return, is as central as the journey itself. No wonder Benjamin succeeds—he has a specific goal in mind (like Jewish emigrants to Eretz Yisrael), in contrast to Don Quixote's less focused adventures.

To understand how important the deviation in endings is, imagine how different the meaning of *Don Quixote* would be if it included a prologue asserting that Don Quixote had succeeded in revising the knightly system and had become a real knight in the real world. It would make the world described in the novel one in which the fantastic could be made real. By making Benjamin succeed in his mad quest, Abramovitsh may be satirizing the Jewish community for believing that the fantastic can be made real and for being unable to differentiate fact from fiction.

Yet Abramovitsh counts on his readership's being sophisticated enough to differentiate the fantastic and the real and therefore catch the humor. He counts on readers to share Mendele's realistic perspective, rather than Benjamin's fantastic one. Where Benjamin represents a negative archetype of the male shtetl Jew, Mendele is his positive, clear-sighted antithesis. Through his ironic comments Mendele effectively subverts all of Benjamin's fantastic claims while also showing that the Jewish proclivity for self-delusion is, in part, the result of an oppressive, anti-Jewish system. This system has, to some degree, forced Jewish traditional life to stagnate and has created the figure of Benjamin. The culture is dominated by inflated rhetoric because real action often seems impossible.[42]

Therefore, whereas in *Don Quixote* the knight errant must slay villains that are generally of his own making, in *Kitser masoes Binyomin hashlishi* the villains seem to be real. Rather than dragons or knights, they are, seemingly, the non-Jews who inhabit the world just beyond the shtetl. Or so that is what readers expect. However, in Benjamin and Senderl's every encounter with a Christian, the Christian assists them in some way. This is typical of maskilic fiction, which seeks to encourage Jewish–Christian relations and to show the Jews that the broader (modernizing) world is a safe and good place that is not filled with Jew-hating Christians. What Abramovitsh may be suggesting is that the collective Jewish psyche needs to transcend its nearly paranoid entrenchment because the dangers that Jews create in their heads are often worse than the reality. (Remember, this was written before the massive 1881–1882 anti-Jewish pogroms, which put a stop to many Jewish intellectuals' attempts at Jewish–Christian rapprochement.)[43]

Christians not only help the pair but throughout the novella they are the characters that challenge Benjamin's madness and serve as "reality principles." The Christians are completely unable, or unwilling, to understand Benjamin and Senderl's mad talk of Lost Tribes. Here Benjamin goads Senderl to ask a Ukrainian for help:

> Freg, Senderl, oyf a tshikavet, dem orl vegn di berg Nisbon un dem koyfer al turak? Tsi veyst er epes mikoyekh di aseres-hashvotim? A kashe oyf a mayse, efsher hot er epes gehert. . . .
> —Iz tshervoni zhidkov ya zna leybku, shmulku bagotie zhidki.
> —Aza tshuve flegt Senderl bakumen fun zayn kapitan.
> —Ni Leybko, ni, ni! Vin tshervoni zhidki pitaye tamotshka, vi zogt men epes, ni, tamotshka, nebn bernele nisbon.
> —Nisbona, zhidko nisbona?
> —Zog im, Senderl, flegt Binyomin shrayen, zogn zolst du im a barg! Mol im oys vi du kenst.
> Senderl flegt tsunoyfshteln hoykh di hent, oystsumoln der-mit a bergele un shrayen derbay: het visoko!—
> —Tfu! Flegt der orl oysshpayen, oysbetlen oyf Senderlen khaloymes un im opshikn tsu al di shvertse yor.

(Ask the goy, Senderl, if he happens to have heard of Mount Nisbon and the heretic el-Torak? Ask him if he knows anything about the Ten Lost Tribes. . . . Go ahead, maybe he does. . . .

("*Vin zahubleni zhidki vin pitaye?*" Senderl might say, asking if their captain knew of any lost Jews.

("*Zahublenikh zhidkov ya zna Leibko, Shmulko,*" would come the answer, viz.: "Aye, two of them, lost and gone forever, Leibko and Shmulko."

("*Ni Leibko, ni, ni!*" Senderl would expostulate. "*Zhidki* on Mount Nisbon."

("Explain to him what a mountain is, Senderl," Benjamin would urge. "Go on, use your hands."

(Senderl would raise his hands and begin to draw a mountain; their captain would spit and wish them all the bad dreams in the world; and so they sailed on.)[44]

The Christian cannot understand Benjamin and Senderl's gar-bled Ukrainian. Moreover, he does not live in the same bipolar mythic landscape of the Jewish characters.

The use of Christian characters as "reality principles" should be measured against Benjamin's decision to set out on the journey, which is a reaction to hearing the townspeople discuss the increasingly anti-Semitic moves against them. The townspeople's talk about the Lost Tribes is in many ways a symbolic and literal attempt to have a form of escape from the increasing number of anti-Jewish occurrences in the town. In dreaming, talking, and constructing mythic fantasies, escape becomes possible, because real action, real movement, has become largely impossible for the passive, ignorant shtetl Jews. On the one hand, Abramovitsh is suggesting that Jews need to increase their mobility and enter the real world because the obstacles are less the anti-Jewish actions than Jewish paranoia, while he is also implying that the original cause of Jewish fantasy weaving and stasis may be the way that others treat Jews.

Until Benjamin sets out, the only movement in the shtetl is discourse, which takes on a life of its own and becomes the one principle of motion in the stagnant shtetl:

> Der shmues mikoyekh dem dozikn inyen kayklt zikh fun shtub tsu shtub, vi a koyl fun shney, un vert kayklenkik zikh alts greser, greser, biz er kayklt zikh arayn in besmedresh same untern oyvn, in dem ort, vos ahin farkayklen zikh ale shmuesn fun alerley inyonim hen soydes fun shtubzakhn, hen politike mikoyekh Stambul, mikoyekh dem toyger umikoyekh kirhen, hen gelt gesheftn, mikoyekh Rotshilds farmegn in farglaykh mit di groyse pritsim un di andere gevise negidim, uhen potshtn mikoyekh di gzeyres umikoyekh di royte yidelekh ukhdoyme. (8)

> (Rumors grow like snowballs, getting bigger and bigger until they roll right into the synagogue and stop before the cast-iron stove, where all things reach their final destination: family secrets, business deals, Turkish and Austrian politics, the wealth of Rothschild, the latest mail delivery with news of recent pogroms or the discovery of a tribe of lost Jews, and so on and so forth. [305])

In *Cervantine Journeys*, Steven Hutchinson asserts that this principle of discourse-as-movement also arises throughout Cervantes' works "where there is no end to the variations on speaking as moving along pathways, or of speech as directed along pathways."[45] Yet in *Kitser masoes Binyomin hashlishi*, the movement of discourse becomes *the* central form of movement, with the real world as something to debate and discuss rather than a space in which one's life unfolds.[46] Benjamin and Senderl become principles of movement themselves, not only because they are traveling from one Jewish town to another but because they are fodder for gossip and are catalysts for the movement of discourse.[47]

We know from the prologue by Mendele Moycher Sforim that after the narrative ends, the pair achieve their dream of reaching Eretz Yisrael.[48] (The story itself, however, focuses on the pair's travels through Poland.) Benjamin succeeds in his return to the mythic, although what exactly he has succeeded at, beyond making it to Eretz Yisrael, Mendele purposefully leaves unclear: "Ale englishe un daytshe gezatn zaynen far a yorn ful geven mit der vunderlekher nesiye, vos Binyomin, a poylish yidl, hot gemakht in di artsoys hamizrakh ergets. . . . Binyomin hot di velt tsu danken far di khidushim, groyse zakhn, vos zaynen durkh im entplekt gevorn un fun itst on vet di mape oder di landkarte bakumen gor an ander ponim" (4). (For the past year all the English and German newspapers have been full of dispatches about a most wonderful journey to [Israel] undertaken by one Benjamin. . . . The world is indebted to him for his many prodigious discoveries, in consequence of which no atlas will ever be the same [302].) The reader is uncertain whether Benjamin has found the Lost Tribes or if he has just made it to Eretz Yisrael. Moreover, the British and German press may be just as gossip filled and untrustworthy as the shtetl.[49] However, if he merely reached Eretz Yisrael, he would not have been heralded as a great explorer. But Abramovitsh never tells readers exactly what Benjamin's "prodigious discoveries" are.

Yet Mendele also sarcastically asserts that Benjamin differs from

der gantser khevre noysim, vos vandern haynt bay unz arum. Un bikhdey maflig tsu zayn di nesiy fun undzer itstikn Binyomin, hobn zey, vi der shteyger iz fun yidn, dervayl fun yene blote gemakht un gezogt az di gantse knufye hayntike noysim zaynen take nor proste shlepers, veysn nisht fun zeyer khiyes, di gantse nesies zeyere, mshteyns gezogt, bashteyt nor drinen, arumtsushlepn zikh, vi mekablim, iber di hayzer. Zey hobn ale a ponim vi malpes akegn itstikn Binyomin, akegn Binyomin dem dritn, dem ekhtn emesn noyseye. (4–5)

(All our innumerable compatriots currently roaming the globe and typically compared by our Jewish correspondents, for the greater glory of Benjamin, to a pack of poor stumblers, a hapless herd of footloose tramps, the roads taken by whom, set beside those of our intrepid adventurer, are so many blundering from here to there, like beggars' rounds or the scamperings of monkeys. [303])

Throughout the novella Benjamin comes across as one of the "poor stumblers" or "footloose tramps," of the type found in *Fishke der krumer*. The prologue, however, asserts that in the end Benjamin succeeds, transforming himself from "footloose tramp" into a heroic figure able to succeed where even the mighty English explorers have failed. Without the prologue's assertion of Benjamin's eventual success, Benjamin would have come across as a Don Quixote whose fantasies were deluded or as just another tramp. The prologue has instead seemingly shifted Benjamin from a Don Quixote to a great Jewish explorer in the line of Benjamin the First and Benjamin the Second.[50]

Mendele, however, will never let Benjamin truly rise above a comic figure. Benjamin's eventual successes stand in jarring contrast to Mendele's representation of him as a schlemiel beggar in the story. This leaves the reader with a sense of disjunction between the heroic successes that Mendele describes in the prologue and Benjamin's actions in the rest of the text. Here are some ways that we might interpret the disjunction:

1. The reader is meant to understand that the last scene—in which Benjamin and Senderl are successfully talking their way out of enforced military service and achieving their first notable success—is a turning point for the characters. They have finally

learned to assert their will and can now make the transformation from Don Quixote and Sancho Panza to real Jewish heroes.

2. This is an incomplete work, and Abramovitsh intended to return to it eventually. In a later version he would have explicitly portrayed the transformation from schlemiel to hero.[51] However, Abramovitsh did release it as it is and thus intended that it would stand on its own, at least for a period of time.

3. The disjunction between the heroic Benjamin of the prologue and real Benjamin of the text is a satiric tool for making the text outwit itself, causing the reader to be uncertain because the heroic Benjamin overshadows all Benjamin's idiocy, and his idiocy subverts his heroic qualities. Thus Abramovitsh might have used the disjunction to destabilize the entire text and subvert both a heroic and comic reading because neither makes full sense in light of the vast disjunction.

A fourth interpretation of the disjunction comes from Mikhail Krutikov:

> In the *maskilic* conceptual system, the attributes of the Russian state signify solid reality, which was opposed to the world of dreams and fantasies associated with the old Poland and Hasidism. Traces of this conceptual framework can be seen in Abramovitsh's novel *The Brief Travels of Benjamin the Third* (1878), where the positive state authority is represented by a Russian official who appears at the end of the story and puts things straight, in the deus ex machina manner. A Russian general saves Benjamin and Senderl from the nightmarish future in the military. . . . This intrusion of reality comes into a sharp contrast with the dream world in which Benjamin and Senderl live, but does not destroy it altogether. The final episode of the novel leaves open the possibility of further development and can be read as an open end, suggesting another cycle in the potentially endless chain of adventures.[52]

This is to say that in the end the Russian general, as a reality principle, recognizes how unfit the pair are and is not taken in by Benjamin's delusions of grandeur. Nevertheless, the adventures will continue, and the pair will eventually be successful.

The disjunction is intensified by the complex interlayering of Mendele's commentaries on Benjamin's first-person accounts of his travels. These two narratives intersect, collide, and continually challenge one another: Benjamin's grandiose reckonings of the journey and Mendele's ironic subversions of Benjamin's inflated rhetoric.[53] Consider the following example:

> Di zun iz dervayl oyfgegangen zeyer sheyn un hot aropgekukt mit ir likhtikn ponim oyf der velt. Eyn kuk irer hot tsugegebn a shtik gezunt, mekhaye geven itlikhe zakh bazunder. Beymer un groz hobn epes vi zis geshmeykhlt eyder di groyse trern toy fun baynakht zenen zey nokh nisht oysgetriknt, akurat vi kleyne kinder tselakhn zikh plutslem freylekh in mitn geveyn fun a blishtshedik tsatskele, beshas trern vi di bob shteyen zey nokh in di oygn. Di feldfeygelekh hobn geshvind zikh getrogn in der luft, geshpilt un gezungen arum binyonim, glaykh vi zey voltn ge-zogt: "Kumt, lomir zingen un shaln un derfreyen dem faynem parshoyn lebn der vintmil, dos iz binyonim aleyn, dos iz binyo-nim der tuneyadevker, der Aleksander mukdoyn fun zayn tsayt, vos er farlozt zayn foterland, varft avek vayb un kinder un geyt in shlikhes, vuhin di oygn trogn!" (34-35)

> (A fine sun had risen and was beaming down on the world, its every glance a wholesome tonic. As an infant will go from tears to laughter at the sight of a shiny bauble, so the grasses and trees smiled through the night's dewdrops that had yet to dry on other leaves. Frolicking birds took to the air with a song as if to say: "Come, let us chant our matins for that fine-looking fellow by the mill! Why, 'tis Benjamin—Benjamin of Tuneyadevka, the latter-day Alexander—the stalwart soul who has set out from his native land, leaving behind his wife and children, to follow God's path where it leads him!" [326-27])

Although the culture and Benjamin himself consider him to be a hero, Mendele constantly portrays Benjamin as a fool. Neverthe-less, like Cide Hamete Benengeli, Mendele takes on the guise of a serious chronicler. However, unlike Cide Hamete Benengeli, who is only *occasionally* sarcastic, Mendele's voice is highly ironic throughout *Kitser masoes Binyomin hashlishi,* and he cuts down all Benjamin's delusions of grandeur. The danger that the readers of *Binyomin hashlishi,* like the townspeople in the story, will escape into flights of fantasy about Benjamin's heroism is offset by Mendele's comments that suggest that Benjamin is as much a fool as a hero.

Benjamin and Senderl are traveling by foot (rather than by horse, as with Don Quixote, or by horse and cart, as with Mendele). Throughout the novella the author thus asks the reader to view Benjamin in two contrasting lights: a near mythic hero, akin to great Jewish explorers of the past, and a half-mad beggar. He is both a grand Jewish character of the past (when Jews could still aspire to the mythic) and a representative mid-nineteenth-century Jewish beggar with delusions of grandeur. The use of a premodern setting intensifies the critique that Abramovitsh is leveling against Jewish communal stasis, by suggesting that stasis and a premodern reality are tied to one another. A release from the stasis would bring on a move to the modern.[54] However, if the city represents the modern landscape, then, as Benjamin finds while traveling, instead of being a locale of movement, the city is as mired in stasis as the shtetl.

According to the logic of the novella, Jewish movement is often reactive movement. Benjamin and Senderl symbolize this: Their roaming from town to town in nearly all cases is impelled not by the urge to get somewhere but by the urge to flee something (in most cases they are fleeing their wives, which strengthens the pair's satiric representation as emasculated men).[55] Their movement can thus be read as reactive and negative rather than noble.[56] The pair can therefore be seen to symbolize diasporic movement: fleeing one spot after another while creating the idea that they are running toward something. The Jews are not the movers; instead, they are those who are moved, and their placement is the result of displacement. The image is the inverse of imperialist movement.

The public setting of the road, with "its heightened contact between different strata of society" (versus the train or ship, where passengers are divided according to class), enables Abramovitsh to present Benjamin in a series of situations in which strangers of all types react to him.[57] By showing how strangers deal with Benjamin and Senderl, Abramovitsh comically establishes a border between the "sane" (the Christians, the wives) and the "deluded" (shtetl Jews), between those that believe the characters and those that see them as losers.

Where the towns that Benjamin describes represent the Galut, his own movement is away from the Galut and toward a return to the home of Eretz Yisrael. However, his partner, Senderl, like Sancho Panza, is never fully comfortable with this and instead asserts that it is better to stay home. For Senderl the big towns pale in comparison to his hometown shtetl (where he suffers regular, fierce, physical abuse by his wife). Senderl thus represents the figure of the "happy beggar" Jew from the shtetl, impoverished and seeking nothing better. For Benjamin, in contrast, everything that he encounters in his travels dims in comparison to his imaginings of Eretz Yisrael, where he plans to become the king of the Lost Tribes. Their perspectives match two stereotypes of passive Jewish men: the oblivious shtetl Jew and the Luftmensch, the impractical Jewish dreamer.[58]

Benjamin and Senderl's relationship is built on these stereotypical traits, and their relationship represents one of the greatest diversions of the text from *Don Quixote*. In *Don Quixote* the title character's asexuality stands in counterpoint to Sancho's earthy lusts. Although Don Quixote creates an imaginary love quest in Dulcinea, in reality he is unable to act within the realm of relationships. The world of sexuality is totally foreign to him. While his relationship with Sancho Panza is intimate, it is within the sanctioned, hierarchical structure of the servant-master relationship. *Kitser masoes Binyomin hashlishi* offers a radical departure from the central theme of an asexual, single Don Quixote: Benjamin has left his wife to undertake a coupling with Senderl. Their relationship can be seen a mock marriage that parodies the degenerate state of Jewish marriage in the shtetl, and it has definite homoerotic overtones.

Benjamin and Senderl's romance begins after Benjamin has a frightening experience in the forest beyond the shtetl. In what

Dan Miron and Anita Norich label "a scene of seduction," Benjamin entices Senderl to join him on the journey.[59] Their honeymoon starts when Senderl arrives at their rendezvous point transformed into a woman: "Senderl iz gegangen ongeton in a tsitsn khalatl. Untergebundn beyde bakn mit a farsholtsene tikhl, unter beyde oygn bloy, tsugrablt, a shtekn in der hant un oyf di pleytses a hipsh pekl. Er hot in Binyomins oygn gehat denstmol dem zibetn kheyn vi a sheyne oysgeputste kale in di oygn funem khosn" (37). (It was indeed Senderl in a calico smock and a grey kerchief clinging to his cheeks. He had a gash beneath each eye, a stick in one hand, and a large pack on his back—but to Benjamin he was as beautiful as a bride [328].) The narrative voice switches to Benjamin's. He describes his feelings toward Senderl by using comically overblown erotic imagery (that plays off medieval love poetry): "'Vi a hind vos glust oyf kvaln vaser, vi a dorshtiker in dem midber, vos gefint lebedike, kvelndike vaser, vos rint arop shpits skale, azoy hot mayn glustike layb zikh geton ton derfreyen oyf Senderlen, mayn basherten, may getrayen gezelen'" (37). ("As a hart [red deer] longing for a spring, or a thirsty man in the desert, when water gushes from a rock," he has said, "so I leaped for joy to see my trusty companion!" [328].)

In contrast to Don Quixote, who fears women, Benjamin dislikes them and is comically infatuated with a man. Benjamin's misogyny pervades the entire story. However, Mendele constantly points out the hypocrisy of Benjamin's misogyny, by contrasting it with the reality that women are the only members of the Jewish community who are accomplishing anything. Of Benjamin's relationship to his wife, Mendele thus writes:

> Bay im aleyn hot keynmol zikh nisht gefunen keyn groshn in keshene. Er flegt tomed zitsn leydik in besmedresh un zayn ployniste iz geven di eyshes-khayel, di parnose-geberin fun a nas apteykl, vos zi hot zikh gemakht bald nokhn kest aropgeyendik, intshteyns gezogt, vos dos gantse kleytl hot ongetrofn, ven zi zol der bay nisht geven arbetn zokn, nisht flikn vinter biz shpet in der nakht federn. Nisht preglen oyf tsu farkoyfn peysekhdik shmalts, nisht aynhandlen amol in a marktog bay ire bekante poyerim keyn metsies, volt nisht geven mit vos di neshome tsu

derhaltn. . . . A yidene, az zi iz shoyn afile gor di eyshes-khayel, iz zi dokh fort nisht mer vi a yidene. Vos der mindster mansbil hot in nogl, hot es nisht, un ken es gornisht hobn di faynste un di kligste yidene afile in ir kop. (24)

(He didn't have a farthing to his name, having spent all his days in the study house while his wife struggled to make a living from a little store she had opened after her parents ceased supporting them as newlyweds[.] [T]he entire stock . . . consisted of the socks that she knit, the down feathers that she stayed up plucking on winter nights, the chicken fat that she fried and rendered before Passover, and the bit of produce that she haggled for with the peasants on market days and resold at a scant profit. . . . How much, after all, could a Jewess from Tuneyadevka understand? She might be a brave breadwinner, but she was still a woman, and there was less in the head of the canniest female than in the little finger of the most doltish man. [318–19])

Mendele thus satirizes a system in which the role of men and women is strictly divided, with women symbolizing productivity (earning a living, taking care of the family, giving birth to children), and men denoting total lack of productivity. In the mock marriage of Benjamin and Senderl, Benjamin seeks to renew this division of male as spiritual, female as material: "'Senderl!—hot Binyomin zikh ongerufn, geshtarkt fun Senderl's verter,—mir beyde zaynen a ziveg min-hashomayim, mir beyde zaynen vi a guf mit der neshome. Ven du zorgst in neshomes mikoykh esn un trinken oyf undzer nesie, akegn zhe zorg ikh in rukhnies'" (44). ("Senderl," said Benjamin, heartened by his friend's words, "the two of us are a pair made in heaven. We go together like a body and its soul. You'll be in charge of the physical half of our expedition, eating and drinking and all that, and I'll be in charge of the mental half" [333].)

However, Benjamin's abandonment of his family is not unique but something that shtetl men indulge in by shirking their familial responsibilities to inhabit the empty realm of discourse. Benjamin is thus a symbol of all that is wrong with male shtetl culture: a constant denial of reality, an avoidance of material responsibilities, and the elevation of the spiritual in order to perpetuate a system in which women do all the work. While his relationship with Senderl mimics the idealist-realist dichotomy of Don Quixote and Sancho Panza, it also satirizes an entire cultural system.[60] Perhaps this is why Abramovitsh does not describe Benjamin and Senderl's travels beyond the parameters of eastern Europe: It would shift a collective image of static Jewish life into the story of a dynamically mobile pair. That would represent real movement, instead of total physical inertia and the false movement of gossip. Yet even when he is moving beyond the shtetl, Benjamin does not rise above a comic figure. The promise of "self-liberation" remains elusive.[61]

At the end of the story, Benjamin and Senderl are forced into military service by some wealthy Jews who do not want to serve and who trick Benjamin and Senderl into going in their place. In preparation for military service, their beards are shorn and their *payes* cut off. This echoes the opening of the novella, when Benjamin describes the arrival of the anti-Semitic provost, who shaves off a Jew's *payes*. However, it was Jews who tricked Benjamin and Senderl into serving in the military.

After a failed attempt to escape, Benjamin convinces the military to release them by giving a speech to the tribunal. In his speech he attempts to use the family that he has abandoned as the reason why he should not be forced into military service: "'Mir zaynen aykh moyser-meydoe, az fun takhsisey milkhome hobn mir nisht gevust, mir visn nisht un mir viln nisht veysn, mir zaynen borkhashem, bavaybt, hobn in zinen epes gor andersh un mit azelkhe zakhenish kenen mir lakhlutn zikh nisht opgebn, zey geyen undz afilu gor in kop nisht'" (117). ("We hereby declare, the two of us, that we are, have been, and always will be ignorant of all military matters; that we are, God be praised, married men with other things on our minds than your affairs, which are totally alien to us" [389].)

Some critics have interpreted this speech as the moment at which Benjamin "vindicates" himself. For instance, Ruth Wisse writes in *The Schlemiel as Modern Hero* that Benjamin's "passivism becomes a pacifism exposing the absurdity of married men who *do* engage in the foolishness of war."[62] And Miron and Norich note that "the dignity of Benjamin's farewell bow, with which he leaves the tribunal as well as the story, is beyond comic histrionics. It is a dignity of an individual who, although overpowered by a repressive system, could see through it and understand its essential baseness. He can leave with a sense of self-respect because he knows that the power he had to face lacks moral authority of any kind. It can crush the body but it cannot and should not be allowed to crush the spirit."[63]

I would argue that Benjamin's seeming vindication must be measured against Mendele's negative portrayal throughout the novella of Benjamin's desertion of his family. It may be that Benjamin asserts "family values" to manipulate the officers, when in truth he wants to escape the military in order to return to the road and perhaps has no intention of returning to the family that he has deserted.[64] In the course of implicating the military system, Benjamin negatively implicates himself as well (by seeking to use the wife he has deserted as an excuse to be released). Benjamin's speech to the tribunal can thus be read in two ways (as with everything he does): as heroic or cowardly. Or it can be seen as having aspects of both, slipping between the two valid readings while not falling squarely in either.

In *Kitser masoes Binyomin hashlishi*, Abramovitsh succeeds in masterfully appropriating *Don Quixote* to present a subtle yet powerful critique of the premodern and static elements of eastern European Jewish life. *Binyomin hashlishi* builds a dialectic between motion and settlement and thereby creates a host of questions about the relationship between the diaspora and the world at large, where roads lead to towns and small cities but where the small cities are no better, and in fact in many ways worse, than the shtetls. It is as though no road is the correct road to a positive modern world, and all the roads endlessly recycle the same stagnant Jewish cultural reality. The only road that does lead to successful movement is the one to Eretz Yisrael, where Benjamin achieves success. However, Mendele undermines the achievement and makes it seem possible that Benjamin's success is a collective Jewish delusion rather than a reality.[65]

Kitser masoes Binyomin hashlishi also raises questions about the tie between discourse-as-movement and physical movement in the Jewish milieu, where gossip moves faster and farther than a body can and where discursive movement can lead to a shrinking of the real Jewish world rather than an expansion of it (in contrast to the way that literature and journalism can sometimes work).[66] In Abramovitsh's setup the more Jews talk and read, the less they do. This is not a critique of intellectualism but in fact a call for more of it and for less fantasy weaving and escapism. Again, though, the story provides no answer, because even the Jew who does set out and physically moves finds that roads lead to a stagnant Jewish world where no one and nothing really changes except the reports and gossip about the one who set out.

"Three Wedding Canopies, Two Red and One Black"

I. L. Peretz's 1901 short story, "Dray khupes: tsvey royte-eyne a shvartse" (Three wedding canopies, two red and one black), shares many structural devices and themes with *Kitser masoes Binyomin hashlishi*. In both works the main characters set out on a journey that seemingly will take them into the broader world for the first time. Where in *Kitser masoes Binyomin hashlishi* the travels are within a closed landscape of physical stagnation and discursive mobility, in "Dray khupes" the main characters move between landscapes that connote the wondertale and the realistic story.

From the opening paragraphs, "Dray khupes" establishes that it is part of the *mayse–bikhlekh* genre of "wondertales" wherein a hero, often a king or his progeny, sets out on a quest and is assisted by someone using magic. Eventually, after a trial of some type the heroic figure returns home and marries. Peretz uses a stock wondertale framework, with a central variation that instead of engaging in physical combat with an adversary, the pursued king escapes the situation by fleeing. This lack of a physical showdown is typical of Yiddish folktales, in which the protagonists often prefer intellectual to physical confrontations.

In the story, Peretz is also relying on Jewish folk images, such as the establishment of the Sambatyon River as the border to the utopian fantasy world (as we also saw in *Kitser masoes Binyomin hashlishi*): "Vayt, vayt, hinter di hore-khoyshekh, oyf yener zayt sambatyon, iz faran a medine mitn nomen 'vunderland,' vu di royte yidn voynen." (Far far away, beyond the mountains of darkness, on that side of the Sambatyon, is a city with the name 'Wonderland' where the Red Jews live.)[67] Peretz's decision to set a tale on the "other side" of the river Sambatyon suggests that he is using an intertextual folk reality. Furthermore, the name of the place, Wonderland, reiterates Peretz's ironical use of the folk material. As Michael Riffaterre writes, emblematic names such as this "are especially blatant indices of fictionality" and are used to stress the artifice of the tale, as Peretz is doing by showing his heavy-handed use of the wondertale genre.[68] In this tale, unlike the open-ended Nahman story, which also has stock folk images, things will apparently be reduced to an emblematic meaning.

Wonderland is like the garden of Eden, with everything in happy harmony:

> Un fartsitert, vi fun groys libshaft, hobn zikh arum dem alem geflokhtn di faynste, vunderlekhste shotn fun di blumen un geviksn, vos hobn geblit oyf beyde zaytn fun taykhl. . . . Un az es hot zikh nokh derbay gelozt hern der shpilfoygl fun tsvishn di tsvey tsvaygn, vos hobn zikh geboygn unter der last fun goldene peyres, hot men virklekh gemeynt, az es iz gor keyn gortn nishto, keyn palats nishto, — az es iz in gantsn a kholem, a farkishefter kholem. . . . Un dokh iz es keyn kholem nisht geven. (15)

> (And trembling, as if deeply in love, wove around all these things the finest, most wondrous shadows of the flowers and plants that blossomed along both sides of the water. . . . And the song of the nightingale could be heard among the branches, which were bending under the weight of golden fruits. Anyone might think that there was no garden here, no palace here—that it was all a dream, an enchanted dream.
> And yet it was not a dream. [61])

According to Mikhail Bakhtin's topology, this type of setting, intrinsic to many folktales, is a chronotope ("time-space") of the idyllic. For Bakhtin, the idyllic chronotope has the following components (all of which appear in "Dray khupes"): It is a familiar territory where the inhabitants know all the nooks and crannies, the focus is on the basics (love, birth, death), and life is harmoniously conjoined with the rhythms of nature.[69] In Peretz's version of Wonderland, all aspects of life have a basic joyful harmony, a natural simplicity of rhythm, and a unity between humans and the natural world.

What is remarkable about Peretz's story, however, is that while he will first present the idyll, as the story progresses he will also portray the destruction of the idyll. According to Bakhtin, destruction of the idyllic is one of the "fundamental themes of literature toward the end of the eighteenth century and in the first half of the nineteenth." With increased urbanization and industrialization, writers begin to show the demise of the idyllic premodern spaces and the advent of the urban landscapes. Bakhtin says these portraits of destruction carry the binary of the idyllic "little world" and the other, larger, more real world: "Opposed to this little world, a world fated to perish, there is a great but abstract world, where people are out of contact with each other, egoistically sealed-off from each other, greedily practical; where labor is differentiated and mechanized, where objects are alienated from the labor that produced them."[70] In "Dray khupes" two characters from the idyllic world head out, cross the border, and enter the larger world, whose features match Bakhtin's description of the anti-idyll. In contrast to *Kitser masoes Binyomin hashlishi*, in which one finds in the broader world small Jewish cities that are merely larger versions of the premodern shtetl left behind, in "Dray khupes" one finds a clear separation between the shtetl as a premodern utopia and the city as a modern dystopia.

In "Dray khupes," we thus find that Peretz is representing on one terrain simultaneously, the idyllic space and its destruction, with a stark line down the center. He portrays the idyll as the "world fated to perish" by having two characters travel to the "great but abstract world" and experience profound alienation and the shock of its anticommunal reality. Peretz uses these naive characters of the idyll to mark out exactly what has been lost. In the end

Peretz has the characters return to the idyll after undergoing terrifying experiences in the broader world. Upon returning home, they
discover that things have changed and the destruction has begun.

By mapping the terrain of the idyll and its concomitant demise, Peretz appropriates the wondertale to express the transition
from the premodern landscape, where things make sense, to
modern alienation. Moreover, his ironic use of the wondertale
framework, as shown by its emblematic name, serves to under-
mine utopian fantasies about the premodern otherworld beyond
the Sambatyon. In the same way that Mendele undercuts the
proclivity for fantasy escapism by making fun of Benjamin's and
the townspeople's obsessions with Jewish adventure, Peretz re-
duces the fantasy by presenting it in an ironic way. Both works
thus teach the audience not only about the broader world but
about how to read literature by ascertaining what is truth and
what is fantasy. Peretz, like Abramovitsh, indicts equally the real
modern world and utopian fantasies of escape into the imagined
idyllic world.

The story is about a wise king and devoted father, Solomon
the Twenty-Seventh (another stock image of Jewish folklore used
ironically in the ridiculously high yet specific number 27), his
beautiful, kind, devoted, and absolutely perfect daughter, Princess
Shulamit, and her best friend, the equally perfect Deborah. The
young women have devoted their lives to helping the poor and in-
firm. On Lag B'omer the two "golden girls" enter the nearby forest for a stroll. The forest, like the entire setting, is right out of a
Disney cartoon. The birds are in complete harmony, flowers are
blooming, and sweet deer look at "di meydelekh mit getraye, hart-
sike oygn, vi nor sarnes un hirshn kenen kukn" (17) (the girls with
faithful, loving eyes, as only stags and does can look [62]). In the
forest the young women consult with a kindly sorceress about
how long the king, Shulamit's father, will live. After a slightly
comic mix-up in which the sorceress misunderstands the question, she asserts that "'ir foter vet derlebn—dem tog fun ir
khupe'" (19) (her father will only live to see her get married [64]).
Shulamit vows that she will never marry (so her father will never
die), and the young women promise to keep this a secret.

At a banquet Shulamit shows disinterest in the men wooing her because she believes that if she holds off on marriage, her father will not die. She asserts, however, that she is not interested in these suitors because they are interested in her only as a way to become king, not because they are motivated by real love. A wise dove arrives to suggest that the king and Shulamit should disguise themselves as poor Jews and set out on the road, because whoever falls in love with her while she and her father are wandering will love her for herself, rather than because she is a princess.

They are overheard by the scheming, evil grand vizier, Joab, who "wears a mask on his face" of devotion, while in reality he is plotting to get the kingdom for himself. His mask disguises his manipulative bent, whereas the king and princess will wear masks of poverty in order to find a kind husband for her. The vizier plots to have two robbers follow the king and princess in order to kill the father. They will, however, allow the princess to live if she will marry the vizier and agree not to reveal to anyone what he has done.

Once the king and princess have departed, Joab "di maske fun ponim aropgevorfn" (pulls the mask from his face), starts to drive all the poor out of the kingdom, raids the king's treasury, and replaces all the honest community leaders with lackeys. When his daughter, Deborah, tries to get him to stop, rather than kill her (which he would prefer but the townspeople would never allow) he decides to marry her to a sleazy wealthy businessman who will remove her from Wonderland. Deborah escapes and, like her best friend and the king, sets out on her own quest.

The journey of the king and princess begins with an interesting consideration of the nature of exile. According to the unnamed narrator, while for most Jews exile has been a harsh punishment, in Wonderland the road and all public realms are entirely safe because people everywhere are hospitable, not hostile. The road, then, is not a space beyond the safe domestic realm but an extension of the domestic into the broader space. Yet as Peretz has made clear from the start, Wonderland is a utopian ideal that must be viewed ironically. He uses the construct of Wonderland as the positive idyll to construct a dichotomy, with the city as Wonderland's antithesis. The pair cross the border, and the folktale characters describe the landscape of a city. The description mimics the travelogue passage that describes the arrival of the country bumpkins Benjamin and Senderl in Glupsk. However, whereas in *Kitser masoes Binyomin hashlishi* the border between the real and the mythic is not a literal space but inside Benjamin's head, here the characters of one genre, the fairy tale, move into the modern space of the urban narrative. Everything in the city is the opposite of the Wonderland idyll. There travelers were at home everywhere; here they are despised strangers. There the woodsmen and peasants (the locals) helped travelers, here they curse them out. Most important, wandering was a pleasure in Wonderland because travelers chose their own path; here in the city wandering is not a choice but a necessity, the result of being homeless and unable to stop moving. Where Wonderland is the mythic rural utopia, its opposite is the urban dystopia. The city is the place of the modern narrative, Wonderland of the premodern *mayse-bikhlekh*.

In the rural landscape of Wonderland everything is in harmony with everything else; the urban space is unnatural. It has neither nature nor animals, only humans. It is a nihilistic, anticommunal reality of unbridled and ferocious individualism and no community to speak of. This critique is all the more powerful because while the shtetl still existed in Abramovitsh's time, although it of course was peopled by deluded bumpkins, by the time that Peretz was writing, he posited that the positive alternative to the city is a purely fantastical space called Wonderland. The ideal, holistic, rural terrain now exists entirely within the realm of fairy tales and fantasies.

Although the king and princess, the two main characters, have come from the fantastic Wonderland, the city to which they have traveled has no space for mythical utopian narratives. Thus the characters from these narratives, the king and princess, learn that city inhabitants completely deny Wonderland's existence. In the urban space one must live entirely in the "true" real world, which excludes the Wonderland narratives of *mayse-bikhlekh* fantasies. When the king and princess ask the locals about Wonderland, they just laugh and say: "'Es iz in keyn geografye keyn "Vunder-land" nisht batseykhnt! Alte vayber flegn a mol ploydern fun Vunderland, altertums-forsher hobn a mol azoyne alte kinder-lider gefunen vos hobn fun oysgetrakhte Vunderland gezungen, nor haynt hot men dos ales farvert. Dem kleynstn kind tor men haynt keyn shekorim nisht dertseyln; emes gilt, reyner, naketer emes'" (43). ("There's no 'Wonderland' in any geography book! Old women used to ramble about Wonderland, scholars of an-cient history once came upon some old children's songs about an imaginary place called Wonderland. But today, all those things are forbidden. You're not allowed to tell such falsehoods to even the youngest child. All that counts is truth, pure, bare truth" [82].) The urban is a space without fantasy and imagination and with-out a literary means of escape from the harsh material world. Whereas in *Kitser masoes Binyomin hashlishi* the setting has char-acters oversaturated with folktales and escapist fantasies, Peretz set his work within a one-sided reality (as one-sided as the fairy-tale world of Wonderland) of harsh materialism where imagina-tion and art have all but disappeared.

As they continue on their way, "Der meylekh mit der basmalke zaynen emese shmate-kloyber gevorn" (44). (The King and the Princess became real ragpickers [82].) Where the wandering in Wonderland is that of a free people, the wandering of our two characters, once they enter the space of the real, is impelled by negative forces: They find no place where they are welcome and need to keep moving in order to beg and stay alive. Their move-ment is reactive rather than free.

In "Dray khupes," Peretz thus shifts the narrative from that of a mythical quest to a real exile. When the king and princess were on a quest in Wonderland, their options were unlimited. How-ever, now the narrative becomes the tale of two Jewish beggars in the harsh city. As winter comes, their lot worsens and their wretched existence is starkly out of place within a fairy-tale genre. Readers aware of fairy-tale conventions (as Peretz was as he wrote this tale) may expect that at some point the suffering of the king and princess will end, because at the end of fairy tales "conflict is resolved, and happiness, joy, and contentment become the optimistic expression of hope for a world as it should be."[71] Readers unaware of the conventions of fairy tales (which probably was true of many of Peretz's readers) may have had no expectation of an easy resolution.

Finally, the kind, devoted king cannot take it anymore. He and his daughter are freezing while desperately picking through garbage, and he lashes out at her, mistakenly blaming her for their dire straits, saying she was too proud to take any of the suitors who wanted her. She, however, finally acknowledges the real reason why she wouldn't marry: the fortuneteller's prediction that he will die if she takes a husband. When the daughter lays bare her secret (secrets are a great force of disorder in the fairy-tale genre), the father asserts that God cannot allow anything to be wrong in his universe and he will quickly mend things. God of course immediately does fix things, for in the fairy-tale genre to which the narrative has now returned, disorder is eventually suppressed, the good win, and evil perishes. This, of course, is to be contrasted against how things work in the locale of the real city, where there is no divine plan, and where the innocent suffer unjustly. Only in the narrative of a wondertale can God act so speedily to relieve the suffering of the innocent and punish the wicked.

In fact, Peretz makes this even more overt by ironically asserting: "Un Shloyme der zibn un tsvantsikster un zayn tokhter, di basmalke Shulamis, zoln geven, khasvesholem, umkumen fun gazlonishe hent, volt keyn mayse nisht geven, oder es volt geven a shlekhte mayse, un shlekhte mayses dertseyln nor shlekhte farbiterte mentshn" (46). (If Solomon XXVII and his daughter, Princess Shulamit, had died at the hands of the murderers, God forbid!, then there would have been no story, or at best a bad story, and bad stories are told only by bad, embittered people [84].) A text that falls within the genre of the wondertale must have a happy ending. Yet this also suggests the opposite result: If this were not a "story" but reality, the king and Shulamit would die at the hands of murderers. But this would make it a "bad" story told by a "bad" person — a sarcastic assertion that shows the absurdity of reading simplistic, fantastic, fairy tales as real stories. Moreover, the statement makes it again clear that this is a fictional world mediated by an author who is entirely responsible for it.

The story continues with a sequence of convoluted tales-within-tales as the pair make their way back to the kingdom. It culminates in the discovery that Shulamit and Deborah are changelings, and the king is really the father of Deborah, not Shulamit. With the discovery of the true condition of the two young women comes redemption and the end of exile. Surprisingly, Deborah decides that, instead of taking her proper place as the princess, Shulamit should continue in that role. Deborah assertively rejects the blessing wrought by magic and enchantment and instead chooses her own destiny. It reflects a belief in the individual's ability to transcend her situation and seek out her own true path.[72] However, the emphasis on individual freedom is countered by the reality that the characters faced beyond Wonderland's border, where they lost their freedom in the harsh survival needs of city life.

While the trio has been away, the evil Joab has become a modern leader, wreaking destruction on the natural world of the rural kingdom and by so doing causing its demise by making it similar to what the king and princess encountered in the city. In fact, by the time the king returns, Joab has nearly, if not totally, destroyed the earthly paradise, leaving only a couple of old crows.

Unlike the typical fairy-tale ending, the transformation of the home is negative. This wondertale has no positive conclusion because the destruction wrought on the paradise is most likely irreversible. In the final sentences of "Dray khupes," in place of a magical upbeat return to goodness, things are left highly uncertain and unfinished:

> Di alte kro farshvaygt un pikt zikh in ek shtark farklert.
> —Un haynt, fregn di yunge, veln zey poyln?
> —Ver veyst? Der hayntiker Shloyme iz erlekh un gut. Er barimter kinstler iz zayn eydem, Dvoyres man mit di shternlikhtike oygn zol vern mishne lemeylekh.
> Zi fartrakht zikh vayter un pikt zikh in ek. (72)

(The old crow fell silent and wistfully pecked at her tail.
"Will they succeed this time?" asked the young crows.
"Who knows? The present Solomon is honest and decent. The
famous artist is his son-in-law. Deborah's husband with the
starbright eyes is to become grand vizier."
   The crows began musing again and pecking at their tails.
[104])

In other words, the pieces are in place for another happy tale, as
they were at the start of the story. However, as the old crow says,
who knows what will happen? (Remember that the vizier has already destroyed the idyll.)

   In "Dray khupes" Peretz subverts the basic conventions of the
wondertale in order to forcefully establish a realistic rendering of
the destruction wrought upon the idyll, or idealized shtetl, by urbanization and modernization. Yet the critique is not wholly negative, because it also asserts the possibility of individual initiative
against outside forces. And the ironic nature of the entire story
calls into question whether the idyll was really as great as it
seemed, or if it only seemed great to self-deluded eyes. (Remember, the ones who most loved the idyll were the wealthy elite—the
king's family—who knows how the peasants really felt about it.)

   Peretz has rendered the critique through a creative use of dual
genres, the wondertale and the realistic tale, and by constructing a
geography that entails both; the main characters pass from one to
the other and suffer the fates prescribed to those located wholly in
one of the two disparate systems. In "Dray khupes" genres become mapped into spaces: the wondertale as the enchanted royal
premodern utopia and the realistic tale as the urban dystopia. In
Kitser masoes Binyomin hashlishi Abramovitsh constructs the terrain of the real as the "outer world" and the fantastic as the escapist "internal world" of the Jews. Peretz, instead of giving his characters any internal landscapes whatsoever, externalizes both
places into spaces that the characters move through.

   For both authors the premodern road is a space on which to set
narratives about the dual locales of the fantastic and the real and to
present forceful critiques of escapism versus individual initiative

and action. The works actualize geographically a Jewish perspective wherein both *exiles* and *home* connote "here," in contrast to the mythical realm, which might be located in gossip (*Kitser masoes Binyomin hashlishi*) or in a wondertale ("Dray khupes"). In both instances the fantastic narrative is located in the *mayse-bikhlekh* that the Jews read simplistically, without differentiating fact from fiction. *Binyomin hashlishi* and "Dray khupes" therefore serve not only to differentiate the geography of the rural versus the urban Jewish landscape but to teach the Jews how to read. Literature should be approached with a critical eye but not to such an extent that readers become the unimaginative sour urbanites of "Dray khupes" who have no appreciation of the arts. Instead, while the Jews should still give themselves over to the humor and fun of the literature, they should also be wary of using literature to withdraw completely from the real work to be done in the real world.

Der Nister's Quests

Like Abramovitsh, who made the traveling figure of Mendele the central narrative tool to anchor his literature, Der Nister used the wandering figure as a key trope. Where Mendele explored the binary of the road versus the shtetl but made both Jewish terrains, Der Nister universalized the road as a setting for the artist to examine how in the modern world the individual finds meaning when forces pull at her from all sides. In Der Nister's early stories the quest resonates with the symbolism in which he believed. In stories that he wrote after Russian Jewish writers denounced Yiddish symbolism in 1925, the quest comes to symbolize Der Nister's difficult break with symbolism.[73] My analysis compares a quest tale from his symbolist period, "Tsum barg" (To the mountain, 1919), and his 1929 story that subverts symbolism, "A mayse mit a lets, mit a moyz un mit dem Nister aleyn" (A tale of an imp, of a mouse, and of Der Nister himself).

More than any of the authors I discuss, Der Nister's life story is central to unlocking the meaning of his cryptic stories. This is true not only because his ambiguous stories make the reader search for extraliterary tools to understand them but also because Soviet critics had such a large influence on his work (as they did on all writers in Russia of the 1920s).[74] As Khone Shmeruk writes of interpreting Der Nister, "Literary analysis of works produced under a totalitarian regime must depend, even more than any other critical enterprise, on reading between the lines."[75] Der Nister's biography offers one tool for doing this.

Der Nister was born Pinkhes Kahanovitsh in Berdichev, Russia, in 1884 to a Hasidic father.[76] He took his pseudonym, Der Nister, the hidden one, when he published his first book of poetry in 1907. The "hidden one" suggests cabalistic imagery and the symbolist notion of the elusive self and symbol but also may have resulted from his having to go underground to avoid military service in 1904. Der Nister made his way to Kiev and joined the Kiev literary group that included David Bergelson, David Hofshteyn, and Peretz Markish. Der Nister's first book of poems, *Gedanken un motiven: lider in prosa* (Thoughts and motifs: Poems in prose, 1907), was followed by *Hekher fun der erd* (Higher than the earth, 1910). Once established as a Yiddish poet, he made the requisite pilgrimage to see I. L. Peretz in Warsaw, whom Der Nister held in the highest esteem.[77] Der Nister married, had two children, and lived in Berlin, where he briefly edited the journal *Milgroym* (Pomegranate) with David Bergelson. In 1922 and 1923 Der Nister published two volumes of symbolist stories, *Gedakht* (Thoughts).

In 1926 Der Nister decided to return to Russia; his inability to see the impending destruction of Yiddish culture still baffles critics of his work.[78] In 1928–1929 Der Nister published *Fun Mayne Giter* (From my estates) and in 1929 brought out a new edition of *Gedakht,* which included a new story, "Unter a ployt" (Under a fence). *Fun mayne giter* and "Unter a ployt" document in part his struggles to renounce symbolism, as Soviet critics were pressing him to do. In 1939, after searching for a new artistic outlook devoid of symbolism, he published the first volume of his masterpiece, the novel *Di mishpokhe Mashber* (The Family Mashber). Der Nister died in 1950. Throughout his career, Der Nister was influenced by many trends, including symbolism, folk tales from Yiddish chapbooks, stories by Nahman of Bratslav, the neo-Hasidic stories of Peretz, and the tales of Hans Christian Andersen.[79]

It is difficult to accurately describe the beliefs of Russian symbolism, the movement that had such a strong influence on Der Nister, because it encompassed such a disparate group of Russian writers. There is no "symbolist" manifesto but instead a number of varied statements by leading members of the movement who were trying to work out what it represented.[80] As an umbrella movement, Russian symbolism predominated from the late 1890s to the 1917 Revolution, when Russian literature shifted toward its ideological and literary opposite: socialist realism. Uniting the disparate elements of Russian symbolism was the belief, garnered from the French poets of the nineteenth century, that the symbol was a tool to evoke, rather than to outwardly suggest, the inner workings of the individual psyche.[81] In contrast to realists, who found the world fixed and readable, the symbolists saw the internal world as transient and so personal that it could not be described outright but only represented by using suggestive symbols. In discussions by and about Russian symbolists, four central themes arise repeatedly that artists laid claim to in different degrees: aestheticism, decadence, pessimism, and mysticism.[82] Although Der Nister was explicit that he considered himself a symbolist until 1929, it is not clear which trends he directly associated himself with.[83] Yet to varying degrees we see all four at play in his writings. The symbolists were also heavily influenced by the writing of Friedrich Nietzsche, who, I will suggest, also inspired Der Nister's story "Tsum barg."[84]

The main trend differentiating Russian from French symbolism was the attempt by some artists to tie symbolism to mysticism.[85] As a major symbolist, Vyacheslav Ivanov, described the trend of mystical symbolism in 1910: "The new poetry seems like the first, vague reminiscence about the sacred language of the priests and magi, who at one time gave the words of national language a special, secret significance, which could be revealed only to them because of the correspondence that only they knew between the world of the secret and the boundaries of popular experience." This special language of the priests was conflated with the poet-as-prophet motif, so that art was elevated to be unknowable to the uninitiated. Interestingly, the mystical notion of symbolism resonates with Nahman of Bratslav's cabalistic imagery; the symbols in his stories connote a higher mystical order that he has access to and that the reader seeks access to. In fact, the Nahman tales seem to be a paradigmatic model of a mystical symbolic tale, and Der Nister's attraction to symbolism may have been partly influenced by how it resonated with the narratives of Nahman of Bratslav.[86] Moreover, the evocative, unique narrative style of the Nahman tales may have inspired Der Nister's own equally unique and strange writing style.

Russian symbolism was also a "neoromantic" reaction to realism and positivism.[87] Dan Miron gives a succinct definition of neoromanticism in Yiddish. Neoromanticism regards "folklore as a source of inspiration, as a 'folk truth' that should be pondered by the alienated modern intellectual who wants to be reconnected with the inner spring of the life and energy of his people."[88] Peretz, the great neoromantic Yiddish writer whom Der Nister greatly admired, mined earlier Hasidic literature and reworked it to present a humanistic framework for the modern Jewish experience.[89] The neoromantic bent of Peretz is seen throughout Der Nister's writing, where Der Nister turns to folklore in his settings and symbols. Der Nister, however, does not use folklore as Peretz does, to give meaning to a Jewish humanistic ideology with extra-literary resonances. In Der Nister's literature folklore becomes manifested in suggestive tropes that are accessible to the artist but often seem just out of reach of the reader.

"Tsum barg" (To the mountain) involves a symbolic quest narrative in which an unnamed wanderer heads out on a journey with no clear purpose in mind. Along the way he comes up against obstacles that are unreadable, vague, and suggestive. In the end the narrative returns to the opening moments, with the protagonist about to get out of bed to start another quest with no clear goal. "Tsum barg" uses symbolism to subvert the traditional fairy tale or romantic quest in which the goals are clear and the end brings success. In Der Nister's symbolist tale nothing changes, no growth happens, and the obstacles are not steps on the path to eventual completion of a goal, but instead represent that the wandering is everything and that the goal is unimportant.

The second tale that I will analyze, "A mayse mit a lets," was written years after the demise of symbolism in Russia but while Der Nister was under extreme pressure to denounce a movement that he still believed in. Instead of subverting the quest drama, it subverts symbolism.[90] The path of the wanderer no longer leads up the clean serene mountain of "Tsum barg" but to a stinking, decrepit, and grotesque world of decaying meanings. In "A mayse mit a lets" the wanderer causes the people he encounters to begin an endless series of transitions from starvation to obesity to starvation. The elevated mountain path of the one-time symbolist is now a road leading to a world of urinating, farting, and breakdown. In "Tsum barg" the wanderer finds on the mountain evocative symbols that are keys to his psyche, but these now are replaced by unstoppable movement. In "Tsum barg" a symbol is a still thing, a rock in the road, but in "A mayse mit a lets" the world is largely devoid of symbols, and there is little but motion—endless, destructive motion.

Both tales unfold in a series of evocative landscapes that have no explicit tie to the real extraliterary world but nevertheless suggest extraliterary themes. In "Tsum barg" the landscape is positive and evokes something, although the reader is not sure exactly what. In "A mayse mit a lets" the landscape is negative and evokes little but decay, breakdown, and the loss of meaning. Moreover, the extreme grotesqueness of the later story, which reads like Rabelais in many instances, has comic elements that are missing completely from the heavy, serious "Tsum barg." Der Nister's difficult break with symbolism becomes comically, and perhaps subversively, rendered, as if to show that if you scratch the surface, symbols do not necessarily evoke anything deep about the psyche, because the psyche is corrupt and rancid—humans are little more than debased corporeal beings. The body of the second story replaces the soul of the first. And if there is no soul, symbolism has little meaning. It is not clear, however, and likely will never be, which came first for Der Nister. Without symbolism the soul of the art disappears, and all that remains is decay.

Or the soul of the artist and art dies and with it the possibilities of symbolism.

Der Nister's quest tales bring together three schools—symbolism, mysticism, and neoromanticism—all of which are interrelated in how they express the motif of movement. Their common ground is that they represent freedom from the rigid forms of the realistic novel and a preference for evocative discourse. The forward movement of the quest meets obstacles along the way that help or hinder completion of the goal. If we read the obstacles on the quest as reflecting symbolism, as we will see in "Tsum barg," we can see them as evoking the inner workings of the psyche. Jewish literary influences often are felt when the symbols suggest the Nahman narratives, where they bring a move toward mystical truth, or the neoromantic Peretz quest, where the obstacles are mined from the folkloric imagination. While the symbol resonates with the larger mystical or humanistic meaning of Nahman or Peretz, within the context of the Der Nister tale the ultimate meaning seems wiped out or inaccessible. The obstacles become oblique symbols that show the wanderer's search, yet their ultimate meaning remains unclear to readers because they do not have access to the psyche of the wanderer/artist. The intentional vagueness of the meaning elevates Der Nister to priest of a magic language, much as Vyacheslev Ivanov described mystical symbolism. In "Tsum barg" the priestly role suggests positive aestheticism, whereas in "A mayse mit a lets" it suggests the fallen state of the priestly class.

A fairy-tale quest generally relies on the reader to give it a cohesive interpretation by decoding the symbolic obstacles that the protagonist faces. Der Nister seems to use a fairy-tale–coded text, but the codes themselves are so personal that they resist any overall decoding by the reader. In Der Nister's quest we have the symbolic geography without any clear interpretive key to decipher the mysticism/symbolism, and only the poet-prophet has the interpretive key. Because the larger meaning is the internal vague framework of the individual psyche (which is constantly in transition rather than static), no general unified meaning can arise. The interpretation is, instead, highly individualistic.

Moreover, the Der Nister quests can cause in the reader an extreme feeling of discomfort, the feeling that, on the one hand, the stories do seek to generate some type of larger cohesive meaning. On the other hand, readers at the same time sense that they are not expected to fully understand the symbolic code. This results as well from Der Nister's conflation of Nahman's cosmic quest (which does support an interpretive code of mystical redemption) and the mercurial lack of a universal code of symbolism. The stories show the influence of Nahman's tales, yet rather than imparting Nahman's cabalistic meanings, the Der Nister stories contain quest symbols that seem elusive and cannot be used to construct any clear principle.

Perhaps Der Nister's quests are so unsettling for the reader because this conflation of mutually exclusive systems of interpretation leaves the reader without any clear "external referents" for interpreting the narrative. In Der Nister's tales, according to Roskies, "to live is to wander."[91] To *read* is also to wander. If we return to the idea of the quest as the realm of the transitive (using Todorov's equation of equilibrium and disequilibrium), for a writer such as Der Nister, whose interpretive system is based on the notion of the symbolic discord between external and internal referents, the quest is the ideal mode for expressing this disjunctive state.

For a writer interested in dislocation, disjunction, the in-between states, the quest is thus a good narrative for constructing spaces of "border realities."[92] Der Nister's use of genre can be seen as a manifestation of his personal philosophy and vice versa. Before the Soviet crackdown on the symbolist movement, the border state was a positive expression of the artistic temperament. After the crackdown the border state reflected the artist's precipitous loss of meaning.

Der Nister was using the same type of narrative framework as many modernist writers—the movement of the protagonist is matched by a narrative style that pushes the reader to construct an individualized, open interpretation (*Ulysses* is the most obvious example). Der Nister's narrative style of the wandering, displaced symbol is matched by the plot of the wandering, displaced subject. The indistinct meaning is embedded in the narrative style and vice versa. For Der Nister, whose aesthetic sensibility ran to multivalent symbols, his quest, like his symbolism, posits individualized interpretations. The quest narrative for Der Nister is in a large part a means to express not only a personal outlook but a narrative system of intransigence and dislocation. More than any of the second-generation writers that I consider here, the text of Der Nister's narratives destabilizes itself by playing with a number of generic formulations and then using them to show their opposite. In particular, in "A mayse mit a lets" the motion of the character in his quest is matched by the motion of the meaning; together they destabilize a cohesive reading.

"To the Mountain"

Der Nister's "Tsum barg" (To the mountain) was probably influenced by Nietzsche's *Thus Spake Zarathustra* (written between 1883 and 1892), in which the Persian philosopher Zarathustra is a mouthpiece for Nietzsche's philosophy of the Ubermensch, or superman.[93] Nietzsche had a strong influence on Russian symbolists. For instance, the major symbolist Andrei Bely wrote a 1903 poem about the mountain quest based on *Thus Spake Zarathustra*:

> The mountains are in bridal crowns.
> I am in ecstasy, I am young.
> Here on my mountains
> There is purifying cold . . .
> But here to me on my cliff
> a grey-haired hunchback has come clambering
> Brought me a present
> of pineapples from the underground
> greenhouses.[94]

Der Nister's "Tsum barg" is similar to this Bely poem. Der Nister describes the mountain as a purifying realm where one encounters strange and indecipherable characters and symbols.

In Nietzsche's original, Zarathustra leaves his hermitlike abode to spend ten solitary years on a mountain, at the end of which he decides to "descend into the deep" and wander the surrounding lands to be a prophet for the people, to whom he proclaims that he will teach the philosophy of "the superman."[95] What is particularly relevant for my analysis of "Tsum barg" is the section of *Zarathustra* entitled "The Wanderer" in which Zarathustra makes this proclamation:

> I am a wanderer and mountain-climber, said he to his heart, I love not the plains, and it seemeth I cannot long sit still.
>
> And whatever may still overtake me as fate and experience—a wandering will be therein, and a mountain-climbing: in the end one experienceth only oneself. . . .
>
> And one thing more do I know: I stand now before my last summit, and before that which hath been longest reserved for me. Ah, my hardest path must I ascend! Ah, I have begun my lonesomest wandering. . . .
>
> To learn to look away from oneself, is necessary in order to see many things:—this hardiness is needed by every mountain-climber.[96]

Nietzsche's allegory imparts the following themes: existential wandering is best done alone; the mountain is the symbol of the most difficult and most lonely obstacle; in order to "see many things" one must learn to "look away from oneself"; and, most important, the lesson of the search is that "in the end one experienceth only oneself."

In Der Nister's tale, we also have the story of a solitary male wanderer who learns these same lessons when, in the end, he discovers that one must look away in order to truly see one's self. Yet unlike Nietzsche's didactic and prophetic prose, which leads to a specific philosophical system of the Ubermensch, in Der Nister's narrative, which superficially shares the same plot and simple philosophy of the quest as a return to self, the state of dislocated wandering is the total state of being. While Nietzsche can eventually arrive at a summit of being, in Der Nister the end circles back to the beginning and there is no sequential movement of soul, spirit, or being, only a permanent state of flux. Where Nietzsche is goal directed (the development of the Ubermensch), Der Nister uses both a prose style (the multivalent symbol) and plot (the circular structure) to subvert and destabilize any linear progression. According to Robert Maguire and John Malmstad, Bely believed that Zarathustra erred by looking down from the mountain rather than continuing on a permanent circular path.[97] Whether Der Nister knew Bely's view of Zarathustra or not, Der Nister's story becomes the exemplar of circular return that Bely thought was lacking in Nietzsche's *Thus Spoke Zarathustra*.

"Tsum barg" is delivered in the first person, a voice that differs from the impersonal folk narrator of the Nahman and Peretz quest. Here, instead, we have an individual telling us his experiences. Yet Der Nister does not make explicit the identity of the narrator anywhere in the story; we learn only that he must undergo the wandering. He is a symbol of movement rather than a being with a history. Other characters will influence his movement, and this is the only way that he will be acted on and will act in the world. The narrator thus becomes a dislocated voice of action, without history, without psychology, either assisted in or deflected from his vague desire to "find a mountain." Within the tale the locales of stasis, or, more precisely, the forces of deflection from the narrator's movement to the mountain, are characters and symbols that the narrator must confront before regaining his momentum.

"Tsum barg" begins with the narrator describing a cozy domestic setting. (I am using a literal translation for this passage in an effort to impart Der Nister's incantatory prose style of repetitions and poetic inversions, which are not always logical.)

In yener nakht bin ikh in gevisn, groysn un vildn vald geven, bay der bobe in ir shtibele an oyrekh gezesn, un shtil un shvaygndik in eynem mit ir in ovnt un in shtilkayt oyf ir altn gevart.

In droysn iz a vint geven. Gedreyt un geton zikh hot in vald, epes far der tir un bay nakht far tir, un in shtibele hot a kanitsl gebrent, shvakh un tsugeshlogn oyf di vent ufgeshaynt, un shtil un umetik di Bobe un ir altkayt balaykhtn. (49)

(That night I was in a certain great and wild forest, with the grandmother in her cottage as an eating guest, and still and quiet together we sat in the evening and in the stillness of her old waiting.

(Outside it was windy. A whirling in the forest was before the door, and the night was against the closed door, and in the cottage a candle-stub burned, weak and affixed on the wind rising, and still and sad was the grandmother in her old age illuminated.)

The inversions, and bidirectional nature of the prose, like a wind blowing back and forth, matches the endless undirected wandering of the main character. This prose style is heavily mediated by the authorial hand, much as in *Thus Spoke Zarathustra*. However, where Nietzsche's prose mimics the King James Version of the Bible to make Zarathustra like an Old Testament prophet, in Der Nister the stylistics mimic wandering without a clear goal.

The reader gains a clue about who the narrator is when, upon getting into bed to rest, the grandmother, the Bobe, comes over and says, "Azoy yung, azoy yung un shoyn in geyers gegangen" (50). (So young, so young and already he wanders as a wanderer.) The Bobe then calls out the door to an "Elter" (Elder). After three calls the Elder arrives. He is the Wanderer's guide, complete with walking stick in hand. Moreover, he is a nature man with "bord un ponim funem vald" (51) (a beard and face from the forest wind). As the Elder stands on the threshold to the cottage, he tells the Bobe that he has brought a message from the wind that they must "set out for the mountain." When the Bobe asks who must set out, the Elder asks who is sleeping in her hut. The Bobe shows the Elder the sleeping youth, and the Elder responds, "This is him." The Bobe seems surprised that the chosen one would be so young and unproven, to which the Elder replies that he is worthy of this, and he will be tried.

When the Bobe asks what the Wanderer's first trial will be, the Elder gives an interesting answer that reflects Zarathustra's reasoning about his own journey. The Elder says, "Er vet visn ver er iz un visn az men pruvt im" (52). (He will know who he is and know he is being tested.) The Elder further states that the trial is terrible because "veyst er, hot men bay im dos heylike nisht visn tsugenumen" (52) (he [the Wanderer] will know [of the trials], but others will deprive him of his holy unknowing). The Wanderer's first trial will be to know himself and his role as the Wanderer (although others will not know what he is). Yet throughout the tale others await him, call him the Wanderer, and are aware of his quest.

Upon being roused from his bed, the narrator complacently agrees to go on his quest (he has passed the first trial of acceptance of his fate). As the Wanderer and the Elder prepare to depart, the Bobe asks how long the journey will last (the Elder replies, very long) and whether the Elder will lead him there. The Elder replies that "neyn, im dem veg visn" (53) (no, he knows the path himself). Yet the narrator still does not tell us the meaning of this journey. The pair go deeper and deeper into the forest. The geography that they are covering is devoid of history, politics, or any cultural specificity. It is clearly a reflection of the author's mind, rather than an attempt to render a specific external reality. The wandering takes on an eternal, structureless aspect, as in the following paradigmatic description of the journey: "Un fun yenem tog iz shoyn a tsayt gehat avekgegangen un ikh bin nokh alts in vald gegangen, fun ort tsu ort, fun vald in vaytern, keyn teg un vokhn nisht getseylt, khezhbn fun khadoshim farloyrn, vald oys un vald ayn, alts mer un mer, un tsu vald nokh keyn ek un tsu frayen keyn oysgang" (59). (And from then, time had passed and I was still moving on through the forest, from spot to spot, farther and farther, losing track of days, weeks, and months, moving here and there, farther and farther, through the endless forest, without any paths out.) The wandering is timeless, ahistorical, eternal, and cut off from real time or space. There are no signposts of intention; it is simply motion without respite.

The motion is curtailed by encounters with a variety of characters and symbols that present the Wanderer with an encoded text, a riddle or rhyme that in some way is meant to teach him something. While in each case the Wanderer asks what he is meant to learn, the meanings are left vague and just out of reach—much as they are in Nahman's quest, where the significance is often hard to specify. With Nahman, however, the reader knows that the decoding can be based upon a cabalistic system, while the meaning for Der Nister's internal panorama is as varied as the whims of the individual mind, a prime example of the symbolist at work. In Der Nister the obstacles are thus not spots for decoding the author's intent. Rather, he is decoding the whole notion of the coded text and overriding the literal interpretation of symbols with the force of narrative movement.

The characters whom the Wanderer encounters are aware that he is on a quest to reach a mountain. They do not discuss the reason for the quest, but each character does reassert the narrator's role as quest seeker: "Geyer, mir hobn gehert, s'iz tsu undz dergangen: du host zikh tsum barg gelozt, tsum altn barg, oyf grenets shteyt, fun undzer zayn un sod fun zayn . . . m'hert dayn nomen umetum, men zogt: du geyst oyf zikher . . . du fregst nisht nokh, du forsht nisht gor bay geyers shoyn" (75). (Wanderer, word has reached us: You had set out to the mountain, to the old mountain that stands at the border of our existence and the secret of our being. . . . Your name is heard everywhere, people say that you go with certainty. . . . You seek no direction, you do not question other travelers.) Upon being asked how he has gained the self-confidence to set out, the Wanderer gives an answer that offers the reader a clue to the larger meaning of the journey:

> Ikh hob zikh azoy getrakht: vayl alts, vos faranen, dos alts iz gegebn tsu mentsh far zayn breyre, far heyliker breyre, oykh eygener lebn un lebn on breyre, un ikh hob ayngeshtelt.
> —Un ver iz dayn orev?
> —Mayn malekh un mayn betukhes.
> —Un vos tut er dir dayn malekh?
> —Er hit mikh.
> —Fun vos?
> —Fun ale sfeykes un fun beyzn alem. (76)

> (I thought thus to myself: because of all that is available; all that is given to humankind for their choice—a holy choice—including one's life and life without choice, I had risked this.
> —And who is your protector?

—My angel and my self-confidence.
—And what does your angel do?
—He protects me.
—From what?
—From all doubts and all evils.)

The Wanderer thus asserts the following: (1) his ultimate answer to the question of what life will bring is hidden from him; (2) in the choice-filled reality, all the Wanderer has is his self-confidence to ward off doubt. Beyond that he knows nothing.

For the Wanderer his quest is a manifestation of the myriad, uncertain, illogical choices of life. There is no larger prooftext to the world. All is motion and movement with obstacles that are self- rather than extrareferential. The Wanderer is one who can face them confidently without recourse to a static code. Der Nister's landscape and the Wanderer exist in a godless realm, without larger meaning and without communal discourse. (However, the presence of an angel suggests that the quest may have a religious meaning.)[98] This reality has myriad choices and few guidelines. Der Nister seems to be suggesting that the deepest parts of the psyche resist static ideology and instead are so individual as to be atemporal and ahistorical.

Der Nister uses the goal-oriented structure while wiping meaning from it. The reader is reading the tale via the "pretransformation text" of the quest, which Der Nister seems to use as his model while drastically reshaping it by dropping the goal. To use the quest genre yet wipe out a meaningful goal impels the narrative into an expression of an individual's symbolic universe. It thus matches the modernist reorientation of the quest in which "one of the founding gestures of literary modernity has been the problematizing, if not the debunking, of the quest."[99]

The Wanderer reaches the mountain, rests on the side of it (like Zarathustra), and awaits the next occurrence in his journey. He soon encounters a skull that teaches him the lesson that we also find in Zarathustra—that one must look up from one's path to see the world and therein one's self. This notion changes the Wanderer's perspective, and as he continues on his path he now looks up and around more. Finally, toward the end of his journey, the Wanderer sees a man atop the mountain who is looking at him. Upon nearing, he sees on the horizon a "kleyn yishuv" (97) (small community). This is his first view of a community of any type. It is also a reality independent of him rather than yet another of the characters caught up in his journey.

Nearing the mountain, the Wanderer comes upon an ibex (98). The Wanderer asks the ibex what he awaits, to which the animal replies that the Elder has asked him to wait for the Wanderer (as the Elder has led all the other characters to him) in order to give him a document. Finally, it seems as though the reader will have something to explain what the quest means. The document is written in the following simple rhyme style: "Der geyer undz—er shteyt undz nisht, er geyt shoyn lang un vet ersht geyn, a sakh gezen un baygeven, er vet ersht zen . . . mir vartn im, getroyen im, un keseyder oyf im kukn—in vaytn dort, in vegn dort, oyf torbe un oyf rukn." (99-100). ("Our Wanderer—he doesn't understand us. He's already been going a long time, yet he'll go first. He's seen much and witnessed much, yet he will see it first. . . . We await him, trust him, and constantly look for him—in distant places, in roads, in sacks, and on backs.")

The document explains the role of the other characters—to patiently await the Wanderer—and restates the Wanderer's actions—to go and go, high and low. Yet again the significance of the quest is not explained. However, the key to comprehending it is given in the central sentence describing how the Elder has explained the going: "Nisht trakhtn zol der geyer zikh in geyen, er iz farlozt oyf veg aleyn, fun olem un farzen" (100). (While on his way, the walker should not contemplate his walking, he should rely on the distant and solitary road itself.) In other words, what matters, again, is not the meaning but the perspective, the journey rather than goal of the quest. In the end his purpose is not a destination but a way of being.

Unexpectedly, however, the narrative does not end with this meaningful discovery. The narrative continues, with the Wanderer saying how he suddenly heard a call of "Geyer, Geyer" and he opened his eyes to see: "Un az ikh hob zikh tsum kol un vi tsum volkn-mentsh oysgedreyt, hob di oygn geefnt, un gor derzen: shtil un in halber nakht bin bay der bobe nokh in vald-shtibele oyfn bankbetl gelegn, tsugeshlogn un nakhtish hot dos kanitsl dos shtibele baloykhtn . . . un azoy un shteyendik oyf mir mitn kop geshoklt, geshoklt un mikh badoyert: 'azoy yung, azoy yung, un shoyn in geyers gegangen'" (100). (And as I turned myself to the voice, turned to face the Cloud Man, I opened my eyes and fully saw: I was still with the grandmother in the half night in her forest cottage, lying on the bench-bed while a candle-stub burned weakly. . . . She was standing above me sorrowfully shaking her head, saying, "So young, so young, and already he is a Wanderer.")

The narrative has returned full circle to the opening. Typical of a quest, the search has brought a return to the home. Atypically, the final words start another quest. Thus this is not a circle, as in Nahman or Peretz, but an endless loop. On the second loop the Wanderer will set out with a clearer concept of how to approach the quest (as gained by the document that he read at the end of his first journey). Although he finally had caught a glimpse of an independent, exterior community while he was on the mountain, in the end he returns to the terrain of the self from which no roads lead out.

Perhaps the story is an allegory of the modern person who searches for meaning on the myriad paths of life and finds that ultimately all paths lead to the home from which one started. This interpretation reflects a neoromantic vision of the past as the material of the present search for meaning. As a symbolist reading, the mountain quest translates to a journey into the deepest parts of the psyche, where the obstacles encountered are symbolic pathways to the internal search. This refutes the type of answers that Nietzsche offers for questions and wanderings. The universal search for meaning is overlain by the individual grid of symbols that are impossible to interpret.

Der Nister repeats the endless circular quest of "Tsum barg" in his later tale, "A mayse mit a lets." In this story the path leads not over a high mountain with clear air but past bodies that are decaying in endless grotesque loops of intransitive movements.[100] Symbolism elevates the mountain path, but in the later story the path moves through shit and piss.

"A Tale of an Imp, of a Mouse, and of Der Nister Himself"

In 1929 Der Nister published *Fun mayne giter* (Of my estates), a collection of stories, some subtle, some explicit, that present his struggle with Yiddish writers' renunciation of symbolism as decadent.[101] Where "Tsum barg" exemplifies his former embrace of symbolism, the stories in *Fun mayne giter* generate a feeling of pessimism—broken meanings, grotesque couplings, and in general a world shattered in part by the breakdown of his belief in symbolism. Whereas in the symbolism of "Tsum barg" the obstacles on the quest are evocative of a psychological journey, here there is no psyche, merely an anarchic and decaying world. I would suggest that Der Nister's decision to denounce symbolism also meant that the Yiddish literary tradition of Nahman and Peretz that I described earlier was lost to him. Thus his decision to turn his back on symbolism was a double blow, affecting his creative arsenal for telling both universal and Jewish stories. If "Tsum barg" is about the existential search of the soul, in "A mayse mit a lets" the world is largely corporeal and soulless.[102]

The story is divided into two main sections. In the first the protagonist, Der Nister, and his donkey travel to a city of glass people who have no physical needs or desires. When the glass people see Der Nister's donkey urinate, they begin the process of becoming physical—the flesh from their belly buttons spreads out over their glass bodies. This physical process, however, does not end with the transformation from glass to flesh, for they quickly become fat, then so obese that the city becomes overtaken by their oozing flesh. In the end the obesity is a punishment as bad as their glassiness. In reaction to what has happened, the inhabitants stone the donkey to death and drive Der Nister out of the city.

In the second section Der Nister enters a city that is seemingly the opposite of the earlier one—the inhabitants are out-of-control consumers living a life of unstoppable Dionysian excess, and here again Der Nister is driven out of the city once he brings on the unstoppable reduction of flesh to hunger. In the end, destitute and hungry, Der Nister decides that he will head off to a distant land.

On first reading the narrative style of and use of extremely vulgar descriptions in "A mayse mit a lets," appear to be quite similar to Rabelais' *Gargantua and Pantagruel* (1532–64). Although Roskies calls "A mayse mit a lets" the "first X-Rated Yiddish fantasy," the constant use of grotesque images, from characters digging through donkey feces for kernels to farting to orgies, makes it part of a tradition in Western satiric literature that runs from Rabelais to Jonathan Swift (although it is not clear whether Der Nister was intentionally working in satire).[103] (We also saw this type of grotesque imagery in *Kitser masoes Binyomin hashlishi* in the descriptions of the refuse- and muck-filled towns that Benjamin and Senderl travel through.) In the writing of Rabelais, as in Der Nister's postsymbolist tales of 1929, the traditional structural hierarchy of people and things is flattened, making a new "place for human corporeality."[104] Where Rabelais was the model for literature of the corporeal, its later manifestations in the modern tale (as in Der Nister) resulted in "what we might call a narrative aesthetics of embodiment, where meaning and truth are made carnal."[105]

Although "A mayse mit a lets" seems to match the satiric narrative style of writers such as Rabelais, Rabelais in large part used satire to unify the writing and to impart a specific commentary on the world. Der Nister's departure from the Rabelaisian text is that in Rabelais the text is subversive and challenges the ascetic medieval worldview. Rabelais used a narrative composed of intersecting series, and a concomitant destructuring of the traditional hierarchy, to build a new world in which a more humanistic relationship to both the body and the world replaces the medieval outlook.[106] In Der Nister we have no such clear intent.

Instead, he flattens the "priestly" with a perspective devoid of philosophy.[107]

In other words, while Rabelais and Der Nister use similar narrative styles, they should be read differently. Where in Rabelais the flattened world is unified by a humanistic philosophy, in Der Nister we have the world spinning into the madness of a solipsistic vision unconnected to a communal philosophy. In Rabelais, as is in Pope, Voltaire, and Swift, satire, used as a challenge to traditional society, controls what would otherwise be a spin into madness. For instance, Swift sprinkles throughout *Gulliver's Travels* a series of clues that tie the narrative to his indictment of the political institutions of the time. Or, in Yiddish literature Dan Miron and Anita Norich have shown that Abramovitsh's *Kitser masoes Binyomin hashlishi* is a satiric rewriting of the Benjamin Disraeli story and a critique of Jewish stasis in a period of imperialist motion.[108]

However, in Der Nister, in contrast, the world is shattered into a grotesque series of intersecting narratives without any clear oppositional world of meaning to structure it. His story is of fragmentation and fracture rather than unity and reflects the fantastic narratives of Balzac and Poe in the nineteenth century, as described by Deborah A. Harter.[109] All these writers are breaking down the unified world of the realistic novel, which for Der Nister can be read as an artist's challenge to the increasingly repressive Soviet regime and the push for socialist realism. Der Nister is thus not only deflating the symbolist movement but challenging socialist realism by deconstructing the possibility of a cohesive world that can be described "realistically."

The Der Nister story also uses primitivism, a perspective revived by the Russian writer Boris Pilynak in 1915, which was important to Yiddish critics at the time and that stands in stark contrast to the symbolists' elevation of aesthetics. Primitivism, says Maguire, makes an "attempt to destroy beauty with nonsense, dissonance, ugliness, formlessness, or artlessness."[110] Here Der Nister is likely evoking an oppositional trend to counteract the earlier symbolic, aestheticized, and "purified" perspective of the artist as prophet. The primitivism is a debased state that stands in contrast to the elevated symbolism.

In "A mayse mit a lets" Der Nister is breaking down a world not only of things but of symbolism and putting in its place a primitivism that challenges order of any type. However, his primitivism is not elevated as earthy but debased and anarchic. Perhaps he is implying that without the freedom to choose his artistic outlook, be it symbolism, neoromanticism, or something else, the best response is anarchic, primitive disorder. Or he may be pessimistically rebutting the symbolists of his youth as ridiculous in a modern world without god and prophets. Another possibility is that Der Nister is pushing the modernist endeavor to its ultimate extreme. If "a major dynamic force behind modernist movements across Europe was a rejection of the positivistic mode of cognition that relied on the surface reality of empirical facts, subject to realistic representation," Irina Paperno writes, when the empirical world beyond the self disappears, as in "A mayse mit a lets," the world becomes a space of solipsistic lunacy.[111]

The story is built on a series of circular narratives that collide and therein serve as literary catalysts to their repetition. The narratives act like a Rabelaisian series in that how they work depends on when they are brought up.[112] However, although certain characters may appear again and again, the story does not contain the layers of meaning that one would expect in such a self-referential text. Instead, the characters remain for the most part flat, caught in their own repeating plots.

In Der Nister, the expansive body is a marker and measure of the world. It is not a symbol but a making of the world into a body. Both spirit and matter can, and do, become caught within spirals of out-of-control motion, which leads to similar extremes. Yet the vision of the endless cycle of unstoppable and out-of-control movement points as well to the narrative style, the self-referential structure of the tale, which is composed of a series of circular loops that are endless catalysts for one another. For instance, throughout the story Der Nister and others repeatedly become caught in the following series of actions: "Un der-nokh lakhn zikh gekratst, un bam kratsn, vi gezogt, gelakht, un nokhn lakhn geveynt, un nokhn veynen troyerik gevorn" (66).

(And afterward he laughs himself to a scratching and from scratching to laughing and from laughing to feeling great sadness.)

The description is of a series of intransitive actions, of self-focused movement, of verbs of action on self, not on others. These are self-referential narrative loops that offer no space for either the Other-as-character or the Other-as-discourse. In this reality, much like the oft-repeated series of intransitive actions that I have just cited, one action leads to another action, which leads to another action. There is no starting or stopping point, because there is no Other of any type on which to build structures of differentiation.

Moreover, the series of actions is basically nonsensical and often quite funny in a dark way.[113] The comedy of the nonsensical can be seen to represent Der Nister's self-satire of his earlier symbolist approach. The loss of footing, disorientation, and a search for a new style, be it primitivist or otherwise, mark out his transition from the artist as priest to the artist as a realist who is trying to present a world that he clearly sees in markedly darker terms than his youthful, idealistic symbolism.[114] Whether this work is a protest about the loss of his symbolism or an exploration of his loss of footing is unclear. Either way, the story shows a shift from the mountain to the gutter.

By making the protagonist Der Nister himself, the self-referentiality is complete. Not only does he, Der Nister, create the story but he is the story. Der Nister's panorama is that of the intransitive action, the constant self-referentiality, the endless narrative loop. Jewish travel becomes for him an endless march of the self into the self into the self. Yet unlike in symbolism, where the self can be evoked through the vague symbol, here the self is corporeal and primitive, accessibly grotesque, and utterly alone.

Conclusion

The road for modern Yiddish writers often led from the shtetl to the city. The city was a symbol of modernization, progress, and cosmopolitanism in contrast to the parochial Jewish shtetl. How the authors described the road to the city reflected their perspective on the forces of change and modernization that the city represented and whether it was positive or negative for the Jews. In the maskilic era the trajectory to the city was positive and represented the modernization and Europeanization of the Jews. This we see, for example, in Yisroel Aksenfeld's *Dos shterntikhl* (The headband) where Michel becomes worldly, educated, and modern through his experiences in Breslau. In contrast, the stories of Nahman of Bratslav turn the maskilic ideal city on its head. Here the city represents the false promise of money and commerce contrasted with the faith of the shtetl. While the city is the place to gain worldly knowledge, that knowledge often leads Jews to stray from their faith, as in "The Hakham and the Tam" (The wise man and the fool).[115] Whereas the road for the *maskilim* led from the shtetl to the city, Nahman's stories project the positive road as heading from the city to the shtetl.

Although Abramovitsh wrote *Kitser masoes Binyomin hashlishi* when he was still influenced by maskilic idealism, the city or large town as he represents it does not fulfill the promise of the *maskilim*. In his rendering the city is just a larger version of the shtetl, and its stagnation is problematized through a physical rendition of the refuse-filled mud that encompasses it. While all roads lead to the city, the city is a recycled, larger version of the shtetl. The road does not represent a trope of movement but a connective path between locales of stasis, some small (the shtetl) and some large (the city). Only gossip has the ability to travel and move, but, again, it does not effect real progress.

Peretz plays with the shtetl-city binary in "Dray khupes" by making the shtetl wholly positive and idyllic and the city wholly negative and destructive. Yet by using an ironic narrative structure, both representations are subverted and destabilized, rendering a challenge to the simplicity of the binary by showing that both the positive shtetl and negative city are mythic caricatures. The road in his rendition moves in both directions between the two extremes, while the work calls for them to move closer together.

For Der Nister in "A Mayse mit a lets," the city is a panorama of the community as it is being hit by unstoppable changes. The changes are corporeal and so physicalized (oozing bodies moving between starvation and obesity) that the spiritual realm is utterly negated. The city represents the forces of change that, when unbridled, lead to unstoppable, destructive movement. Although Der Nister probably was not writing a critique of the city-as-modernization, his story suggests that the city is a catalyst for a type of change that can drown a community.

The trajectory from the shtetl to the city was problematic for all the writers that I discussed in this chapter, because the forces of change represented by the road could be destructive for the Jewish community. By problematizing that road, these writers critiqued the effects of modernization. For Jewish modernists who wanted to escape the parochial shtetl, the city offered great promise. Yet each of these writers showed that the promise was not always fulfilled.

The Yiddish road tales also subverted another trajectory: the Galut trope in which the path eventually leads from Europe to Eretz Yisrael. In this trope wandering is a temporary state before eventual Jewish redemption and the return to Eretz Yisrael. In the Yiddish road tales, in contrast, all paths lead back to the starting point, and all routes are circular rather than linear, so even in *Kitser masoes Binyomin hashlishi,* in which the road eventually goes to Eretz Yisrael, the story itself is overshadowed by the framing narrative of *Don Quixote,* where the town is the start and eventual finish of the movement, and by Mendele's commentaries suggesting that little has changed.

Jewish travel on the road could take on a romantic or teleological form by being either travel for its own sake or goal oriented. Most stories that I have discussed shared aspects of both, where the search for something—the Lost Tribes, a mountain, a husband—was the excuse for undertaking a journey that would bring the characters out of the shtetl and into the broader world. The broader world, however, was clearly patently fictional in all the stories, from the way every character is tied to the Wanderer's movement in "Tsum barg" to the dual wonder-realistic landscapes of "Dray khupes." When the goal was Eretz Yisrael, however, anything was seemingly possible, and a parochial fool like Benjamin could become a great explorer.

For all these writers, the road was a terrain that could be reclaimed as a safe Jewish space by manipulating certain genres into patently fictional settings. By so doing, these writers appropriated "the road" into their fictional geographies and turned it into a symbol of a variety of notions, from the mystical system of Jewish restoration to the claustrophobic, solitary quest of the modern person to a representation of the breakdown of the shtetl and the advent of destructive urbanization. But for all the writers, while modernization offered great promise, it was also a destructive force that broke apart and shattered the world and word to produce the entrenched muddy stasis of Abramovitsh and the solipsistic, grotesque vision of Der Nister. The road for these writers, while it led out, also clearly let in the forces of destruction.

3

The Train

I never travel without my diary. One should always have something sensational to read in the train.

—Oscar Wilde

As the apocryphal story goes, when in the 1840s Tsar Nicholas I decided to develop the railroad in Russia, he placed his hand on a map and used the edge of his palm to trace the line that it would follow. However, the line inadvertently included the ridge of his thumb, and the ridge became part of the train system. The story is an unlikely one, but it underlines the tsarist nature of the Russian railroad. It would transport the gentry between St. Petersburg and Moscow, move soldiers to the front, and carry merchants around the country. Clearly, the last thing that the tsar had in mind was that the great Russian train system would become something that many Jewish writers regarded as Jewish rather than Russian.

The third-class train car was where Jews from the shtetls and cities of eastern Europe would typically become acquainted, conduct business, speak Yiddish, and talk about their families.[1] The car would be full of Jews fleeing violence, Jews starting their transatlantic passage to the United States, Jewish merchants, Jewish horse traders, and even Jewish horse thieves. In *Kim* Rudyard Kipling describes how the trains of the great British

Empire became Indian trains inhabited by Sikhs, Muslims, Sipoys, and Hindus, speaking their languages and making it *their* train as it chugged through the continent. Similarly, Russian Jews often made the Russian train into a Jewish train through their conversations, their fights, their gossip. Yiddish writers used this Judaization of the train car to make it an ideal setting for Jewish storytelling.

As Jonathan Crary has observed, "Modernization is a process by which capitalism uproots and makes mobile that which is grounded."[2] Because the railroads generated unprecedented economic and social mobility, and by so doing broke down many premodern socioeconomic constructs, railroads became emblematic of modernization. Thus Yiddish writers found a natural binary that they could use in their works, of the railroad as a symbol of mobile modernization and the shtetl as a symbol of premodern stasis. Opinions varied, however, about whether the change wrought by the trains was good or bad for the Jews.

In this chapter I consider three tales of train travel spanning nineteen years: Sholem Abramovitsh's 1890 "Shem un Yefes in a vogn" (Shem and Japheth on a train), Sholem Aleichem's 1911 *Di ayznban-geshikhtes* (The railroad stories, written between 1902 and 1911), and David Bergelson's 1909 novella, *Arum vokzal* (At the depot). My analysis contrasts these stories and examines them against European literary portrayals of train travel to demonstrate how Jewish writers used the motif of the train to problematize modernization and urbanization. As I show, Yiddish literature portrays the train as a vessel that brings the tides of change into and out of the shtetl.

In 1865 the popular Yiddish poet and songwriter Elyokum Zunser (1836–1913), better known as the Badkhn, or Jester, published a poem entitled "Der ayznban" (The railroad).[3] The poem was a typical maskilic piece, highly idealistic about the new railroad system of Russia. It explained to the Jews that the new invention would modernize their lives. All the aspects of the train that many Jews undoubtedly found frightening became, in the poem, positive symbols of the "new age." However, Zunser wrote "Der ayznban" when the train was a new form of transportation in

Russia (train travel came to Russia several decades after it came to western Europe).[4] By the time of Zunser's second railroad poem, "Lid fun ayznban" (Railroad poem), a mere ten years later, the train was no longer a novelty; for Zunser it was now a negative symbol of bureaucracy and class stratification.

"Lid fun ayznban" humorously depicts the negatives of train travel in a step-by-step breakdown of the roles of each train official, from the director to the mechanic to the telegrapher. All the officials are portrayed ironically, as gods deciding the fate of the masses of poor Jews under their jurisdiction, with the ultimate arbitrator, or God, as Zunser calls him, the train director.

Zunser's critique of train travel is unusual because its focus is none of the aspects usually associated with the new mode of transport: its frightening speed, massiveness, or ability to carry numerous passengers. Instead, this ballad portrays the train as a force that creates unfair and discriminatory class divisions and a space within which train bureaucrats usurp the free will of the passengers:

> Di konduktorn bakukn di biletn
> Un tsezetsn di pasezhirer yedern in zayn klas,
> Vemen in erstn—mit divanen gebetn,
> Un vemen in dritn—vu eng un vu nas. (lines 17-20)

> (The conductors examine the tickets,
> And seat every passenger in their class,
> Those in first—with comfy recliners,
> And those in third—so crowded and damp.)[5]

Zunser's first railroad poem was optimistic that the train would be a democratic, positive force that would literally transport the Jews into the modern world. The later poem shows that instead of a being a democratizing force, train travel, unlike earlier modes of transportation, stratified the classes and discriminated against the poor (seen here as Jews). As Nicholas Faith has written: "The class structure of the trains themselves showed the railways as social reflectors, rather than innovators."[6]

The rapid development of railway systems across Europe in the mid-nineteenth century was an event unprecedented in history. The railway system, by its sheer size and the effect that it had on the development of capitalism and industrialization, marked a "revolutionary transformation." More important for this study is that the train "introduced the notion of a gigantic, nationwide, complex and exact interlocking routine."[7] The railways were a vast, impersonal, mechanized system that placed the passengers under the jurisdiction of officials and created new centralized, bureaucratic spaces. For Yiddish writers at the turn of the century the train showed that modernization brought the loss of individual freedoms, because many Russian Jews equated bureaucracy with arbitrary anti-Jewish edicts.

Yiddish stories such as Sholem Abramovitsh's "Shem un Yefes in a vogn" expressed the notion that the train was like a prison because it positioned Jews in dangerous "official" spaces. The train was thus perceived to be an oppressive invention because it extended bureaucracy into the space of travel. Now, instead of dealing with officials only at border crossings or at entrances to and exits from cities and towns, they accompanied travelers for every step of their trip. Nevertheless, the writers made the train car into a Jewish space as much as they could, considering the bureaucratized arena that it represented. However, at the same time attempts to create a Jewish space were impeded by the regular interruption of train officials and by the constant sight from the train window of lands inhospitable to Jews.

For turn-of-the-century eastern European Jews, who had experienced waves of pogroms, the train was a reminder of their relative lack of safety in public spaces. On a train Jewish passengers had to constantly deal with officials, and if any problems arose, they had no real means of escape. The train heralded Jewish alienation from the relatively safer space of the closed shtetl. Yiddish literature between 1870 and the 1930s thus challenged the widespread notion that the railroad was a positive development. Whereas in England, for instance, the railroad was generally viewed as an invention that would bring beneficial changes, such as making travel and vacations possible for the middle and lower classes, Yiddish literature often portrayed the train negatively.[8]

Russian literature of the second half of the nineteenth century also made the railroad a central theme (particularly after the Moscow–St. Petersburg line opened in 1851).[9] For example, in Tolstoy's *Anna Karenina* (1873–76) the train represents the breakdown of the agriculture-based economy. The central character, Levin, argues that the railways "produced an exaggerated centralization in the cities, a growth of luxury, and the consequent development of new industries, and the credit system with its concomitant Stock Exchange speculation, all to the detriment of agriculture."[10] Tolstoy symbolized the negatives of train travel in the character of Anna Karenina. Her adulterous affair is sparked by an encounter on a train, and she commits suicide on its tracks. Anna Karenina also represents a modern pace, expressed in her intense sexuality, that is destructive to traditional life. However, Tolstoy critiqued the train system from the perspective of the landed gentry, who saw industrialization as the beginning of the end of their era of dominance. Anton Chekhov's *The Cherry Orchard* (1903) offers a similar view of the train, which its characters constantly mention as heralding the end of the era of the landed gentry. (However, Chekhov probably viewed the demise of the landed gentry as much less problematic than Tolstoy did.)

Thus the train caused a split between progressive Russians, who saw it as representing positive aspects of "collective" movement, and those who were more conservative and did not want the change that the train symbolized.[11] Overall, in Russia "the vast majority of literary works of the second half of the nineteenth century—including works like Dostoevskii's *Idiot* and Tolstoi's *Anna Karenina*—used the railroad as a symbol, harbinger, or backdrop for death, destruction, disaster, immorality or evil, often implicitly linking the new machine with the devil and even the anti-Christ."[12] In western Europe, in contrast, where railways arrived earlier and social stratifications were different from the peasant-gentry class system of tsarist Russia, the trains were generally seen as a positive, democratic development. Nowhere in European literature did trains represent a means of transportation that was particularly problematic for the poor, yet that is how Yiddish writers often regarded them. Both Yiddish and Russian writers would make the train a central motif, but their critique of the train was very different. Where Russian writers saw the train as a harbinger of the breakdown of a conservative system of values, Yiddish writers saw the train as promoting class stratification and as especially dangerous for Jews.

The Yiddish narratives that I consider in this chapter portray the shift from the "closed" shtetl to the "open" train with varying degrees of optimism. In Abramovitsh's "Shem un Yefes in a vogn" (1890) the narrator, Mendele, attempts to transform train travel into a positive experience by Judaizing the train ride. However, by the time of Sholem Aleichem's *Di ayznban-geshikhtes* (1902–1911), the train car is a symbol of the breakdown of community. In Bergelson's *Arum vokzal* (1909) the setting has shifted from the mobile train to the static station, and the shtetl has all but disappeared. In each of these stories the demarcation between Jewish and non-Jewish forms of train travel is clear. Jewish train travel is marked by the bureaucratic, and thus negative, anticommunal processes of modernization, whereas non-Jewish train travel is a pleasurable experience, because Christians do not find official spaces to be dangerous in the same way that Jews do.

Yet although Christian train officials occasionally intruded, the little world of the train was for the most part isolated from the outside landscape and the other people inhabiting it. In these train stories real life and the real problems of Jewish oppression are examined much more than they were in road or ship tales. Ship travel could hold the real world at bay to some extent because the sea was an "international landscape," whereas the train moved over national spaces.

In two of the works the train is the mode of transportation for fleeing Jews ("Shem un Yefes in a vogn" and *Di ayznban-geshikhtes*). They use the train because it is inexpensive, fast, and can hold a large number of passengers. In none of the stories does the train become the positive model of travel-as-holiday, as in countries such as England.[13] The purpose of train travel was, instead, generally utilitarian and served some greater need (escape, business); the journey itself was not important, pleasurable, or a form of "good travel," as James Clifford puts it. The train was a means of transportation that was like a traveling minicommunity, moving over lands from which the passengers were cut off. As Roger Green writes, "When the train carries passengers, it carries them doing things: eating, sleeping, reading, writing, thinking, gazing, talking, walking, standing, sitting, lying down, making love, murdering, dying; practicing these and other pursuits while passing through, by day or at night, industrial cities or deserted landscapes with which they have no connection whatsoever."[14] Yiddish writers conceptualized the train as a minicommunity of Jews. Jewish travelers, such as the train passengers, lived their lives, and underwent considerable hardship, while passing over a terrain from which they were cut off. This Jewish community was both positive, as in "Shem un Yefes in a vogn," and negative, as in *Di ayznban-geshikhtes*.

The train, a symbol of modernization and the impersonal, anti-Jewish bureaucracy associated with it, became a negative trope of the breakdown of Jewish communal life: pogroms, exile, loss of meaning, alienation. In general, the train marked the path away from the Jewish community and toward the anonymous, meaningless, and arbitrarily oppressive rhythms of modern life.

"Shem un Yefes in a vogn"

In Abramovitsh's short story Mendele takes his first train ride and initially finds it an unnatural and frightening experience.[15] Mendele prefers premodern forms of transportation, such as the coach and buggy, and is extremely uncomfortable on this new contraption. For him the train is a symbol of modernization, urbanization, and industrialization: negative forces that cause individuals to be disconnected from the Jewish community and their spirituality.[16]

In the opening passage of "Shem un Yefes in a vogn" Abramovitsh weaves two linguistic threads into his description of a bustling train station. These linguistic threads work against the literal description. The first thread relies on intertextual resonances with the Bible, and the second is the poetic use of language as the merger of sound and meaning. Both models, working together, impart the total schism between exilic, or Jewish, and bourgeois, or Christian, constructs of travel.

Unlike third-class travel, which Abramovitsh symbolically ties to exile, first class is often associated with a bourgeois realm in which travel is a form of tourism. Bourgeois travel does not have the mythic undercurrents of exile. As Caren Kaplan shows in *Questions of Travel,* the paradigms of exilic travel and (first-class) tourism travel contrast sharply: "The commonsense definitions of exile and tourism suggest that they occupy opposite poles in the modern experience of displacement: Exile implies coercion; tourism celebrates choice. Exile connotes the estrangement of the individual from an original community; tourism claims community on a global scale."[17] Where the third-class experience is filled with the overwhelming tension of displacement in the global sense, the first-class experience is pleasant, because it is tourism and "tourism celebrates choice." Mendele's main reaction to train travel is that it crushes his free will. Mendele's personal experience in the opening paragraphs is a reflection of the larger paradigm of exile as estrangement.

Abramovitsh's poetic use of language emphasizes the schism between the poor Jew and the upper-class Christian, as imparted both in the overt description and the intertextual resonances. The poetic use of the Yiddish in the opening paragraph conveys the intense chaos of the train station in the moments after the train has arrived and passengers are battling to find a seat.[18] The search for a place is the overriding concern of the moment. To impart this Abramovitsh packs the opening paragraph with a series of words that all have the same suffix, in order to stress the frantic nature of the moment and the repetitive mechanical sounds of a chugging train: "S'iz a loyfenish, a shrayenish, a shtupenish, an ontretenish oyf fis, a shtoysenish in rukn." (There is a running, a yelling, a squeezing, a stepping on feet, a pushing and shoving.)[19]

The frantic search reaches a crescendo in the final stanza of the description: "a kleternish oyf ale fir, a drapen zikh oyf di glaykhe treplekh vogns fun drite klas, aynshtelndik zikh dos lebn, kedey tsu farkhapn dort erter batsaytns" (3). (A climbing on all fours, a scramble up the stairs of the third-class wagon, gambling with your life in order to grab a spot in time.) The word *kedey* (in order to) is the poetic break, both in sound and meaning, stressing that the opening paragraph climaxes in the search for a seat. This poetic use of language matches the search for a literal and figurative "place" (even if just for a train ride).

The second paragraph starts with "un ikh" (and I), which is followed by "Mendele Moykher Sforim," the narrator's full name. Mendele is part of this chaotic reality. The poetic use of language emphasizes his merging with the bustle. In the first paragraph Abramovitsh conveys the frantic activity by using a series of words with the same ending and a buildup of short sentences; here he uses the constant repetition of the accented word *mikh* to convey the frenetic scene that Mendele has become part of: "Un ikh, Mendele Moykher-Sforim, balodn mit khfeytsim . . . un yog mikh un kni mikh un buk mikh un klamer in eynem take mit ak-heynu bney-Yisroel" (3). (And I, Mendele the Bookseller, bur-dened with goods . . . hurry myself, knee myself, bow myself, and hold on for dear life together with my brethren, the children of Is-rael.) The crescendo of choppiness breaks with the unaccented words *in eynem,* leading to the ironic assertion that he is "in eynem take mit akheynu bney-Yisroel" (together with our breth-ren, the children of Israel). Mendele is now fully a part of the frantic crowd of Jews, and his language matches this reality.

The paragraph ends with Mendele's description of how first-class passengers are proceeding, and the sound of Yiddish again matches the mood of the passage: "Ot denstmol grod shpatsirn zikh yene pasazhirn fun di umes-hooylem gants ruik ahin-aher farbay dem tsug, farleygendik di hent ahinter, un ersht nokhn dritn klung geyen zey zikh arayn dafke gelasn" (4). (All this while, the gentile passengers are strolling up and down the hallway in front of the station with their luggage and waiting until the bell rings for a second or even a third time, when they will mount the train at leisure, and each proceed to his appointed place [123].) The poetic use of language punctuates the reality that he is now describing. The whole sound is even, level, and fluid. It can be seen as expressing the notion of bourgeois travel as a positive experience, implying that Jewish travel is essentially negative. The calm, fluid language matches the pace of the bourgeois first class, whereas the choppy, repetitive language matches the image of the third-class Jews frantically searching for a place.

Upon taking his seat in the cramped car, Mendele is so overwhelmed by the experience, and so hemmed in by luggage, that he is unable to move at all and instead sits there fearfully "shvitsing" (sweating). The experience of train travel is terrifying and "unnatural." As Faith has pointed out, the feeling of unnaturalness that the train engenders, as opposed to the "natural" carriage, was a common reaction of first-time passengers because the "perceptual and temporal dislocations of railroad travel" caused them to feel a profound loss of footing.[20] This is manifested in Mendele's extreme discomfort and his need to find some meaning in the uncertainty.

He establishes equilibrium by linking his first train ride to the larger Jewish story of Galut. The language that Abramovitsh uses to convey the experience resonates intertextually with the corpus of Jewish narratives of exile. Intertextual discourse requires readers who understand the symbolic and literary meanings resonating below the surface of the text. From the fractured, anonymous modern world symbolized by the train, Abramovitsh builds a community of readers who understand the tale's Jewish meaning.

Mendele quickly realizes that his negative feelings are not the result of a change in him but in his mode of transportation: "Nor dos bageyn zikh fun dem konduktor mit di pasazhirn, di oyffirung fun di pasazhirn eyner mit dem tsveytn, un dos agmesnefesh, vos ikh hob ayngenumen in der kurtser tsayt, hobn mir gegebn tsu farshteyn, az di enderung iz nisht kholile, in mir zelbst, in mayn natur, vos den? Der art forn hot zikh umgebitn" (5). (But the treatment the railway officials accord to the passengers, and the passengers to one another, together with the experiences I have just undergone, combine to persuade me that the change is not in my own disposition, but in this strange mode of travel [124].)

According to Mendele, although the premodern coach is filled with everyone "ayngeprest vi hering in a fas" (packed together like herring), any discomfort is mitigated by not losing one's free will. No matter how crowded it is, "men geyt tsu fus, di gantse erd iz far undz fray" (5).[21] (They could always get out and take a walk, there was nothing to stop them and they had the world at their feet [124].) Whereas passengers in a carriage can exercise free will, train passengers are like prisoners: "Ikh fil mikh epes vi in tfise, nisht tsu torn aroysraysn zikh funem engenish fray afile oyf a rege. Un dos eygene take iz oykh mitn shvitsn. Es iz nisht glaykh, az men shvitst mitn gutn viln tsi az men shvitst, vayl men muz shvitsn" (5–6). (I feel like a prisoner, not allowed to rip myself free from the packed crowd for even a moment. And that, of course, is why this perspiring is so unpleasant: Sweating freely is not the same as being forced to sweat.)[22]

For Mendele two factors cause the lack of free will on the train: Train passengers cannot leave the train to take a stroll, and passengers are always under the jurisdiction of train officials, who are like prison wardens. Mendele is responding viscerally to the processes of mechanization: The speed and ordered stops take him out of human control and into arbitrary and fixed mechanization. As in Zunser's poem "Lid fun ayznban," the train brings an increase in centralized bureaucracy, which forces the passengers into the hands of officials—anonymous automatons who steal free choice and are especially dangerous for Jewish travelers.

Mendele's other reason for disliking the train is that it is un-natural. In contrast, in a carriage life moves slowly and at pace with nature: "Men fort zikh pamelekh, pamelekh, nisht geaylt—vayhi erev vayhi boker, un es vert ovnt un es vert morgn—yom ekhod, eyn tog, tsvey tog, dray tog, i. i. vi es iz genug tsayt tsu kukn zikh, tsu batrakhtn alsding oyfn veg. Der himl iz vi a bloyer forhang oysgeshpreyt iber di kep, felder vi sheyne panorames farnemen di oygn mit tvues un kraytekhtser alerley" (6). (Time flows on for them, evening and morning, one day . . . a second day . . . a third. . . . There is world enough and time to meditate on all things, to satisfy every desire in the course of their travels. The sky is a tent over their heads, the earth spreads its bounty before them, they watch the glorious pageant of God's creation, they rejoice in its variety [124].) Mendele's ironic use of the creation myth ties the coach colony to a holistic framework in which time is natural and everything has its place.

For Mendele the speed of the train makes it dangerous and disconnects the passengers from the real world. As Wolfgang Schivelbusch has pointed out, this was a common perception of early train passengers, who often perceived the speed of the train as a manifestation of its being totally disconnected from "real time" and the "real natural world" that one experiences in a carriage.[23] On a train passengers lose their connection not only to the natural world but also to natural time.

Whereas the coach is like an homogeneous family or the closed social units of the premodern world, the train is like a heterogeneous city, with myriad class divisions and class hatreds. Whereas the coach moves in natural time, the train moves in city time, which is frantic, compartmentalized, and disconnected from the natural world: "Men flit, men fort oys a velt, nisht rekht ontsukukn di sheyne natur, un nisht tsu visn di erter, vu men iz flink durkhgeforn, mit altsding vos iz dort" (6). (Such passengers may traverse the whole world without regard to the grandeur of nature, the beauty of mountains and plains, [and all that is out there] [124].) The train is thus a symbol of the breakdown of the unified natural world into fractured parts of the industrial machine. The machine is anonymous and inhuman. It lacks familial, natural, and spiritual ties.

"Shem un Yefes in a vogn" chronicles the search to find a unified system of meaning in the atomization and meaninglessness of modern life as represented by the train. The title of the story suggests this, by using the word *vogn* (wagon or carriage) rather than *ayznban* (railroad). In the course of the tale Mendele's interpretation of the situation transforms the negative train into the positive carriage.

The train whistle blows, and the description shifts from Mendele's ruminations on the unnaturalness of the train to his immediate surroundings. The minute the train starts moving, the "groyse shtot" (large city) of anonymous disconnected strangers becomes a cohesive community of Jews who interact with one another as if they were all members of an extended family.

In the midst of the bustle, Mendele begins to examine the family that is sharing his train car, and he is at first disappointed to find himself with such a strange group. However, after he notices their dire poverty, his disappointment shifts to compassion. Mendele finds himself intrigued by the sad family and manages to get various members to tell their story. Everything about them points to a larger symbolic meaning, from their names (the father is Reb Moshe; his son is Yankele, or Jacob) to their eternally sad countenances. After the conductor takes their tickets—and by so doing keeps the official, anonymous world of the Russian bureaucrat out of their immediate vicinity—Mendele asks the father to tell his story. However, Reb Moshe's tendency is to deliver his tale in narrative spurts. After Mendele implores him to tell it as a cohesive whole, the father begins to deliver a coherent narrative. This marks a shift from a discordant voice (exemplifying the pandemonium of Mendele's first train ride) to a flowing, unified, narrative that matches Mendele's increased comfort once he finds a larger Jewish meaning in the train ride.

At the start of Reb Moshe's monologue Mendele acts like a comically isolated premodern character, because he does not understand Reb Moshe's references to how Bismarck's edicts have recently brought on more hard times for the Jews. Mendele does, however, understand the religious intertextualities: Reb Moshe likens the new exile to Bismarck's expelling "Shem's kinder, nisht keyn geborn daytshn" (15) (the sons of Shem who were not of German nationality [128]). Reb Moshe's speech is peppered with numerous Jewish references. So when Mendele misses the present-day political commentaries, he nevertheless catches the Jewish meaning.

Reb Moshe's story about how his family has been kicked out of Prussia, along with all Polish nationals and Jews, "profoundly affects" Mendele. For him the story symbolizes the Jewish exile, or Galut, and the family members are different aspects of it. The father represents passive acceptance of the exile, and the infant son symbolizes the lachrymose dirge of the Galut.

As the trip gets under way, the ticket taker completes his rounds, and, as usual, a number of passengers crawl out from under the seats. Typically, the hidden passengers would be poor Jews, but this time a strange figure emerges from beneath the cluttered bench: a Pole. This is probably Mendele's first encounter with a Pole, as opposed to the Ukrainian peasants of his own region.[24] The Pole is a fallen member of a class of artisans; he wears "alte farlatete hoyzn, in a poylishe poyerish svite mit meshene heklekh, farshpilet bizn halz" (10) (ragged trousers and a Polish cape that fastened with brass hooks across the chest [126]). Mendele is intrigued, not only because it is a Pole traveling with a clearly traditional Jewish family but also because the family greets him so warmly. Mendele sits back and finally lets Reb Moshe tell his tale with little interruption. The place in which Mendele had been so uncomfortable has now become a locale for conversing and making personal connections.

Reb Moshe explains to the puzzled Mendele that the Pole with the comically long name is in fact an adopted member of his family whom they have renamed Japheth. The intertextual reality becomes even more deeply symbolic as Reb Moshe and the Pole become Shem and Japheth. Their story is a retelling of a midrashic tale about "Noah's two sons, Shem and Japheth, who represented the future division of the world into Jews and gentiles. The rabbis envisioned the two sitting together under the same tent, studying Torah," according to David Roskies.[25]

As in the original tale, the story of Reb Moshe and the Pole is of two men dealing with life "after the flood"—in this case the flood is Bismarck's expulsions. Although before "the flood" the Pole abused Reb Moshe for being a Jew, after the expulsion they became like brothers. Reb Moshe rescued the Pole and adopted him into the family. His family taught the Pole the Torah of exile: how to live with dignity as a displaced, impoverished person. It is a "Torah" that the Jews have mastered. The reconciliation of the archetypal hatred between a Christian and a Jew comes about because their common exile breaks down the hierarchy of aggression and flips the traditionally powerful Christian into a disempowered (Jewish) exile. Through their shared experience the Jew and the Pole become Shem and Japheth in the tent, studying the Torah of survival.

The Jewish exile has, however, left a positive mark on the Jews: "Ot der goles hot zey gemakht andersh fun ale felker, mit di eygn-shaftn, mit di feyikkaytn zeyere, un hot zey gegebn a bazunder forme in zeyer tsdoke gebn un in zeyer tsdoke nemen" (33). (It is exile that has given them special characteristics that mark them off from all the other peoples, has taught them special contrivances to gain a living, and has set a special stamp upon their charity, too, from the point of view of both giver and receiver [135].) The exile has taught the Jew to be both resilient and charitable. As a young man, the Pole had been abusive, but by getting to know this Jewish family, he has become a kind, gentle friend.

Mendele transfers the story of the family from the immediate historical reality to its larger religious significance as the Galut. This is a shift to symbolic and mythic discourse. By turning their experience into the larger Jewish Galut, he gives a larger significance and meaning to the mundane, yet terrible, reality. Moreover, by feeling compassion toward this family, Mendele establishes communal ties, thus transforming the anonymous train car into the familial carriage. At the moment that the family in the train car becomes symbolic, the train car stops being a disconnected unnatural force of modernization that seizes control of the passengers, who in turn submit their free will to it. As the family becomes a symbolic entity, the train becomes a part of the Galut.

Mendele has claimed the train within his symbolic system (which is the Jewish system) and made it part of a larger framework of greater meanings. By Judaizing the train, Mendele is able to end the story on an optimistic note. Mendele declares: "Es zol zayn der viln fun far dir Got, mayn Got, es zol nokh zayn fil, fil talmidim azelke—vet zayn Shem mit Yefesn brider, sholem oyf der velt, un fridn oyf kol Yisroel, omeyn!" (36). ("[If it is your will God, my God,] Grant us but a few more such disciples—and Shem and Japheth will be brothers—and peace will come to Israel. [Amen!]" [136]) This is not to say that the horror of the current exile is overlooked or downplayed. Rather, the story suggests hope in community, even during extremely hard times.

Moreover, although Abramovitsh wrote the story after the pogroms of the 1880s put an end to the maskilic era, the optimistic
belief in Jewish-Christian relations is a throwback to maskilic
idealism. The difference from a maskilic outlook is, however, that
rather than the Christians showing the Jews the way, now it is the
Jews showing the Christians the true path by serving as a "light
among the nations."

"Shem un Yefes in a vogn" describes the junction of the premodern and modern, with Mendele as the former and the train as
the latter. Yet by the end of the tale the train has been appropriated into the sphere of the premodern by the symbolic and mythic
"reading" of the whole experience, thus transforming expulsion
into exile. This appropriation is possible because the train experience is still novel and not yet a permanent part of the cultural
landscape.

The train, which at first had been for Mendele profoundly uncomfortable, becomes something he has mastered. This has occurred, in part, through Reb Moshe's teaching Mendele how to
put a symbolic reading on the train and to see it as part of the Jewish exile. Mendele has also come to understand that the train is a
place of contact with the broader world and is thus a compartment for learning. In the new age of technology sacred tomes are
not the only texts about how to live. The train enables new contacts with people, both Jews and non-Jews, that serve as learning
experiences. The train has made this possible by putting Mendele
in a small compartment with strangers whom he would never
have encountered in his day-to-day life. Through his encounter
with "Shem and Japheth" he has learned about political anti-
Semitism and how to master the new times by sanctifying them
within specifically Jewish readings of the event.

The Railroad Stories

Sholem Aleichem's *Di ayznban-geshikhtes* is a collection of tales
by a self-described traveling salesman who tells of his encounters
with the other passengers in a third-class train car.[26] The stories

are important within both Sholem Aleichem's corpus and the development of Yiddish literature for the groundbreaking way in which they critique Jewish communal life at the turn of the century.

At a time of profound personal dislocation for the author and the Jews he was describing, the railroad car became a setting for telling stories.[27] The salesman-narrator seeks to make the stories that he hears in the car into *peklekh* (sob stories) that he can sell, whereas the collection as a whole reflects Sholem Aleichem's mature and dark vision after his own exile. The reader is put in the uncomfortable position of being both entertained by the tragic tales, much like the other passengers in the train car, and feeling compassion toward the characters.

A train would seem to be the ideal locale for storytelling: a group setting, disconnected from a grounded location, and representing the archetypal Jewish community. Yet the train is also a symbol of the encroachment of the machine on rural spaces. It is thus a space in which one can enact stories that reflect the ascendancy of industry and the concomitant breakdown of the rural, enclosed, isolated shtetl. The path of the train matches the decline of the shtetl and the erosion of the ideal Jewish community. Rather than a settled, entrenched shtetl (so satirized in Abramovitsh's *Kitser masoes Binyomin hashlishi*) as the backdrop for the tales, we have the dislocated moving space of the train. The stories told to the salesman thus reflect the hard times associated with urbanization and the decline of the shtetl.

The salesman-narrator conceives of the stories that he has collected as his "mayse soykher" (story merchandise). The wrenching stories are not only entertainment but also something to exploit by turning them into a type of goods that he will later sell. He reflects a notion of literature as merchandise that is bought and sold. In the era that Sholem Aleichem is describing, people give little freely, and individual needs often override communal ones. Help is given in exchange for goods; one listens to another Jew's stories to be entertained rather than to be empathetic. *Di ayznban-geshikhtes* thus marks the end of Sholem Aleichem's use of the idealized communal discourse of the "Kasrilevke" genre or shtetl tales, and the ascendancy of the ever-duplicitous individual voice of the salesman. Although the passengers telling the stories seek out a community of listeners who will sympathize with and support them, many other passengers listen to the tales as brief, exciting respites from the boredom of the trip—in contrast to the real compassion in "Shem un Yefes in a vogn" when Mendele feels so deeply for the poor family's suffering.

The overpacked train car increases the opportunities to be entertained and becomes the reason why the salesman suggests that the best form of train travel is in the third-class car, not first class, where only bourgeois silence reigns.[28] Whereas the "bourgeois space" is segregated and polite, the third class, the locale of the masses, offers "continuous communication."[29]

In the final section of the collection, "Third Class," the salesman-narrator recounts a few other reasons why the third-class cars are preferable: Although they are loud and crowded, they are also friendlier and a good place to conduct business. And if someone needs something, the others can provide it. However, the assistance of the other Jewish travelers is not based on communal friendship and the free giving of help but on the barter system (which, it seems, is the central type of business in this Jewish space). The interactions with strangers are motivated by a mutual desire to exchange something, unlike in first class, where it is assumed the talk will instead be conversational. Moreover, many stories in *Di ayznban-geshikhtes* are about the oppressive nature of public discourse, be it bureaucratic or otherwise, and how removed the communication of the period is from communal storytelling found, for instance, in the "Kasrilevke" stories.

In the third-class car one can gain valuable advice and folk cures from other travelers. However, this positive notion is subverted when the salesman recounts how he nearly died after using one of the folk cures that another passenger told him about. At the very least, riding in the third-class car provides access to information from locals on where to stay in their towns. But, again, this also has its dark side, because those who offer to help may be thieves.

At first reading, the folksy tone of the salesman seduces the reader into believing that traditional Jewish travelers can feel at home only in third class, whereas only self-hating assimilated Jews could like the first- and second-class cars. Upon closer reading it is clear that each positive aspect of the third class is undermined by a negative: This is not a home but a business setting where every assistance is rendered in exchange for something else; information offered may not be good information but dangerous advice; and the car may not offer safety but the constant possibility of being robbed. There is no community in the positive sense of mutual support. The Jewish community has become a community only in the negative sense of the word. To be sure, the third-class car may be entertaining, but the narrative suggests that the price is dear: So many stories are fraught with profound suffering that only a sadist, or someone seeking to use the stories in some way, could "enjoy" them. Thus we have the salesman-narrator, who wants to sell the stories as a form of entertainment for a modern readership rather than accept them as expressions of the community's lives, anguish, hopes, and dreams.

Di ayznban-geshikhtes portrays a distressing picture of Jewish life at the turn of the century. The desperate plots of the storytelling passengers are matched by the cynical perspectives of the listeners. As Miron asserts, the "selection of the railroad coach as the setting of the cycle symbolizes the end of the intimacy of shtetl literature." Thus the collection of stories "does not continue the shtetl experience, but rather undermines it."[30] According to Schivelbusch, rail travel is "experienced as participation in an industrial process," and for Jews in turn-of-the-century Yiddish literature the train setting is symbolic of the new industrial age and the collapse of any community.[31]

Instead of throwing away all the stories that he has collected, the salesman has decided to "aroysgebn in a bukh oder opdrukn in a blat" (8) (publish them in a book or newspaper). However, he chooses to remain anonymous. The traveling salesman's plan is to "record" the encounters that he has with other passengers. The train is a choice setting for narratives relying on chance encounters with strangers. The stories that he hears represent a collective image of Jewish life in a state of ever-worsening suffering, where families are struggling day in and day out to take care of their children while facing anti-Jewish government edicts.

Within *Di ayznban-geshikhtes,* however, a pair of tales offers respite from the suffering described in the other stories. These are the tales about the Leydikgeyer (the Slowpoke Express). The Slowpoke Express connects isolated shtetls and is part of the rural landscape. Its stories, following the logic of *Di ayznban-geshikhtes,* are more uplifting because they are enacted in a landscape in which the destructive forces of modernization have not yet led to the breakdown of the shtetl. It is called a slowpoke, because it is slow and nearly always empty. The emptiness of the train car reflects the demise of rural life and the smaller concentration of people out in the country. However, the train's emptiness also makes it an ideal setting for slow storytelling versus the frantic, often prematurely ended, stories of the regular train where new characters constantly intrude with new narratives. On the Slowpoke Express storytelling can take a pace akin to the slow-moving train. The humorous contradiction of terms in its name matches the humorous contradictory tales told about it. The contradiction rests in the conception of the Slowpoke Express as miraculous because it seems to assist the Jews, when in actuality it is a machine that merely follows its own mechanical logic, and its slowness is the result of human ineptitude rather than anything otherworldly.

We soon learn the history of this rural train: when the Jewish community heard that the tracks were going to be built, they were pessimistic. (As later events show, their pessimism was well founded, because in one of the two stories about the Leydikgeyer, the train carries anti-Semitic hooligans to the shtetl to start a pogrom against the Jews.) The Jewish community's pessimism soon gives way to greed, and "railroad fever" takes hold as everyone seeks to make a fast buck from the new railways. Yet as with nearly everything described in *Di ayznban-geshikhtes,* Jewish initiative leads to disaster—all the investors lose their money.

The first story about the Slowpoke Express, "The Miracle of Hoshana Rabba," is a comic tale about an adventure of a Jew and a priest that gives the naive Jewish reader a solid grounding in steam mechanics.[32] The plot is about the adventure of Berl Vinegar and the local anti-Semitic priest, and the story is set when "the train was still new" and locals would come to watch this strange machine. Berl Vinegar, the Jewish character, strolls up and down the platform, focusing his attention on the train, while the priest focuses his attention on the Jew. One underlying critique, then, is that Jewish energy is well spent on learning new things, but Christian energy is wasted on harassing Jews.

Berl explains to the priest that this new machine is wondrous because it is so simple: By merely flipping a few switches, the train starts. The priest is incredulous and cannot believe that a Jew could know how this huge machine works. Berl, and the story, will prove the priest wrong by showing that a Jew is capable of understanding fairly complicated steam mechanics, whereas a priest is completely ignorant about them. Berl tells the priest to get on the train and that he will show him that he knows his stuff.

Not only does Berl get the train to move but he gets it to run faster than it ever has. Berl, the Jew, has used his brains to get the massive machine to run more efficiently, in contrast to the regular train crew, which is nothing but lazy, ignorant drunks. The real fault for the train's slowness is not the train itself but the inefficient way that it is used.

Berl's mastery of the machine soon ends when he is unable to get it to stop, and he imagines the horrible impending crash. However, Berl then remembers the other facet of a steam machine—the brake—and reaches out to pull it, only to be stopped by the anti-Semitic priest, who is still too filled with hate to acknowledge that a Jew may in fact be more capable than he is. Berl responds to the priest's ignorance with a simple, truthful statement against anti-Semitism:

> "Dayn lebn?—Makht tsu im der galekh mit gal. Vos for a vert hot a hintish lebn? . . . Mit vos iz mayn lebn, lemoshl, erger baym Reboyne-sheloylem fun an anderens lebn?
>
> ". . . Na ze, foterl, dem khilek, zogt er, fun mir biz dir. Ikh tu vos ikh kon, der lokomotiv zol zikh opshteln—heyst dos, az ikh zorg far undz beydn; un du, zogt er, bist azoy oyfgetrogn az du

bist kapabl mikh nemen un aropvarfn funem lokomotiv, dos heyst—hargen a mentshn!" (123)

("Your life?" said the irate priest. "Who gives a damn for the life of a dog like you?"

(. . . [Berl responded] "What makes you think that my blood is any less red in God's eyes than yours? . . . Just look at the difference, Father, between you and me. I'm doing my best to stop this locomotive, because I'm trying to save us both, and all you can think of is throwing me out of it—in other words, of murdering your fellow man!" [192-93])

Although the Jew may be more moral and the intellectual victor, the real control of the situation is still with the priest. Berl can certainly hold his own verbally and outwit the priest, but he can do nothing physically with a non-Jew who refuses to allow him to pull the brake. In the end a crash is averted when the train runs out of coal.

This tale is told not by Berl himself, or by the traveling salesman, but by a passenger who heard it from someone else. Its structure takes on aspects of a folk legend.[33] The folktale is comforting for the Jews because it has a character able to show up an anti-Semite and keep his faith while mastering the modern world. The train is also seemingly on the side of the Jews because it stops before an accident can occur and because it is the setting in which a Jew morally surpasses an anti-Semite. In reality the train merely follows the same machinery logic that Berl had deduced earlier. Yet Berl, the believer, puts a spiritual spin on the logic of the machine by declaring that it is God's will that the train has stopped, sparing their lives (194). The miraculous element of the story reflects not what has occurred in it—the train adventure followed real logic in its unfolding and had nothing overtly miraculous about it—but how people understand what occurred. Berl decided that it was God's will (not a drunk rail hand's shoddy work) that the train would be low on coal. That was the primary miraculous act.

In the second tale about the Slowpoke Express, "The Wedding That Came without Its Band," the train again "miraculously" helps the Jewish characters. In this story as well, the theme of escaping from anti-Semites is central—the train "saves" the Jews from "a horrible fate." The framework for this story, like the previous one, is a folktale told by the same traveler to the salesman about an event "back in the days of the Constitution" when pogroms were frequent.

As the speaker describes it, massacres were occurring everywhere, though none took place in his shtetl. Soon enough, however, a local decided it was time to start one and sent for outsiders to assist him. In response, the Jews tried to get a Russian prefect to help them. In return for a large payment, or bribe, the prefect ordered "a company of Cossacks from Tulchin" to protect the Jews from the pogromists. (The speaker is aware of the irony of Jews getting help from Cossacks.) The Jews, knowing the catastrophe that awaits them, beg the prefect to at least have his police force meet the train. In like measure, the local wealthy residents, whom the speaker sarcastically calls "our local patriots" (because they are leaving the dirty work to others), also head off to meet the train. The race is on. The Cossacks are coming on horseback, the pogromists by train. The question is which group will arrive first. Logically, it seems that the pogromists on the train will, but the Jews are pinning their hopes on "their train," the Jewish train, the Slowpoke Express (197). The imminent arrival of the train and the Cossacks transforms the train platform into a multiethnic gathering.[34] The Jews are fearfully awaiting a pogrom; wealthy Polish residents are gleefully awaiting a pogrom; the Jews have bribed a Russian prefect to keep the peace; and a Cossack has hired thugs who are arriving by horse to serve as bodyguards for the Jews. On the train are the Ukrainian pogromists. This multi-regional hodgepodge has gathered tragicomically to await or to enact a pogrom.

With the platform packed, the train pulls into the station. As the engineer steps down, the tragicomic moment reaches it peak: the onlookers realize that the inept engineer has forgotten all the passenger cars! There will be no pogrom.

As in the other tale about the Slowpoke Express, trains are machines that follow their own logic and are on the side of whoever can master them. The stupidity of non-Jews has again led to the Jews being saved. Both tales suggest that Jews of the period need to balance their faith with awareness of the machinery of the new age. To reject the new invention will make them as short-sighted and ignorant as the priest.

The Leydikgeyer stories show how to balance faith and science by using characters such as Berl, who offers spiritual interpretations to mechanical occurrences. In these tales the train becomes "Judaized," whereas in the rest of *Di ayznban-geshikhtes*, the train is a symbol of a host of negatives related to the advent of modernization and the breakdown of shtetl life.

Berl stands in contrast to the salesman-narrator of the collection, who represents the current period. The salesman feels no real empathy or connection with the other passengers. Instead, he seeks to be entertained or to exploit the suffering of others. In place of a deep spirituality we have a figure who is repeatedly taken in by surface appearances. Instead of Berl, with his ability to start a train by making a leap in logic, we have a character of marked naiveté. Yet unlike the salesman, who comes across as a real character, Berl exists only within a folk legend, where the wondrous can occur and where good always wins out in the end.

In the Leydikgeyer tales the train becomes a comic Jewish machine that delivers great punch lines by running out of steam and arriving without the pogromists. In these stories, unlike those in the rest of the collection, the train is not the setting for stories that Jews tell about their lives. Instead, the train is the story, a Jewish story about using comedy to outwit oppressors. In the end, however, these stories are merely comic relief from the majority of the tales, in which the train is a negative symbol containing a negative Jewish community whose dark stories match the dark times.

At the Depot

David Bergelson (1884–1952) wrote *Arum vokzal* (At the depot) in 1909.[35] He was born in the Ukraine to a middle-class family. He received a traditional Jewish education but also was well read in

Russian and Hebrew. By 1909 he had switched to Yiddish and was seeking to have his first major work published, the novella *Arum vokzal*. After publishers rejected *Arum vokzal*, he published it himself. The work was met with strong, positive reviews, as critics heralded this unique voice.[36] Bergelson sought to create a unique prose style that broke with classical Yiddish literary traditions.[37] Whereas the classical writers made the train a symbol of the modern breakdown of community, Bergelson's novella turned this equation on its head. Instead of a train, he described the train station. Instead of a construct of movement, he examined notions of stasis. Instead of the positive shtetl-like community that Mendele created in the train car, or the antishtetl of *Di ayznban-geshikhtes*, the shtetl now existed in the memories of the main character.

The setting of the novella is a Ukrainian railroad depot that is a symbol of stasis and inertia:

> Un shteyn shteyt er do fun yorn a fargliverter un toyter un vayzt der gegnt oys, vi a farkishefter hiter, velkhn s'hot amol emets af a shpitsl farshlefert mit an eybikn melankholishn driml. . . . Drimlendik hit er op di vegn, vos bukn zikh tsu im, di noente un vayte berglekh un toln mit yenem sheynem un tsevorfenem dorf, vos ligt in der tif fun a langn tol, un drapet zikh shoyn fun yornlang af di shipuim fun di tsvey shkheynishe berg un kon zikh nokh alts biz zeyere shpitsn nisht aroyfdrapen. (15)

> (Petrified and inert, it dominates the countryside like a spell-bound sentry, cast by some prankster into everlasting, melancholy sleep. . . . Somnolently it stands guard over the incoming roads, over the near and distant hills and valleys, and over the pretty village, scattered at the bottom of a long valley, that has spent years clambering up the slopes of two adjacent mountains without ever reaching the top. [84])

The station is a character awaiting the arrival of a hero to "makht tsum lebn umkern alts" (15) (recall to life everything languishing and dead [84]).

Bergelson is playing with a convention found in numerous nineteenth-century novels, wherein the arrival of an outsider interrupts the bucolic charm of village life. (Examples are Thomas Hardy's *Return of the Native* and *The Woodlanders,* Jane Austen's *Pride and Prejudice,* and Nikolai Gogol's *Dead Souls.*) Bergelson alters the tradition: In place of a character we have a personified station awaiting the change. Yet the gloomy setting is going to remain gloomy: No hero will emerge.

In the opening of *Arum vokzal* Bergelson flirts with literary expectations and then refutes them to subvert the neatly structured world of the nineteenth-century novel. Instead of a hero to lift the eternal, imperturbable gloom, a train arrives, as the opening passage continues: "Derfar hot zi oft a nudnem genets geton, gekhapt pamelekh ir groys, alt un leydik moyl un mit groys foylkayt oysgeshpign a langn un loyfndikn pasazhir-tsug. Fun vayt iz der tsug gelofn un getrogn hot er mit zikh a gute un freylekhe psure farn vokzal un far der gegnt, un geaylt hot er zikh di psure tsu brengen" (16). (Occasionally its toothless old mouth opens in a weary yawn, and out spits a long rushing passenger train. The train comes from far away and is eager to impart its good tidings to the station and the surrounding countryside [84–85].) Again, the reader's expectations are raised: Perhaps the train will be a literary tool heralding change, as is typical of the nineteenth-century novel.[38] Instead, the train also falls victim to the eternal sleepiness of this countryside:

> Ober nokh inem ershtn troyerikn ophilkhn fun zayn langn un freylekhn fayf hot er zikh shoyn ibertsaygt, az di moreshkhoyre iz do zeyer tif un eybik. Er iz shoyn tsum vokzal tsugekrokhn pamelekh mit a gefalenem gemit un dortn shteyn geblibn mit a shvern un langn zifts fun der bafrayter un heyser pare funem tormoz.
>
> —Umzist . . . umzist . . . un farfaln . . . alts farfaln—hot zikh a toyber klang tsuzamen mitn zifts arumgetrogn. (16)

(But after hearing the first mournful echo of its expansive merry whistle, it realizes that nothing will ever pierce this region's deep, eternal gloom. The train slows to a dispirited crawl, and comes to a stop with a long heavy sigh of steam. The sigh hangs suspended in the air like a verdict: "Useless, useless, and doomed." [85])

This opening passage establishes that this is not a nineteenth-century novel but a modern one. It has no hero. It has no highly structured plot that will reach a climax of some type. Instead, as is typical of modernist prose, the narrative voice focuses heavily on descriptions rather than straight action. Rather than a plot that unfolds diachronically, everything, including the plot line, is static; it becomes consumed by the shadow of the "petrified and inert" train depot. The depot is the central character, central image, and primary frame of the story, and it reflects the claustrophobic, modernist prose that Bergelson uses. Although each arriving train will bring a momentary wisp of hope and merriness, as soon as the train fully stops at the station, it is subsumed into the dead reality. Nothing can challenge the permanent, austere gloom.

The opening passage is cinematic in scope. It unfolds along paths of motion, like a train car moving through the countryside or a camera shifting its focus in a long shot.[39] In broad strokes the description begins with the roads that lead into the train station and a general description of that station. As a train pulls into the station, the construct of train-as-movement meets with the depot-as-stasis:

> Un ba di rayznde, vos in tsug, hot zikh derfar modne farkvetsht dos harts, un a bloz hot af zey geton mit troyer. Zey hobn bald aroysgeshtekt zeyere umbakante penimer un shvaygndik batrakht dem altn un shleferikn vokzal. Azoy pust, moreshkhoydik un nudne iz do geven; s'hot zikh keynem nisht gevolt redn un funem ort zikh a rir ton. Un di mentshn hobn geshvign, geshtanen on a shum bavegung un shoyn oysgezen azoy melankholish un shleferik, vi aleyn der alter farshteynerter vokzal. Etlekhe fartifte in khaloymes zaynen do pamelekh arumgegangen un shvaygndik gekukt af di farkholemte rayznde. (16)

> (As for the passengers inside one such train, they felt an inexplicable twinge of sadness and thrust their heads out the windows to examine the ancient, sleepy depot. The drabness and tedium were disheartening; no one felt the urge to say anything or stir from his seat. The people on the platform stood motionless, looking as glum and stony as the station itself. Some paced

alongside the train, absorbed in fantasies about the brooding strangers aboard. [85])

Each community — the moving and the static — is momentarily brought into the other's reality. The narrative eye shifts to a view of the station and some of its denizens, after which the narrative eye pans over the station and begins its journey away from the depot. The motion away from the station comes by means of a passenger, who arrives on the train and thus brings with him the positive energy of movement (in contrast to the station denizens as figures of stasis). The depot is thus divided into two areas, the eternally static locale that the middlemen inhabit, and "faran nokh a tsveyte zayt vokzal, vu keyn sokhrim dreyen zikh nisht arum. Zitsndik oyf di ayngeshpante britshkes, drimlen dortn untergegartlte shmaysers un mit ummentshlekher geduld vartn zey af zeyere onkumendike balebatim" (18). (Another part of the depot, free from the bustle of local dealers, where coachmen sat nodding atop their harnessed buggies, waiting with superhuman patience for their masters to arrive [87].)

From a general description of a horse-drawn carriage, Bergelson moves on to a train passenger who is climbing into his buggy and heading home. The passenger quickly becomes part of the slumbering landscape, falling fast asleep while his children are at home eagerly awaiting his arrival and the gifts that he will bring them. For his children the passenger still represents exciting travel and movement, whereas he has already become part of the somnolent landscape. The energy of the train ride has quickly worn off.

The opening passage offers a series of images of movement and stasis; roads in and roads out. It is a complicated, highly literary vision of travel versus habitation, community versus individualism, change versus stasis. Encompassing each moment of the opening description is the larger, forward-moving, cinematic perspective of a train that is coming into a station and a passenger who is departing and quickly becomes ensnared in the landscape's sleepy haze.

In the earlier Yiddish stories that I discussed, the train was a symbol of change, for better or worse, and a historical marker of the new times. In *Arum vokzal* the train is metaphysically sucked into the shadow of the depot. Because the depot is stasis, the train in its environment becomes still. The train suggests the desire for change. But it is a futile desire. All there is, and can be, is stasis. In this modernistic work the motions of change in traditional novels have become the locales of inertia. *Arum vokzal* refutes the genre that it seems to be a part of—the nineteenth-century rural novel—and instead offers us a vision, often cinematic in scope, of an inert, still, dead, sleepy reality. The larger meaning is left deliberately vague.[40] We have the picture and are asked to look at it and to draw our own conclusions. Even though the tale negates a larger cohesive reading, the depot is nevertheless used as the central image that focuses the reader's understanding on the ties between train stations and notions of stasis. The meaning of the depot and the inert landscape is secondary to how they are described.

Although the protagonist, Benish Rubenstein, is a confused, undirected, often hazy thinker, in the larger landscape of *Arum vokzal* most reality is bipolar, with things split into opposites. The train depot and its eternal stasis is the negative half of nineteenth-century literary notions of trains and train stations as symbols of change and energy. Without the depot's eternal stasis the eternal movement of trains beyond its shadow would not exist. Like Benish's relationship with the character Itsik Borukh, the relationship of trains and depot is parasitic. The depot is the land of the dead and a necessary shadow to the land of the living. However, it is more a world of purgatory than hell or heaven.

Economic middlemen inhabit the depot. They are the conduits for the exchange of goods, just as the depot is the conduit for the motion of the trains. In both cases the goods come and go from them. The train station is thus a symbol that marks the conflation of commerce and travel.[41] The economic middlemen are the "mercenaries" of the new economy. The "location of the merchant community at the depot corresponds to its economic position. The merchants are situated at the point where the old world of the shtetl, represented by the horse transport, meets the new world dominated by big cities connected by trains."[42] The depot middlemen inhabit the realm beyond the center, whether of the city or of the town.

The broader story is one year in the life of the station, as conveyed through its most marginal denizen, Benish.[43] His character is the literary opposite of the hero that the horizon awaits in the opening passage. Benish is a petty, mean, and totally unlikable character, very much a reflection of a prototypical "underground man," as presented in Fyodor Dostoyevsky's 1863 *Notes from the Underground.* Like the purported author of Dostoyevsky's *Notes,* Benish is the opposite of the positive hero. Instead of being "proud and forceful," he is completely without forcefulness of any type and has only a negative effect, if any, on those around him. He lives in a hazy reality of constant resentment and alienation. He is much despised and is despicable. In this bipolar world, where the content middlemen of the depot represent an easy acceptance of their position, Benish has a profound dislike of his alienated location. However, unlike Dostoyevsky's Underground Man, Benish seeks to improve his situation yet is unable to carry out the changes that he wants to enact.

In all ways, Benish's negativity feeds the middlemen's contentment because he keeps them from considering the world of movement and change beyond the depot. Benish supplies them with a scapegoat that keeps them self-satisfied and content. He is necessary to their easy acceptance of their middle position, just as the depot is necessary to the movement beyond its shadow. Where the middlemen are happily situated in the middle locale, Benish is utterly homeless, having broken off all contact with his family and home for his endless futile wanderings. For him the wealthy home he came from in the shtetl (before his father lost his money) is the positive antithesis of his disconnected, angry life because it was the site of "alts, alts iz faran dortn" (76) (everything that mattered [128]).

The community of middlemen at the train station is the opposite of that in the shtetl: it is all male, with few Jewish aspects. It has no home or domestic realm; it is an entirely nondomestic, public world, and the middlemen habituate it comfortably. Its new economy, with segmented production, is the inverse of the shtetl's where artisans and petty merchants dominated, and in its idealized form life had a unified meaning. Where the middlemen have managed to forge an all-male alternative to the shtetl, Benish is alone and yearns for the domestic reality that his enemy, Avromchik, has managed to build on the boundaries of the depot, with his nice home and his "feminine" wife, Clara.

For those content with their location, everything is fine. For modern antiheroes like Benish, people who are discontented, life offers nothing but movement and eternal restlessness, the need to always seek something, but in the end, like the depot, they go absolutely nowhere. Much like the salesman in *Di ayznbangeshikhtes*, Benish represents the decline of the communal and the ascendancy of the dislocated individual. Whereas Dostoyevsky's Underground Man inhabits a dank, suffocating cellar, Benish lurks around a depot. The depot, which should be a place of great activity and change, instead is the locale of stasis and decay.

Only at the end of the novella can the principle of movement bring Benish out of his stasis. Yet the movement comes not by a train, which for Benish is as inert and dead as the depot, but by a buggy, which has no tie whatsoever to the ever-static shadow of the depot. As Avraham Novershtern points out, Benish's leave-taking in a buggy ties the end of the story to the opening paragraphs, which concluded with a businessman alighting from the train and heading home in a buggy, thus bringing a cyclical motion into the tale.[44] The story has come full circle as Benish rides off on what is probably yet another failed business venture.

This movement is the catalyst for Benish to finally write to the wife he has deserted (although he may never mail the letter and may instead resort to his former inertia).[45] His riding in the buggy means that the principle of movement has broken Benish out of his inertia to attempt a reconciliation with the family that he has deserted and the domestic realm that he longs for. Yet by repeating in the final paragraphs the carriage leave-taking of the opening ones, the story also points toward the closed, ever-repetitive reality, where no real escape or forward movement is possible.

The only thing in the novel that can really move is the train, which is a personification of the narrative voice. Like the train, the narrative voice passes around and over the still landscape. The author holds the camera and sweeps over the still landscape, focusing on what interests him, skipping over what does not. No wonder that Benish cannot escape, cannot see outside himself and connect with the broader world: The broader world is the moving camera. And Benish, the modern man, is caught in a stifling frame of modernist prose.

Bergelson creates a setting that encompasses both the static, dark locale of the inverted shtetl (the depot) and the space of movement and change (the train), all within the larger framework of a modernist narrative that is not weighed down by place. But Bergelson provides no path to integration, as in "Shem un Yefes in a vogn," where the story returns to the mythic narrative, or as in *Di ayznban-geshikhtes,* which provides the ideal figure of Berl Vinegar. Instead, Bergelson offers a landscape where the paths of motion exist just beyond the reach of the main character, who is desperate to find them but cannot.

Conclusion

In "Shem un Yefes in a vogn" the train car is a meeting space for Jews, as well as a location where for the first time Jews can share a small intimate space with non-Jews. Thus the train is a multiethnic melting pot for a variety of Jews and on occasion for Christians as well. The setting means that Jews come into contact with each other and a variety of domestic tales from all over eastern Europe; moreover, the third-class train car is a new arena for international politics and gossip. The train, then, is a vehicle for new contacts: between Jews, between Jews and Christians, and between Jews and domestic and international tales.

The train is also a negative symbol of how the modern world is bringing about the breakdown of the closed shtetl with its (idealized) cohesive Jewish community. Looked at sequentially in the three stories that I have discussed here, the response to the train-as-modern becomes increasingly more pessimistic. In "Shem un Yefes in a vogn" the narrator, Mendele, is still able to negotiate his own path of return to the mythic, communal, lost Jewish world by inserting a symbolic response to the hardships that he is witnessing. In *Di ayznban-geshikhtes* the mythic, positive space is now contained within two miraculous tales, disconnected from the current reality but still offering a path of hope for the audience. By the time of *Arum vokzal*, the ideal community exists only in the memory of the main character, and the paths of return seem closed to him.

The train is thus a vehicle and force of disruption that brings change and motion to the static shtetl. The disruptive force can be positive: bringing Jews into increased contact with the broader world and enabling Jews to make contacts with one another, thus helping to build a network of mutual assistance. The disruptive force can be negative as well: extending the power of the bureaucracy, bringing non-Jews into the shtetl to instigate pogroms, stratifying the classes even more than they have been previously, and becoming a setting for the Jewish exile.

Thus we have in Yiddish tales of railroad travel a dual vision of the train. On the one hand, when Jews are in it, they make it their own Jewish world. It becomes a Jewish train. The public train car becomes the private domicile of Jews. A shtetl of sorts, for better or worse. On the other hand, when Jews are outside the train, witnessing it, the train is not Jewish but part of the modern European bureaucracy that infringes upon Jewish individuals and communities. Through storytelling, the train could be reclaimed and Judaized, yet by the time of Bergelson even that no longer seems possible.

4

The Ship

Caelum non animum mutant qui trans mare currunt.
(They change their skies but not their souls those who run across the sea.)

—Horace

We have seen how the train in modern Yiddish literature was a force of contact and disruption, a symbol of the modern times, when everything was changing, people were on the move, and the small world of the shtetl Jew was extending with the increased contacts brought by the railroads. Of the three tropes—the road, the train, and the ship—the train is the symbol most emblematic of the influence of modernization and urbanization. The train marks the societal changes of modernization, whereas the ship is a space that represents the Jewish individual in contact with an international community of travelers. The ship thus represents movement from the "closed" shtetl to the "open" broader world.

In general, the ship in the Jewish cultural imagination represented a hopeful symbol of the passage from negative Europe to positive America. Whereas the train was disruptive because it brought forces of change and modernization into the shtetl, the ship was redemptive. For example, in Sholem Aleichem's *Motl Peyse dem khazn's* (The adventures of Mottel, the cantor's son), the Jewish emigrants undergo a symbolic rebirth during the ship journey that the narrator, Motl, likens to the Jews' leaving Egypt after Moses divided the Red Sea.[1] The ship in the Jewish cultural imagination was both the means of transport and the symbol of the rebirth brought about by leaving the Old World for the new. The ship's crossing represented the transitive state between the past in Europe and the future in the United States, and during the journey Jewish emigrants would seek to come to terms with their massive dislocation. Where the train thus represented the Jewish collective that was facing change, both ship narratives that I analyze here—Lamed Shapiro's *Oyfn yam* (On the sea, 1910) and Jacob Glatstein's *Ven Yash iz geforn* (When Yash went forth, 1938)—tell of the effect that the dislocations have on a Jewish individual.

Yet while the Jewish collective often viewed the transatlantic passage as positive, both works chart out the existential dangers that Jews, and other emigrants, encounter when leaving Europe for the Americas. Both writers use the setting of a ship, whose passengers come together by coincidence, to explore assimilation pressures and the "melting pot." In both works the journey thus represents the anguish, and hope, of the Jewish emigrant; the transatlantic passage is a motif of acculturation.[2] In Shapiro's novella a young male emigrant, the narrator, is on a transatlantic voyage to the United States. During the journey the narrator tries to find a way to fully root his identity in his eastern European childhood before he has to face the challenges of living in the United States. In contrast, Glatstein's autobiographical novel takes place during a transatlantic voyage that is returning him from the United States to Poland. During the journey the autobiographical narrator, Yash, recounts his original transatlantic passage from Poland to the United States, where he felt extremely hopeful about his future. By the time of his return voyage to Poland, the narrator has become a mature acculturated American and is no longer a greenhorn. The return voyage is a time to ruminate on what becoming an American has meant for him as a Jew. Where Shapiro's work concerns a young man who is beginning his process of Americanization, Glatstein's work is about an Americanized Jew who is learning how much the process of Americanization has cost him.

The voyage not only expresses the fate of the emigrant but enacts the plight of the modern individual "at sea" in a chaotic and uncertain world. In both novels the protagonist struggles to incorporate the shtetl past as a building block for his new "American" self. The ship is the vessel and the ocean the backdrop for the individual's search to both leave and reclaim the past. The ship, like the train, is also a setting for storytelling. In *Oyfn yam* and *Ven Yash iz geforn*, throughout the journey a series of other passengers tell the narrators stories about their lives and those of others. The narrator's monologue about the journey is thus broken up by interpolated tales of other passengers. Where in the *Ayznban geshikhtes* the stories do not markedly affect the narrator, in both ship tales the interpolated stories are expressions of, and influences on, the narrator's existential search for an authentic self. On the train the stories represent the Jewish communal vision, whereas the ship tales are expressions of the narrators' highly personal rite of passage. In both ship narratives the individual can be seen as a representative of any emigrant but also as someone who must nevertheless face obstacles specifically related to his Jewishness.

For the turn-of-the-century Yiddish writer who probably grew up in an inland shtetl or town, the ocean was often a mysterious, mighty, and dangerous place. Ashkenazic Jewish life had little tradition of seafaring, but sea stories were nevertheless popular.[3] In Yiddish literature of the nineteenth century, both maskilic and Hasidic tales describe the sea in a way that matches such descriptions in European literature of the time: as a wild, dangerous realm in which shipwrecks were common. Thus we have Vitlin's popular rewriting of *Robinson Crusoe* into Yiddish, *Robinzon di geshikhte fun Alter Leb* (1820), in which Robinson Crusoe is the Jewish Alter Leb shipwrecked on a deserted island; and Nahman of Bratslav's story "The Burgher and the Pauper," which describes two tempests during an ocean voyage that lead to two shipwrecks.[4]

By the twentieth century, when ship travel by Jews was often a transatlantic journey by steamship, the ship had transformed from the fragile vessel of eighteenth- and nineteenth-century

European literature to the hearty ocean liner. The ship was now a basically safe vessel that held a community of passengers united in a lengthy voyage across the sea. This made the ship an appropriate literary vehicle on which to create a closed reality that matched that of the shtetl just as the shtetl was in decline as a literary setting.[5] Yet unlike a typical shtetl (and the train car as represented in Yiddish literature), the ship's closed world was inhabited by a mixed group of Jews and non-Jews haphazardly thrown together. The ship thus became a symbol to evoke the Jew's intimate encounter, often for the first time, with the broader non-Jewish world.

The ship was an image of order in the disorder and "uncontrolled arena" of the ocean.[6] Whereas a train passenger rode in a closed, safe, homey compartment protected from the elements, to walk the deck of a ship meant being exposed to the elements where the only landscape was nature in its vast intensity. The ship ride offered a strange combination of feeling that one was alone on a vast sea, while also feeling one's self to be in a closed setting from which no escape was possible. The simultaneous feelings of freedom and imprisonment are juxtaposed with the "built-in directionality and purpose" of the transatlantic journey.[7]

A central difference in the journey by ship and the road or train journey lay in their different purposes. As the poet W. H. Auden describes it, the ship journey in literature arose from a society at risk:

> The ship, then, is only used as a metaphor for society in danger from within or without. When society is normal the image is the City or the Garden. That is where people want and ought to be. As to the sea, the classical authors would have agreed with Marianne Moore. "It is human nature to stand in the middle of a thing; but you cannot stand in the middle of this." A voyage, therefore, is a necessary evil, a crossing of that which separates or estranges.[8]

Thus a journey by ship was often a reactive journey that resulted from a society in transition that was forcing some members to permanently leave their home for unknown lands.

Auden's analysis is particularly insightful because Jews often undertook ship travel in reaction to pogroms and anti-Semitism, and their doing so reflected the impossibility of remaining any longer in eastern Europe. The sea journey represented the traveler's state of total flux—the need to come to terms with the terrible loss of one's home and prepare for the uncertainty of the New World. As Moore said, the sea represents the zone of difficult transition where "it is human nature to stand in the middle of a thing; but you cannot stand in the middle of this."

In contrast to a train car, where the Jewish passengers often rode together, during this period (1910–34) someone traveling by ship was more likely to be traveling with a mixed group of non-Jews from many lands. For this reason the ship in Yiddish literature becomes a setting reflecting issues of hegemonic internationalism versus the homogeneity of the shtetl landscape. The ship thus is more like a minicity than a shtetl. The steamer trip was also much longer than a typical train or carriage ride, with the other passengers remaining the same throughout the trip. This was a setting in which to establish ties that were both deeper and of a different sort than on train or road journeys. Moreover, on a ship each passenger was cut off from her "real" life of home, family, work. This disconnection opened the possibility to recreate one's self for the duration of the journey.

In *Oyfn yam* and *Ven Yash iz geforn* both authors use highly sophisticated and innovative narratives to convey the dislocation and transition of the emigration experience. These authors are comfortable with modernist narratives. Shapiro appropriates the romantic sea quest and turns it into a modernist framework for depicting the alienated artist. In Glatstein's work the modernist approach, as exemplified by a polyphonic narrative, meets the challenge of Jewish history. Both use the framework of the standard emigrant steamship journey to weave their deep ruminations on the existential anxiety of the Jewish emigrant.

Both *Oyfn yam* and *Ven Yash iz geforn* use emigration and the journey to explore larger issues of Jewish diaspora and displacement. The ocean setting is the place for preparing to step onto the "unrestful" shore of the United States, where the immigrant will not have the time, or the poetic space of the sea, for such intro-spection. For the Jewish emigrant in these works, life matches the ocean environment, one of permanent movement. On the ocean the emigrants in both stories learn that to live as fully integrated Americans they must maintain spiritual ties to the Jewish land of their childhood. The path of integration, like the path of the ship, begins in Europe and ends in the United States. Yet according to these authors, to be a mature American is to be ever in transit be-tween the shores of the United States and Europe.

Immigration narratives in native languages were often written by someone recently arrived in America who had not yet acquired English and had little choice but to use the native language. Other immigration narratives in native languages are written by people who have acquired English yet have decided to continue writing in their native language. An author's decision to write in his native language often reflected a decision to write for other immigrants and not the general public. Both Shapiro and Glatstein were adept at English but probably decided to use their native language in order to communicate specifically with a Jewish, Yiddish-speaking audience.[9] The readership either still lived in eastern Europe or had emigrated to the United States. The works document the pressures that Jews faced, or would face, in the United States, and show ways for Jewish readers to hold on to their ethnic and religious identity despite these pressures. As is typical of other works about emigration that were written in Yiddish, the hazards of assimilation are the focus, and Yiddish, a language resistant to assimilation, a tool to fight the pressures of Americanization.

As Matthew Frye Jacobson has suggested, a question that comes to the forefront in non-English narratives is how much the author writes from the perspective of an emigrant rather than an immigrant.[10] By writing in their original language for an audience of native speakers, these authors are speaking as much about the community and place they left as about the specifics of American-ization. Therefore these narratives offer up not only neglected perspectives on the United States but expand our understanding of the lands and communal systems of different ethnic groups.

In American Jewish immigration novels that were written in English, Americanization is frequently a hazardous process filled with struggles to find a secure identity that incorporates both Jewish and American cultural influences. The dilemmas of Americanization are played out in a variety of forms: struggles with parents who are representative of "Old World" values, disillusionment that economic success is not matched by personal fulfillment, intermarriages with Christians that offer an outward sign of assimilation that is often matched by family discord.[11] Most Jewish works in English before the 1920s, although marked by ambivalence, were nevertheless fairly optimistic about the process of assimilation.[12] In the late 1920s and 1930s a shift occurred, and it matched the rise of nativist pressures. A number of works challenged the American dream and the virtues of Americanization.[13] Examples include Ludwig Lewisohn's 1928 novel, *The Island Within,* which documents the discrimination that Jews—even those most overtly assimilated—faced in the United States, and Michael Gold's 1930 proletarian novel, *Jews without Money,* which portrays the abuse of poor immigrants on the Lower East Side by greedy capitalists and corrupt leaders.[14]

When Yiddish-speaking Jewish immigrants chose to write in English, the language may have been a manifestation of their assimilation: They had learned the language of the United States and could even write books in it. For instance, although he was the editor of the most important Yiddish newspaper in the United States, the *Forverts,* Abraham Cahan's decision to write his immigration works in English was partly a means to display, and assert to his readers, the importance of learning English.[15] While a number of critics have shown that Cahan's vision of the United States was highly ambivalent, if not outright negative, I would suggest that, for the average Yiddish-speaking immigrant, reading Cahan's books in English was part of the process of linguistic assimilation.[16] As many Jewish writers began learning English, those who chose to write in Yiddish were fighting to continue the Jewish language, and Jewish perspective, against pressure to Americanize. In an era marked by anti-immigrant sentiment they were stubbornly asserting their right to fight for their own cultural, literary, and linguistic sphere in the United States.

Although written in Yiddish, these works are emblematically American tales. To become American is not to land and "mature" into a new, fixed identity. Instead, the novels present an alternative vision of Americanization that incorporates, and accepts, one's childhood memories as building blocks for maturation. These authors are suggesting that by becoming too stable, too grounded, the immigrant represses the movement of memories. Shapiro and Glatstein are showing their Yiddish readers that transition is positive, symbolizing an acceptance of the full processes of life. In contrast, in the assimilationist model, growth often begins only after the immigrant has taken her first steps on the new shore of the United States. I would suggest that the Jewish audience they were specifically addressing understood that by likening Americanization to a journey by ocean, they were replacing the "landed" assimilationist model with the voyage, eschewing pressures to repress one's old national identity in favor of a fluid acceptance of the unique past of each immigrant.

On the Sea

Lamed Shapiro's novella *Oyfn yam* (On the sea) was published in Warsaw in 1910, the year after publication of his first pogrom story, "Der kush."[17] The five sections of *Oyfn yam* are titled "Nakht" (Night), "Shvaygn" (Silence), "Der ayzbarg" (The iceberg), "Helshtern" (Bright star), and "Der reyakh fun land (The scent of land). The ocean is the landscape for the existential rebirth that the narrator experiences during the journey, as he says in his own closing words: "Yam, o yam, oyf dir hot der mentsh badarft geborn gevorn" (229). (Ocean, oh ocean, on you we are reborn). Throughout *Oyfn yam* the ocean symbolizes a zone of creation wherein the narrator confronts the most elemental aspects of himself and experiences a rebirth in which he discovers how important his Jewish roots are.

Shapiro (1878–1940) was an influential Yiddish writer who, along with other "second-generation" Yiddish authors such as Jacob Glatstein, shifted the focus of Yiddish literature from external descriptions of Jewish life (as with the "first generation" of Yiddish writers—Sholem Abramovitsh, Sholem Aleichem, and

I. L. Peretz) to the workings of the psyche. Steeped in modern Russian and European literature, the second generation of writers experimented with a variety of techniques, from stream-of-consciousness prose to expressionistic poetry.[18] Shapiro developed the impressionist style in Yiddish literature, using symbolic vocabularies to express the internal reality of his characters. He emigrated to the United States in 1905, returned to Europe in 1906, and settled permanently in the United States in 1909. The rest of Shapiro's life was marked by frequent moves, alcoholism, and depression.[19] *Oyfn yam* was followed by a period when Shapiro published his most well-known stories, which use impressionistic techniques to convey the horrors of pogroms.[20]

As was typical of his generation of Yiddish writers, Shapiro combined genres to express the workings of the psyche, and *Oyfn yam* uses a vision of nature and the journey that is very much a reflection of European romanticism. According to Paul Gifford, the journey in romanticism was a means to externalize explorations of selfhood.[21] In *Oyfn yam* the journey that the unnamed narrator undertakes is first and foremost an internal quest for authentic selfhood. Thus the ocean, the ship, and the characters that the narrator describes all in some way reflect his search for self-understanding.

Moreover, not only does the journey reflect a romantic quest of self but the setting of the ocean resonates deeply with its symbolic usage throughout English romantic poetry, in particular in Samuel Taylor Coleridge's *The Rime of the Ancient Mariner*.[22] In romantic poetry, according to Jonathan Raban, "the sea was the realm of man as solitary creature, the hero struggling with elemental forces."[23] The sea as a zone of rebirth appears throughout romantic literature; "the sea becomes the place of purgatorial suffering: through separation and apparent loss, the characters disordered by passion are brought to their senses."[24] The sea is a setting for purgatorial suffering because it is unpredictable and at a moment's notice can shift from calm to gale. The romantics saw that they could use this unpredictable nature to express the shifting passions of the human soul, as in Keats's sonnet "On the Sea":

> . . . Often 'tis in such gentle temper found,
>   That scarcely will the very smallest shell
>   Be mov'd for days from where it sometime fell,
> when last the winds of Heaven were unbound.
> Oh ye! who have your eye-balls vex'd and tir'd,
>   Feast them upon the wideness of the Sea;
>   Oh ye! whose ears are dinn'd with uproar rude,
>   Or fed too much with cloying melody—
>   Sit ye near some old Cavern's Mouth, and brood
> Until ye start, as if the sea-nymphs quir'd![25]

The sea, then, is a constant rebuttal to the "cloying melody" of settled, dull life and a reminder that deep passions can suddenly well out of the most calm surfaces. In *Oyfn yam* the sea journey also represents a purgatory of suffering for the narrator, at the end of which he is ready to make the transition to the new world. The forward journey of the ship matches the journey of his search, whereas the terrain of the search is the chaotic, strong, harsh ocean teeming below him.

To fully appropriate a romantic perspective was difficult in an industrial age because the transatlantic journey took place on a steamer.[26] Part of the romantics' attraction to sailboats was that these are fragile vessels that can break apart under a violent gale, as in Percy Bysshe Shelley's poem "A Vision of the Sea":

> The great ship seems splitting! it cracks as a tree,
> While an earthquake is splintering its root, ere the
>   blast
> Of the whirlwind that stripped it of branches has
>   passed.
> The intense thunder-balls which are raining from
>   Heaven
> Have shattered its mast, and it stands black and
>   riven.
> The chinks suck destruction. The heavy dead hulk
> On the living sea rolls an inanimate bulk,
> Like a corpse on the clay which is hungering to
>   fold
> Its corruption around it.[27]

The fragility of a great sailing ship caught in a tempest became for the romantics a stock image of the fragility of the human soul in the midst of emotional storms. Where the sailboat relies on the forces of nature, and becomes one with them, the steamer plows through the sea. To the romantic the steamboat was thus a machine "affronting the nature of the sea."[28]

Shapiro overcomes the disjunction between the reality that a steamship was the vessel of the emigrant journey and his desire to use a romantic narrative style, which required a sailing ship, by making the ship a combination of the two. For instance, he gives the ship masts: "Farsheydine lider hoybn zikh fun shifdek un vern farshtorbn inem fayfn funem vint tsvishn di mastn" (194). (Different songs arose into the air from the ship's deck to die out in the whistle of the wind between the masts.) Yet he also fills the narrative with the lonely sound of the steamer's horn: "Mu-u-u-u!—hot zikh plutsem aroysgerisn baym shlofndikn shif fun der brust" (196). (Tut-u-u! The sound wrenched out suddenly from the breast of the sleeping ship.) In real time the craft is a steamer chugging westward toward the United States, while poetically it is a sailboat conveying an anguished lost soul through a journey of self. In setting his romantic journey in the period when steamers were carrying emigrants across the Atlantic, Shapiro gives the craft aspects of the sailboat (masts) that make it less of a machine and more a part of nature. Although where the ship is heading is unclear throughout the narrative (to increase the romantic quest aspects), during the final section of the work the reader learns that it is a ship of emigrants heading to New York City.

Until the ending specifies the destination, the ship moves through a nameless ocean, going nowhere and everywhere. This brings the narrative out of a political or historical location and into a totally symbolic reality that marks "a dark night of the soul." The ending, however, forces the reader to reconsider her understanding of the piece. It is not merely a romantic consideration of art and madness and death; it is also tied to the very real processes of exile and migration of the Jews. The ending impels the narrative into this framework and brings all the earlier considerations of creativity and madness into a relationship with exile and migration.

Oyfn yam is built around the narrator's interior monologues, peppered with strange, troubling stories told to him by unnamed passengers. The stories are prooftexts of a sort for the narrator that reflect on the relationship between the individual and his artistic impulses and provide a commentary on the narrator's search for his authentic self-as-artist. The narrator never speaks to other passengers. His silence stresses that this is a highly personal, individualistic journey of self. All the characters that the narrator views silently become part of his image of himself, reflecting his inner journey and lessons of its dangers. The narrative relies on a step-by-step layering of meaning as each passenger's monologue is added to the narrator's search for self at a time of profound dislocation.

Taken as a whole, *Oyfn yam* is a subtle, beautiful rumination on many of the darker forces of life, as represented by the ocean as the symbol of the restless unconscious and the ship as a marker of an individual's attempt to confront the deepest parts of herself. The ship symbolizes the evolution of the artistic psyche, along with larger considerations on movement and exile. The subtle mixing of reality (in the name of a suicide victim, in the sketch of a Gymnasium student) plays throughout the narrative against the larger, vague, highly symbolic panorama of the ocean as the landscape of the unconscious.[29] The narrative constantly fluctuates between the real and the symbolic, the named and the unnamed, while intermingling universal elements (the "artist," the "emigrant") with specific ones (the Jew).

Oyfn yam examines the ties between creativity, madness, and death by using the ocean to represent an area in which the forces come together. The themes of creativity and madness, which arise throughout the collection, subtly echo the narrator's own fears about the tie between his own creativity and the darker forces of madness and suicide. The novella thus is a consideration of how creative forces contain within them the seed of their own destruction because of the close tie between artistry and madness. This perspective marks the work's philosophical tie to romanticism, while the stylistics—stream-of-consciousness prose, polyphonic sections, a weak plot line, and unnamed narrator and setting—are all attempts to use a modernist narrative style.

The collection begins with the section entitled "Nakht" (Night), which establishes what the sea and ship represent. In the opening paragraph the narrator asserts that the ocean is the formless setting for the dark forces of the world (and the unconscious) through which a symbolically lost ship creeps:

> Khmarne, umetik oyfn yam . . . es dukht zikh—nokh hot got di velt nit bashafn. Tsvishn dem koytikn himl un der vister oyberflakh funem vaser, oyf der gantser breyt funem veltlekhn toyevoye, shvebt arum der gayst fun almekhtikn got—a shtrenger, umfrayndliekher un shverfarzorgter gayst. Umruik shlaydern zikh eyne oyf di tsveyte di tunkl-gedikhte veltn mit di groy shoymkep. Shver iz der umet fun fartroyertn yam un groys iz zayn oyfregung. Mentshl, vuhin krikhstu! Mentshl, vuhin rukstu zikh! Oyf a shol fun a nisl hostu zikh gelozn iber di mekhtike vasern. Akh, du nebekh-nebekhl![30]

> (A frothing ocean—as if God hadn't yet created the world. Between the overcast sky and the desolate plane of the water, in the full breadth of the chaos, hovered the spirit of almighty God—a strict, unfriendly, and apprehensive spirit. The dark dense world restlessly slammed itself against the gray, frothy heads: Harsh is the gloom of the mournful sea and great is its agitation. Little man, what are you creeping toward? Toward what are you moving yourself? You have set off over the mighty waters in a transport as fragile as the shell of a nut. Oh, you poor wretch!)

The fragile romantic ship creeps over the stormy unformed ocean. The ocean as a formless void reflects the creation of the world in Genesis 1:2 and the typical literary association of the sea as the material of creation.[31] The ocean, then, is the void where night and day mix, a place without borders, just an endlessly intermingling dark, swampy place. And the ship is part of this landscape, animate and unyielding, like a primordial beast, a great whale arising from the chaos: "Un vi dos krekhtsn fun shif iz dem on-oyfher-geroysh fun di veltn, azoy vert farshlungen di undrey-ste shayn fun di fenster—in tsuzamengegosenem nepel fun himl, vaser un nakht" (193). (And the unceasing noise of the world is like the groan of the ship—as the hesitant beauty of the window is devoured as the sky's fog, water and night melt together.)

In this lost place disconnected voices lose sight of "reality" as they enter the landscape of dreams of the ship. The voices are representative of the polyphonic landscape of the ship and the "melting pot" model, where sounds mingle and collide, and where away from nations and homes different accents are the mark of nationality, be they Scottish, Italian, or otherwise. Each voice marks a different national song, and for the narrator the song with the deepest resonance, his "beloved song," is tied to the ocean, of "Eicha," or Lamentations:

> Italyenishe gratsyeze melodyes, ongezapt mit zunenshtraln un heyse blikn nakht-shvartse froyenoygn. "Got bless di ship." Iz mispalel der gezaltsener, mit yam vaser durkhgeveykter breyt mit a shtarker, nideriker shtim. . . . Un bislekhvayz vert di shtim veykher, di tener—nideriker un bahartster, un a tifer, farboregner tsiter shvindlt unter di verter: "Ikh bet dikh, kler-oyf mayne oreme brider" . . . o, mayn liber eykhe—ikh derken dikh! In fremde verter, in farshidnste melodyen shnaydstu zikh a veg, du eybiker, unshterblekher leytmotiv. (194–95)

> (Graceful Italian melodies absorbed with sunbeams and hot night-black women's eyes: "Got bless di ship" as the saltiness is worshiped and the ocean water drenched wide with a strong, low voice. . . . And gradually the voice becomes gentler, the tones lower and bolder, and a deep, hidden shiver emanates below the words "I beg you, enlighten my poor brothers." . . . Oh, my beloved song of Lamentations—I recognize you! Through strange words and different melodies you cut yourself a road, you eternal, immortal leitmotif.)

While the ship foreshadows the "melting pot" of the United States, the unnamed narrator is not melting into the pot and is instead starting to take on personal characteristics, most centrally that he is a Jew who connects with his people's song—Lamentations—within the cacophony of disconnected voices. Intentionally or not, the melting pot of assimilation is resisted in favor of one where the voices do not merge (although they join together) but remain distinct.

The narrative then shifts to the narrator, who is standing alone on the deck trying to establish a relationship with an ocean that is the mirror of his own unrest: "Aher, guter bruder! Gib mir dayn mekhtike ayz-kalte hant. Vi groys un shtark du bizt, azoy kleyn un nishtik bin ikh. Vi umbagrenetst es iz dayn makht, bin ikh nisht veyniker shvakh un hilfloz. Ober vi shreklekh dayn oyfregung zol nisht zayn, bin ikh toyznter, toyznter mol tseruderter un umruiker. . . . Groys iz di umru fun kleynikn mentshele" (195). (Come here brother! Give me your mighty ice-cold hand. As great and strong as you are, so small and a nothing am I. As unlimited is your might, so I am weak and helpless. But as terrible as your excitement shall be, am I a thousand, thousand times more unruly and restless. . . . Great is the unrest of small men.) The narrator's unrest dominates the narrative, as visions of unrest alternate with moments of calm. The vast, mighty, cold, turbulent ocean is a reflection of the lost individual and, in a broader sense, the existential alienation of all people. Where the sea is the void of creation, the ship is its first creation. The image of creation appears repeatedly throughout the narrative and reflects the narrator's search to understand his own creative impulses.

At the border between night and day, as the ship wakes up, memories come to the narrator as he too awakens from the dreamy night and recalls dawn in his childhood shtetl when the men rushed off to the morning prayers. While he is standing on this vessel, it moves him away, perhaps forever, from the place of his youth, but the same moment life in his town is continuing as usual. The border between night and day matches the collision in him between the present, when he is alone on the distant ocean, and the memories of his past. Yet no matter the distance he has made on his journey, Shapiro's narrator acknowledges that he cannot escape the memories of the shtetl that he has left: "Tsu mayn oyer dergreykhn etlekhe klep fun unzer altn shames' hiltsernem hemerl, klangen, vos zaynen geboyrn gevorn, ven ikh bin nokh a kind geven, hobn mikh yorn lang arumgezikht iber der velt un yetst hobn zey mikh ongeyogt in mitn broyzendn yam" (197). (Several strokes of our old beadle's wooden gavel reached my ears. Sounds that were born when I was just a child, for years had searched me out across the world, and now they caught up with me in the middle of the sparkling ocean.) The past, which fills his mind with both sentimental longing and guilt, is woven into his process of rebirth.

The clash of the past and present is symbolically tied to the binary opposition of the ocean as the locale of the internal world of memories and the land as the space of the real. Standing on deck at sunrise, the narrator is positioned at the border between the contesting worlds of memories and reality, past and present, day and night. It is the place of the artist, on the edge, on unsure footing and filled with conflicting forces. Yet it is also the place of the emigrant, who is trying to look ahead but is caught in an endless cycle of memories of the place she has left behind. The memories of the shtetl impede the narrator's attempts to re-create himself as a solitary artist alone on a vast, poetic sea.

As the day comes and brings to a close the "umruike nakht" (unrestful night) and its border reality, the clipped, disconnected voices transform into passengers. The day brings the building of borders—the conscious landscape—out of the vague borderless night, matched symbolically by the vague borderless ocean. After the long dark night of the soul, the day thus seems to herald rebirth and renewal: "Di velt-geshikhte hot zikh ongefangen oyfsnay fun same onhoyb" (199). (World history started anew from the very beginning.) The creation parable continues: First came the sea of creation, then the primordial ship, and now the formation of a society. On the ship the solitary passengers start making connections: "Tsvishn di pasazhirn hot zikh bislekhvayz oysgevebt a nets fun bashtimte farbindungen un farheltnishn" (199). (Gradually, a net of connections and relationships was woven between the passengers.)

However, in the fresh morning moments instead of rebirth, a passenger commits suicide by jumping overboard (200). After a desperate roll call, the passengers learn that the suicide was a quiet, fortyish, man named Yanko Ravitsh. By jumping into the ocean, he merged with the void, thus demonstrating to readers the profound difficulties of the emigrants' passage (200). By becoming part of the void Ravitsh can be seen as representing the pressures on emigrants to void parts of their identity. This is suggested when the narrator ruminates on the tragedy that Yanko Ravitsh died without anyone knowing much about him other than that he was a young male. His individuality is a "Shreklekher sod" (terrible secret) that the other passengers cannot penetrate (201). The suicide, who went through the same dark night as the narrator, did not emerge reborn at dawn. This image overshadows the rest of the narrative and represents the forces of depression and madness. The suicide is positioned as a real threat to the narrator on his passage through dark realms that he, like Yanko Ravitsh, might never come out of. The suicide is also a concrete example of the profound hardship of being an emigrant. Like Ravitsh, the narrator is young, single, and male. Faced with the uncertainties of the new world, Ravitsh chooses suicide. His death symbolizes the danger inherent in leaving the Old World, where everyone knows you, for the new one where you are just another anonymous immigrant.

Immediately after the suicide the narrator has a conversation with another passenger. During the conversation the other passenger describes to the narrator a neighbor of his who used to paint pictures of the ocean: "Er flegt zogn, az ven der yam redt, kon er im moln. Mer oder veyniker farbn, a veykherer oder a sharferer shtrikh—dos ales iz mentshlekh. Nor ven der yam shvaygt . . . dertseylt er im azoy fil, azelkhe zakhn, velkhe er iz nisht imshtand ibertsugebn oyf der layvnt" (202). (He used to say that when the ocean spoke, he could paint it. More or less color, a softer or stronger tone—all this was human. But when the ocean was silent, it told him so much, so many things that he was then able to portray on the canvas.) The painter eventually became insane from his relationship with the ocean. The tale of the mad artist who speaks to the ocean expresses the narrator's own relationship with the ocean of his creativity, and the constant danger of madness and suicide for the artist. To show the tie between the unconscious (the sea), art, and madness, the narrator superimposes on himself the image of the mad artist who painted the sea and lost his mind, and the man who killed himself by jumping to his death. All three men mix together in the framework of the narrator's inner consciousness:

> Dos shif hot zikh gevigt, ikh hob gedrimelt, un emitser hot mir geredt shtil in oyer arayn:
> —Ikh hob gekent a maler, flegt er moln dem yam. Iz er meshuge gevorn . . . gerufn hot men im Yanko Ravitsh. (203)

> (The ship rocked and I dreamed, and someone spoke softly into my ear: "I knew a painter who used to paint the ocean. . . . He went crazy. . . . He was called Yanko Ravitsh.")

The narrator is struggling with two universal archetypes, the artist and the emigrant. Rather than providing a respite from the long dark night, the day has intensified the struggles of his soul.

The next section is about another of the forces of unrest: love. The new characters are a young couple whom the narrator has been watching throughout the trip. The pair appear as opposites: The young woman is blond, not very pretty, but strong and friendly looking, whereas the young man is beautiful, pale, and fragile. They like to sit on the deck while the man sings disquieting, otherworldly songs.

The songs cause the young woman suffering and pain because they make her long deeply for her own "voice," which she is unable to find. The couple evoke the larger theme of artistic expression and the search for one's artistic voice. As in the previous chapter, wherein a character (the suicide) is juxtaposed with a second one (the mad artist), in this chapter the young woman's search for a voice, and her angst at not finding one, is matched with a tale of a polar bear that is awakening from hibernation.

The story of the polar bear on an iceberg contains aspects of Coleridge's *The Rime of the Ancient Mariner*. In Coleridge, as in Shapiro, the narrator is drifting on a frozen, barren landscape:

And through the drifts the snowy clifts
Did send a dismal sheen:
Nor shapes of men nor beasts we ken —
The ice was all between.

The ice was here, the ice was there,
The ice was all round:
It cracked and growled, and roared and howled,
Like noises in a wound![32]

As in Coleridge's poem, "der ayzbarg" in Shapiro's story intro-
duces an animal symbol after the description of the frozen landscape. In Coleridge's work the animal is the albatross, a Christian
symbol, whereas in Shapiro's it is a polar bear.

The polar bear tale is told as part of a description of the ship's
movement into the cold, empty, northern Atlantic. The narrator
watches the polar bear awaken on the iceberg and search vainly
for something to eat. Wherever the starving bear looks for food,
he finds only water and more water (like Coleridge's "the ice was
here /the ice was there /the ice was all round"). The bear wanders on a futile search for food that will lead nowhere but death.
His quest is another reflection on the narrator's search and an
echo of the voiceless young woman. The narrator is a traveler
through the ocean landscape, and the question is whether he will
navigate properly to find a safe haven or, like the bear and the
young woman, remain in a futile, angst-ridden search with no end
in sight.

The section ends with the passengers on deck watching the
breakup of an iceberg (reflecting the polar bear's futile search).
The narrator watches the young couple react to the death of the
iceberg: The woman watches her man as he alternates between
watching the iceberg and watching her (211). During this peak
moment the couple do not really connect with each other and instead deal with the event in their own way. It is another solitary
existential "border moment" between life and death, love and
loneliness, the domestic and untamed nature. It is another manifestation of the moment earlier in the narrative when the narrator

stood on the deck on the border between night and day. It is the locale of both the artist and the emigrant.

The trip continues with the endless water. The narrator reflects upon the strangeness of a seemingly endless journey that leaves no trace of its passage: "Mir hot zikh dedakht—yorn zaynen farbay, zint mir hobn dem breg farlozn, un undzer shif iz nokh alts gegangen un gegangen, un vi es hot nokh zikh nisht gelozn keyn shpur, azoy hot es, dukht zikh, nit gehat keyn tsvek. . . . Arum un arum iz geven vaser un vaser, vaser un vaser, tog ayn tog oys, un es hot zikh fil beser geleygt oyfn gedank, az undzer shif dreyt zikh arum zelbst" (212) (It seemed as if years had passed since we left the iceberg. Our ship was continuing on and on, leaving no trace, endlessly. . . . Around and around was water and water, water and water, day in and day out, seeming as if our ship revolved around the same point.) This also evokes the suicide who died and left no trace of himself on those around him.

While the ship's journey (like life's passage) leaves barely a trace, the ocean is the eternal void of creation. Where the ocean is endless, life is horribly short: "Un az umet hot ongefilt undzere hertser, un keyner fun undz hot nit gevust, vos iz di urzakh derfun: Di eybikeyt fun yam oder di kurtskayt fun undzer lebn" (212–13). (Sadness filled our hearts and none of us knew the cause: the eternity of the ocean or the brevity of life.) The constant repetition, in different forms, of the theme of creation versus the short insubstantial passage of life matches romantic notions of the sea. As Bernard Blackstone writes, this is a representative romantic motif: "The sea is the area of unlimited possibility and inexhaustible fertility. Her tides, obedient to the moon, invade the solid realm. The succession of her waves figures the mutability of life, the nothingness of human generations, yet also their indestructibility in the primal unity."[33] In Shapiro's romantic vision the individual artist struggles to comprehend and come to terms with the primordial void of eternal creation.

The final chapter, "Der reyakh fun land" (The scent of land), marks the culmination of the quest for an artistic voice and the search to come to terms with the shtetl past. The chapter opens with a feverish vision of a "Feye" (fairy) arising from the clouds:

"A blas, gutmutik ponim iz aroyfgeshvumen oyfn himl, un a blase shayn hot zikh tsegosn ibern yam" (225). (A pale, good-natured face emerged in the sky, and her pale beauty flowed out over the ocean.) The Feye is a positive amalgamation of women from the narrator's shtetl childhood whom he is pleased to meet again (225). The narrator asks the Feye what she has seen on the land of his childhood that he has now left. She offers him a series of three images of the past, each reflecting a state of extreme unrest; the participants do not know if the next moment will bring disappointment and heartache or improvement of their condition. The images are of a baby crying for its mother, a young couple walking along and not speaking to each other after a quarrel, and an old man tenderly watching his sick daughter sleep.

Each image is a peak moment of awaiting a change for better or worse in childhood, adolescence, and adulthood. In the first—childhood—the help will (or will not) come from a parent, in the second from a lover, and in the third from one's child. The three moments of "unrest" reflect the narrator's present state, where he too stands at the precipice between his past in Europe and future in the United States. After presenting each image, the Feye asks the narrator whether he can relate to the pain in each image. She phrases the question by asking whether he is child enough (the first image), young enough (the second), or old enough (the third) to feel the anguish of those depicted. In other words, does he still have a deep enough connection with his own past and the stages of his life to relate to those suffering life-cycle hardships? This question is particularly important for someone leaving the Old World, for it points to the importance of holding on to one's past self in the move to re-create one's self in the New World. It is a subtle indictment of those who have left for the United States and turned their back on both the Old World and their old inner selves. Throughout the journey the narrator has been searching to understand what his self is. He realizes now that these stories from his past are the basic stuff of selfhood, as he states "Mayses, mayses mayn ikh" (227). (Stories, stories my I.) With this moment of realization he can finally arrive at the new land. He has safely undergone the ocean journey and learned that on the ocean, as on the new shore of the United States, although immigrants will find possibilities to fully re-create themselves, they must nevertheless keep hold of an identity rooted in the Jewish past. By not doing this, the self can literally disappear, as happened with the emigrant Yanko Ravitsh. For him, and the Jewish readership that Shapiro was specifically addressing, Jewish cultural memory offers a solid identity.[34] While an artist may seek individual answers to her struggles about her "true self," the journey has taught the protagonist that for the emigrant, the answer is to reconnect with his own people.

As the ship pulls into New York Harbor, the "unrestful" wind of land sweeps over the ship: "In der luft hot arumgeshvebt der umruiker, basheftigter gayst fun land" (229). (In the air hovered the restless spirit of land.) The passengers are awakening from the seascape in the harsh reality of the landed world and are moving from the poetic/symbolic realm into the real.

Suddenly, out of the unrest arises another vision of a massive hovering woman (like the Feye). However, unlike the first vision of the Feye, which was imaginary, this vision is real: It is the Statue of Liberty: "A rizike froyenfigur mit an oyfgehoybner hant hot zikh opgetseykhnt links" (229). (A giant figure of a woman with an upraised hand drawn leftward.) Lady Liberty is now to be met by an integrated self that arose from the long, dark night of the sea passage. As the narrator says in his closing words, the ocean is the realm in which to become reborn.

The journey was not only a romantic one but depicted the real fears and uncertainties of the emigrant en route to the United States. Shapiro chose to convey those anxieties using a romantic journey while at the same time insisting that the reader view the narrator as a Jewish man on a transatlantic voyage to the United States. While he deliberately left the specifics of the journey vague, giving it the feel of a romantic voyage of self, this trip clearly reflected profound anxieties that all passengers felt. The first event thus involved a young male emigrant unable to face his anxieties and choosing suicide. The journey then showed not only an artist seeking his voice but an emigrant seeking to order his inner world before stepping on the unrestful shore. Taken as a whole, *Oyfn yam* expresses in the most sophisticated way possible the profound uncertainty of emigrants during their voyage to the new land.

Yet rather than expressing this in straightforward autobiographical discourse, Shapiro used a romantic and symbolic vocabulary to show the deep unrest caused in the soul of a Jewish passage. By so doing, he showed the readers—those who experienced the journey firsthand, those born to parents who had, or those expecting to undergo it in the future—the existential anxiety inherent in the trip. He also offered a form of advice: To arrive safely one must never fully leave the past and instead must incorporate it deep in one's psyche. Moreover, by turning a tale of emigration into a romantic journey, Shapiro showed that this basic event of modern Jewish life could be the material of high art.

When Yash Went Forth

Jacob Glatstein's 1938 *Ven Yash iz geforn* (When Yash went forth) suggests similar lessons—to live as a fully integrated American one must reckon with one's past rather than reject it, as so many immigrants were wont to do in their effort to stop being greenhorns (195).[35] Like *Oyfn yam*, *Ven Yash iz geforn* covers a transatlantic journey. Yet it is the inverse of the emigrant's trip to the United States. Instead, we have the story of an immigrant's return to the old country after years in the United States. Woven into the narrative, however, is a lengthy memory of the narrator's emigration journey as a youth from Lublin, Poland, to New York (148–72). This memory builds a contrast between the youthful emigration trip, when the narrator could not wait to escape his provincial town for the United States, and his return as an adult who is now aware of how much he left behind.

Glatstein (1896–1971) was at the forefront of modern Yiddish poetry in the United States. He was a leader of the Inzikhistn (introspectivist) movement, which sought to create a "consciously modernist poetics" that would express the junction between the individual in a modern urban world and her internal, chaotic reality.[36]

Glatstein and the Inzikhistn group were dedicated to unsentimental expressions of the modern reality, using experimental, harsh, free verse to show the kaleidoscopic nature of the modern world. Members of the movement were highly influenced by European and American modernist movements from futurism to expressionism.[37]

Published in book form in 1938, *Ven Yash iz geforn* is an autobiographical account of the poet's 1934 return to his hometown, Lublin, Poland, twenty years after leaving for the United States.[38] The purpose of the trip is to visit his beloved mother, who has fallen ill. The novel describes the voyage to Europe, brief layover in France, and the train ride through Germany to Poland. The account ends as the train arrives in Lublin. We never read about the moment of reunion with the mother. In this novel the modernist approach with which Glatstein was so involved the 1910s and 1920s in the Inzikhistn group confronts the challenge of Jewish history. Traveling to and through fascist Europe, Glatstein comes to understand that the internationalist modernism that he embraces is built on tenets that exclude Jews.[39] Glatstein followed *Ven Yash iz geforn* with *Ven Yash iz gekumen* (When Yash came), which describes his stay in a Polish sanatorium following the burial of his mother.[40]

During the journey the narrator faces questions similar to those raised in *Oyfn yam* about how to successfully bridge the two worlds that represent his past and his future. As in *Oyfn yam*, a ship is an ideal setting with which to express the difficult state of transition of the Jewish emigrant. However, where Shapiro's journey is a romantic quest in the framework of a consideration of modernist exile, Glatstein's journey uses modernist narrative techniques to construct a polyphonic vision of Jewish selfhood.[41] In both works the ocean serves as the landscape for delving into issues of bicontinental selfhood, and the trip marks a rite of passage for the narrator as he seeks to reconcile his old self with the new.

Through his travels Glatstein's notion of himself as a free individuated American artist is challenged as he becomes aware of the manner in which an anti-Semitic environment categorizes him as a Jew and marks him as Other. The return to Poland unhinges and essentially deconstructs any univocal notion of himself as American and exchanges it for a more complicated dialogue between the urge for a free universal self and one that is ethnically bound. The work exemplifies an immigrant's new awareness of his inextricable tie to a homeland that constructs him as the Other.

Unlike *Oyfn yam*, *Ven Yash iz geforn* covers two modes of travel, the ship and the train. Glatstein sets up a dichotomy between landed national concerns (the train) and those that arise in a symbolically "international" space (the ship). By using the train as the marker of the local and the ship as the international, Glatstein builds a series of arguments about how local political rhetoric affects attempts to realize internationalist ideals. The work as a whole serves as a commentary on the place of Jews within the broader discourses of nationalism and internationalism during the rise of Nazism in the interwar era.

The journey to Poland and the painful confrontation with the world that he left as a youth has a profound influence on Glatstein's artistic outlook. Until his journey to Poland, Glatstein did not place specifically Jewish concerns at the forefront of his poetry, although he often wove them in. The trip to Lublin heralded a difficult period during which Glatstein sought to balance concern about the horrors to which European Jewry was being subjected and the objective of being true to his art. His struggle to balance his artistic and Jewish self came to a head during the journey and would influence his writings thereafter.

Glatstein therefore rendered a specifically Jewish form of interwar homecoming in which the return home was in all senses the inverse of the standard sentimental account. Yet the plot of *Ven Yash iz geforn* seems to mirror the common motif of a U.S. immigrant's return home to reconnect with his childhood. The return home should be a catalyst for autobiographical remembrances of the protagonist's childhood years in the old country. In his original introduction to *Ven Yash iz geforn*, Glatstein asserts that his novel is a countermodel to this type of immigrant autobiography, as exemplified by Louis Adamic's popular 1934 book, *The Native's Return: An American Immigrant Visits Yugoslavia and Discovers His Old Country*.[42] Glatstein says that his journey and writing are different from Adamic's in three ways: No grand reception awaited him upon his return; descriptions of shtetl life were not exotic to his readers because other writers had already so thoroughly described the shtetl, and, most important, Glatstein was never tied to Poland, as Adamic was to Yugoslavia.[43] Glatstein's return was not that of a native son but of an outsider. His work exemplifies the strange problematic return to a home that never really was a home because he was on the Jewish margin.[44]

Ven Yash iz geforn challenges idealized notions of return, reconnection, and the synthesis of the Old World with the new. In this novel the return home is not a return to a place but to being regarded as the Other. Instead of finding a home, Glatstein finds a new concept of selfhood that he would later liken to the hidden status of the Marrano.[45] Years after the trip Glatstein would assert: "Historically Jews have lived a double life, like Marranos, even in the freest countries. It's a matter only of sensitivity. . . . But we are all Marranos. Even in America we are Marranos."[46] The self-as–Marrano means not only a homeless (or nationless) self but a self that is permanently split between the public and the private. This fissure is expressed in the novels through Glatstein's use of a polyphonic narrative style in which the autobiographical voice is muted, and other voices predominate. Both novels take place entirely in the public realm, in encounters between characters, in their conversations. The polyphonic style resists univocal concepts of selfhood, which state that the self is knowable and unified. Instead, the self-as–Marrano is the meeting point of a constantly shifting relationship between one's private reality and how one is defined as a Jew by the ever-changing outside world.

Ven Yash iz geforn challenges the reigning notion at the time that the post–World War I era was conducive to the construction of the "new man," whether the new Russian or the new American, who was liberated from the old prejudices and constraints and free to build himself and his society in a progressive and positive way.[47] Glatstein's work satirizes the new Russian communist alongside the idealistic American. He does this by contrasting the progressive, universalistic ideologies of the characters whom he encounters during his journey with examples of how Jews are still discriminated against in the Soviet Union, the United States, and Europe.

Jewish "homelessness," according to Glatstein, is the result of dual negative and positive forces: entrenched worldwide anti-Semitism caused Jews to always feel as though they were the permanent Others in exile, and the "Jewish psyche" is universalistic and eschews nationalistic ties. Glatstein's return will thus be to a people, not a place. By constructing a new prototype of "Jewish return," Glatstein's novel undermines accepted notions of nation and selfhood and creates a space for the marginalized by making a full reckoning of their legitimate placement in the vocabulary of return.

Three narratives intersect in *Ven Yash iz geforn:*

A travelogue of the protagonist on a journey to visit his dying mother.
Dialogues (seemingly unmediated by the narrator) in which strangers tell their stories to the mostly silent Yash.
Yash's interior monologues that recall his past. The interior monologues arise in reaction to Yash's dialogues with other characters. The autobiographical remembrances are not a temporal autobiographical sequence. Instead, they are thematic.

All three narratives work together to express the "going forth" of the novel's title and the transitory nature of all the experiences described therein. *Ven Yash iz geforn* has no private space — everything is in public, and everything is in motion. The dialogues, woven into the forward motion of the travelogue, give glimpses of myriad other characters, many of them Jews, who are also in transit toward the European continent of their childhood. The interior monologues represent a break from the constant movement. Yet simultaneous with each moment of reminiscence or dialogue is the narrator on a journey with a real goal in mind: to return to his home and see his mother. Except for a brief layover in Paris, the narrator is moving toward this aim at every moment in the book.

The voyage to Europe is a symbolic and literal journey of selfhood between the dual locales of the United States and Europe. For each character that the narrator encounters and describes, the ship ride is a zone for self-metamorphosis and the place for examining how identity is constructed, because on the ship all are seemingly free of their backgrounds and can re-create themselves.

Moreover, the ship is in the guise of an international landless state with no dominant voice, or nation type, and each character is a microcosm of selfhood and nationhood. Ship life minimizes action and maximizes dialogue while enabling the passengers to take on the guise of being in an "international system" rather than a nationalized terrain. The ship can thus be seen as a microcosm of the United States, in the idealized sense of a pluralistic melting pot. However, as the narrator learns during his journey, on the ship, as on the U.S. shore, what is supposed to be a pluralistic environment in fact has certain cultures that predominate, while other cultures are suppressed. For Glatstein, Jews are pressured to hide their unique cultural traits in order to be accepted into the broader culture.

During the journey each character will present a dual self to the narrator, be it the teacher-bohemian, doctor-poet, or someone else. Questions of identity were central for the post-World War I generation, members of which often felt as though they had lost their way and the world was tenuous and uncertain, devoid of beauty and poetry. As an English pianist asserts about his lost generation: "Nisht nor ikh, nor der gantser nokhmilkhomedor. Fun undz vet shoyn keyn layt nisht zayn. Vi kenen mir gebn der velt sheynkayt, oder afile kinstlerishe mieskayt, az mir zaynen glat durkhgeverimte mentshn" (139). (Not only me, but the entire post-World War I generation. We will never amount to anything. How could we give the world beauty, or even artistic ugliness, since we are all rotten to the core?)

The contrast between the current lost generation and youth before World War I is starkly manifested in the lengthy remembrance of Yash's emigration journey from Lublin to the United States. The memory builds a dichotomy between the current return to a Europe marked by fascism and the more optimistic journey of his youth.

The Journey from Europe to the United States

Yash makes a brief visit to the third-class deck, which evokes his first transatlantic passage. The ensuing flashback covers his leave-taking from Lublin—his sad goodbye to his mother; the train ride to Warsaw with his beloved, gentle grandfather and brief stay at his aunt's home in Warsaw; a train ride to the port to catch the ship to England; the ship to the United States; and the first days in New York. The memory thus fluctuates between ship and train travel and remembrances of stays in Warsaw and New York.

The overriding perspective of the narrative is that of a naive optimistic youth setting out for the first time. The life that he is leaving in Lublin is one of hanging around with a group of friends that emulates the "goyish" world of books while being disconnected from "real Jewish life" around them: "Mir geyen vi di paves un zaynen umreal, vi aroysgenumen fun bikher. . . . Arum undz flakert a goyeshk lebn, etlekhe goyeshke lebns, a poylish un a rusish. . . . Arum undz kokht mit shnayders, shusters, blekher, papirosn-makher . . . ober mir zeen keynem nisht" (151). (We strutted about like peacocks in a false reality taken from books . . . and all around us blazed a "goyishe" life, different "goyishe" lives—Polish and Russian. . . . Yet surrounding us seethed real tailors, shoemakers, metal workers, cigarette-makers . . . but we noticed none of them.) Rather than staying in the false reality of the shtetl gang (as his adult eyes now view it), he decides to leave for the United States and distance himself from the worsening situation of his family and the rising anti-Semitism.

After a sad leave-taking with his family, he catches a train to Warsaw. His memory of the train ride recalls in positive tones the pleasure of an extended journey alone with his beloved grandfather while also conveying the pain he experiences at seeing (perhaps for the first time) proud Jews acting in an undignified manner because they are too poor to pay their train fare: "Es rayst dos harts tsu zen vi groyse yidn mit berd un hadres-ponim, yidn vos kenen derlangen a frask mit der breyter hant, bahaltn zikh unter di benk mit dem zayt-zhe moykhl aroyf, vi in shul erev yonkipur tsu malkes" (156). (It tore one's heart out to see the dignified traditional Jews, Jews who could deliver a smack with a powerful hand, hide themselves under the benches with their asses facing up, all ready for flagellations like in Shul on the eve of Yom Kippur.) The

memory of the train ride is thus marked by a mixture of sentimental longing for his last moments with his grandfather and an
awakening to the difficult situation of the Jews that he is leaving.

Once in Warsaw he experiences the city with the eyes of a
small-town youth awed by the "di groyse vunder fun der nayer
shtot" (158) (the great wonders of the modern city). His journey
has taken him from a shtetl, where the youth pretend to be like
big-city artists and intellectuals, to the big city, which he views
with the wonder of a country boy. After more goodbyes he heads
to Sosnovitz. While there, he has a fantasy of what his life would
be like if he did not leave for the United States: "'Vos mir Ame-
rike? Ver darf zikh arumtlikn oyf aza langer nesie? Blaybn do,
khasene hobn mit dem shvartsers tokhter, geyen ongeton in atlese-
nem shlofrok, zitsn shabes baym tish iber dem shmekndikn koy-
letsh. . . . Di likht in di hoykhe zilberne laykhter flemlen un viln
zikh rateven un in der shtil in der fintster kush ikh half-shleferik
dos yunge, shemevdike un shvangerdike vayb'" (165). (Who needs
America? Who needs to undertake such a long trip? I'll remain
here, marry the dark one's daughter, go around in a satin morning
coat, sit at the sabbath table over the lovely smell of challah . . .
the light in the tall silver candlestick flaming and trying to rescue
itself. And in the dark stillness, half-asleep, I'll kiss our child and
my shy and pregnant wife.) The fantasy presents an ideal portrait
of the traditional male life, with a loving wife and the practicing
of Judaism, all within a safe and sentimental haze. It marks an
emigrant's fears of what the New World will bring and a longing
to return to the safe, familiar landscape of the ideal shtetl.

After a brief disorientating scene in which he becomes lost in a
Polish town, he eventually manages to catch a series of trains to
the port. On the train he is utterly exhausted and is aware that he
is being looked upon as a vulnerable youth. During the disorienting train rides he barely sleeps. In his exhaustion he forgets that he
is now in the outside world and believes himself to still be in the
Jewish milieu. At one point he is shocked to realize the strange
Yiddish that he hears while dozing is in fact Polish and that he is
no longer surrounded by Jews but by "goyim." His passage thus far
has been marked on the one hand by a series of positive images of

the shtetl that he is leaving (his beloved grandfather and mother, the fantasy of remaining) and on the other hand by a sense of total dislocation and disorientation as he finds himself transplanted into the strange, non-Jewish broader world.

Once on the ship he feels more grounded as he connects with the other Jewish passengers and a rabbi who blesses their journey. Yash is part of the broader myth of the Galut, and all the up-rooted Jews share his exhaustion. Moreover, his urge to connect with other Jews is the opposite of what will occur on his return journey to Lublin. Then he will (at first) play the part of the urban sophisticate who hides his Jewishness from the other passengers, as they hide their own Jewishness from him. On the ship single young people hang out with each other, sing songs, and start romances. He falls for a young woman, Sonya, to whom he swears eternal love (while she swears her eternal love for his best friend). These shipboard young people are the reverse of the lost generation on the 1934 journey: They are carried away with optimism and the freedom that they experience on their first solo journey.

Within this memory of his emigration journey, the ship, in contrast to the railroad, is a much safer space for a Jew. Unlike the train, where he was surrounded by Christians and felt disorientated, and that deposited him between legs in predominantly Christian towns where he felt at risk, on the ship he can build friendships, enjoy himself, and be protected from the hazards that the Jewish traveler usually faced. Moreover, the shadow of anti-Semitism that predominates during the 1934 journey, as the ship heads to Hitler's Europe, is nowhere to be found. In fact, the ship's cook is even a Jew who goes out of his way to cook a Sha-vuot feast for the Jewish passengers (170). As Glatstein portrays it, the train journey from Warsaw to the port is quite different from those described in Abramovitsh and Sholem Aleichem. In Glat-stein it is no longer a Jewish space but one where Christians pre-dominate, and he feels in danger. In contrast, the ship of his youthful journey takes on aspects of a Jewish shtetl on the move, as we found in Abramovitsh and Sholem Aleichem.

The only hint that his optimistic imaginings will not be real-ized on the U.S. shore comes from a cynical German American passenger who sarcastically warns Yash that he had better beware and not fall into the typical "Jewish immigration story": "Der amerikaner daytsh tseredt zikh mit mir shpeter oyf der shif un er makht gutmutik khoyzek fun mir un fun dem gantsn yidishn folk. Dos gantse yidishe folk, zogt er, fort keyn New York un dos gantse yidishe folk fort tsu a feter un der feter arbet in a shop bay hemder, tsigarn oder bay hoyzn" (170). (The German American spoke with me later on the ship, and he good-naturedly ridiculed me and all the Jews. All the Jews, he said, travel to New York to an uncle, and the uncle works as a sweatshop worker, cigar maker, or at pants.) The German passenger suggests that instead of following the traditional plan, Yash should head out west. Of course, once the ship lands, Yash completely reprises the immigration story: He will work in his uncle's shop on the Lower East Side.

The disorienting awareness of the real hardship that living in the United States will cause occurs at the moment he arrives, when, rather than being met by loving family members and friends, he finds a note telling him that his uncle cannot meet him (because he must work) and that he must make his way alone to the uncle: "Es hot mir farklemt baym harts. Der gantser onshtel fun mayn veltlekhkayt hot zikh plutsim genumen brekhn unter dem varemen tuml fun kushenish un haldzenish, fur freydgeshreyen, fun borekhabes in nayem land. Mayn araynfor iz vayt nisht geven keyn triumfaler. . . . A gantsn tog iz mir nokhgegangen dem daytshes gelekhter, vos hot aroysgeknalt fun a moyl shvere goldene tseyn—dos yidishe folk zukht dem feter" (171). (My heart clenched with the weight of it all. My entire pretense of worldliness suddenly broke down under the warm tumult of kisses and hugs, of joyful yells, of "welcomes" to the new land. My arrival, in contrast, wasn't triumphant. . . . The whole day the German's laughter, which had snapped out from his mouth of golden teeth, trailed after me: "All the immigrant Jews look for their uncle.") All his worldly pretenses (carried with him from his Lublin days with his literary friends), and all his hope, are met by the painful lonely reality of New York.

The passage to the United States has unfolded along three distinct stages:

The disorienting train ride where sentimental longings mix with a sense
   of total dislocation as he moves through this alien, new, and "goyish"
   landscape
The voyage with other Jews filled with optimism, friendship, and young
   love
The cruel arrival and the crashing of his youthful dreams

Glatstein deliberately describes the journey as archetypal, and
it must have matched the trip of innumerable youth, both Jewish
and not, on their passage from Europe to the United States, filled
as they must have been with optimism — and learning upon arrival
that life would be difficult. In contrast, the return home on his
second journey reflects the much more sophisticated, less archetypal perspective of an adult who is trying to see through the veil
of youthful optimism to the deeper currents. Moreover, the heady
optimism of his youth is no longer appropriate for members of
the post–World War I generation, who often approach the world
pessimistically, with the hardened perspectives of the prematurely
mature.

The Voyage from New York to Lublin

The opening sentence of *Ven Yash iz geforn* establishes that the
ship will offer a unique setting for the narrator with its own set of
rules: "Azoy shnel vi di shif hot zikh opgerisn fun nopl, hob ikh
zikh glaykh derfilt in di hent fun di spetsyele marin-gezetsn" (9).
(As soon as the ship detached itself from the umbilical cord of
land, I straightaway sensed the special laws of the sea.) The ship is
a closed space that will shut all characters off from their personal
day-to-day world as well as the larger sociopolitical climate.

   With the world of land far away during the course of the
journey, the ship is a symbolic "new world," or "little planet," as
Glatstein calls it, where each character is a microcosm of selfhood and nationhood and where as a group they will create a
new united world of the sea: "Antloyfn un shneler iberlozn di
sentimentale dermonenishn fur kroyvim, tsugebundnkeyt un tera-
firma. Di 'Olimpik' hot zikh opgerisn fun der erd un iz glaykh

gevorn a planetl far zikh, mit an eygener bafelkerung, an eygn lebn un afile an eygenem umzikhtbarn manhig" (10). (The sentimental reminders of kinsmen, attachments, and terra firma were quickly dropped. The *Olympic* ripped herself from the land and straightaway became her own little planet, with her own population and life and even her own invisible leader.) The ship as a new society is the ideal locale on which to play out questions of identity. With the characters temporarily uprooted from all the things that make up their day-to-day life, how they talk and what they say is their primary means of self-expression. The narrator's role will be to listen (and constantly note how they speak: what their accents are, how clearly they talk) as one after another of the characters comes to him to tell him her story. At first he is like a journalist, listening patiently and recording what he hears while muting his own voice. Upon finding on the ship a newspaper with a report about Hitler, he is forced from the role of spectator into that of participant.

Many passengers embrace ideologies of one type or another that Yash shows to be hypocritical. For example, Glatstein follows up a description of a group of "new Russians"—the elite of the Soviet Union's young generation—with a statement about how communism has only improved the life of the elite. The ideology of equality and liberation for all does not match the reality, and for Jews to embrace communism is particularly hypocritical. He thus sarcastically says of a communist Jew: "Bin ikh vider mekane mayn bafraytn bruder un ikh vil trinken mit im tsuzamen a tost far dem nayem yidn, vos ruft zikh nisht op krenklakh in moskve, ven men shlogt yidn in alzhirye. A tost for dem nayem yidn!" (105–6). (I am in turn jealous of my liberated brother, and I wish to join him in a toast to our new Jews, who do not scream blue murder in Moscow when the Jews in Algeria are being beaten up. A toast for the new Jews!)

Glatstein does not challenge communist ideological discourse alone. Pro-American sentiments are equally contested. Throughout the novel Glatstein contrasts pro-U.S. slogans with individual autobiographical accounts by American Jews of anti-Semitism in the United States. (This is also a stark challenge to Adamic's pro-American idealism in *A Native Returns*.) These individual accounts present a strong counterargument to sentimental American patriotism. The United States offers unique difficulties for Jews because it impels many to hide or repress their Jewishness in the idealistic hope that they will be allowed to assimilate equally with other immigrant groups. One after another the passengers demonstrate that this is not the case—even when they assimilate, they are still discriminated against. For example: "Er dertseylt mir az der tate zayner iz a doktor in a kleyn shtetl in West Virginia. A mol hot er gemakht gor a sheyn lebn, ober haynt iz shoyn vayt nisht vi a mol. Hinter dem tatns pleytses geyt on a shtiler boykot, di merste kristn geyen tsum tsveytn doktor in shtetl, oykh a krist" (143). (He told me that his father is a doctor in a small town in West Virginia. In the past his father was able to make a good living, but now things weren't what they used to be. You see, behind his back, his father was suffering a kind of boycott, in which the majority of the residents would go only to the other doctor in the town, who, like them, was a Christian.) Where the other passengers have dual European and American selves, the Jewish passengers do not have this freedom of choice. No matter what they decide, the outside world will mark them, and often discriminates against them, for being Jews.

On the ship the narrator seeks out his real brothers: not the idealistic internationalists but the hidden Jews, or Marranos. Yash's search for the other Jewish passengers begins with the arrival of the newspaper report about Hitler. Until that point Yash seems to be like most of the other passengers in second class. The arrival of the newspaper awakens Yash's "Jewishness": "In dem dozikn internatsyonaln gan-eydn oyf der shif iz di Hitler-nays geven dos ershte vos hot mir derlangt dem patsh iber mayn yidishkayt" (37). (In the international "Eden" of the ship, the news about Hitler was the first thing to deliver an awakening slap to my Jewishness.) He begins to seek out other Jews, who, like him, will be profoundly disturbed by news of Hitler in a way that other passengers will not understand:

Ikh hob derfilt eynzam. Ikh hob zikh gefilt baleydikt far der ersht-klasiker nays, vos geyt in nivets un vos vert oyfgenumen azoy kalt un glaykhgiltik. Ikh hob gezukht a "varem yidish harts" vos zol mir helft lakhn, veynen, ober alts mit dem yidishn trop.

Un khotsh der bakser hot zikh baklogt oyf di yidishe besteds, vos bahaltn zeyer yidishkeyt, hob ikh, efsher unter dem druk fun di Hitler nays, ongehoybn zen etlekhe yidn. Es kon zayn az zey hobn tsulib der zelbiker urzakh genumen aroyskrikhn fun bahaltenishn un zukhn kompanye. (37–38)

(I felt lonely. I felt myself hurt by the news that went uncommented on and that was received so unemotionally and indifferently. I searched for a "warm Jewish soul" that would help me to laugh or cry—so long as it was with a Jewish stress.

(And although another passenger, a Jewish boxer, had complained about the "Jewish bastards" that hide their Jewishness, under the pressure of the Hitler news I began to see a variety of Jews. It could be that for the same reason as my own, they too began to creep out of their hiding places and seek out company.)

For the non-Jews the voyage is a bridge to a Europe that they will tour (a group of musicians), pass the summer in (a Wisconsin teacher who takes an annual summer break in Paris), visit the old country (a Polish American passenger), or return home to (a group of Soviet students who spent time studying in the United States). For them the journey is part of Clifford's schema of "good travel." For the Jewish passengers the ocean trip marks a bridge to a very different Europe, one that signifies the ascendancy of Hitler, which they either can choose to actively ignore (as with an assimilated Amsterdam Jew, [47–48]) or approach nervously.[48]

Europe will force the American Jews to focus on their Jewishness, an aspect of themselves many have unsuccessfully sought to sublimate in the United States.[49] For the Jewish passengers the freedom to be whomever they want, to be "new men," is not open to them because once removed from the international capsule of the ship and in the national spaces of fascist Germany and anti-Semitic Poland, their identity will be defined from the outside as the Jewish Others.

However, as Yash will fully grasp when Nazi youth enter the train during the train ride through Germany (208), unlike many other ethnic minorities, assimilated Jews are able to hide their Jewishness. Yash can have two identities: a Jew and an American. His ability to hide his Jewishness is what brings to his attention the false role that he has constructed as a free American. This becomes clear when his interest shifts from pretending to be a bourgeois, assimilated American to gaining a newfound and total respect for a Jewish passenger who does not try to hide his Jewishness (12, 38). The encounter with the dignified Jewish passenger reminds Yash of the quiet Sabbaths that he spent with his parents in Poland and allows him to reconnect with suppressed memories of his childhood.

The ability to hide one's Jewishness and be like a Marrano becomes for Yash/Glatstein a central aspect of what it means to be a Jewish American. The false comfort that Glatstein had once cultivated in the United States, based on his equal status with other Americans, was an illusion because it was only a local construct. As soon as he left U.S. soil, this notion was challenged (181–82). However, the problems of American Jews are clearly of a different sort than those faced by other U.S. minorities, such as African Americans and Chinese Americans. The racial hatred toward blacks and Asians generally was more overt, and certainly more violent, but assimilated American Jews had an option not open to these other minorities: They could hide their Jewishness and pass themselves off as, say, Italians or Greeks.[50] *Ven Yash iz geforn* thus subtly establishes for the reader a specific construct of Jewish immigrants—who encounter discrimination when regarded as Jews but who can choose to hide their true ethnicity. The ability to hide one's true self becomes the special mark of what it means to be a Jew and offers unique problems.

Where the non-Jewish characters use the journey by ship as a space for trying on different masks, the stakes are much higher for the Jews—the decision to keep quiet about their Jewishness is not necessarily one of choice but of self-protection. For the Jewish passengers dual selfhood connotes anti-Semitism, and their dual self is not the teacher-bohemian or doctor-poet but a public as-similated self and (often hidden) Jew.

In each encounter that Yash has with a Jewish character, that character's perspective on what it means to be a Jew is quickly asserted; the Amsterdam Jew (56) expounds on how wonderfully the Dutch treat the Jews; the communist Jew (105) asserts that the Russian Revolution has liberated the Jews of Russia; the young American Jewish student (143) describes his ill treatment in the United States. In each encounter the characters describe how they view their treatment in the varied lands in which they live. In each conversation, from the most idealistic to the most pessimistic, the Jewish characters perceive themselves as a special, separate population within the larger nation where they reside. Their common trait is their Jewish separateness. Where for the other passengers this ship is part of their pathway to a Europe that all see in positive terms as the place they will tour, return home to, or visit for an extended period, for the Jewish passengers the ship is headed straight toward Hitler's Europe. No wonder, then, that for every Jewish passenger Yash encounters, questions of Jewish self-identity are paramount. How each person, Jew and non-Jew alike, reacts to the news of Hitler is the litmus test of true character.

When the ship arrives in France, the illusory freedom of the ship as an "international paradise" becomes painfully, embarrassingly clear to all the passengers (181–82). There is profound awkwardness as the "ship brothers and sisters" break into little national units. All the defenses that passengers seemingly had dropped while at sea are now painfully back in place. Landing in a national space has shifted each into her landed identity and shown up her posturing as an internationalist.

This is a forceful challenge to bohemianism by a Jewish modernist intellectual. The ship is like a traveling "salon" in which passengers meet, argue, drink, flirt, and let their defenses down to talk. However, this bohemian freedom is not an option for the Jewish passengers, who do not have the luxury of forgetting that they are Jews in a world in which Hitler is on the rise. Those in the center can be whomever they want because the world outside is not labeling them as anything.

When the plot moves to a landed, national reality, both in Paris and on the train to Poland, the setting shifts to grounded nationhood. Here there are dominant languages, and the impending crisis is tangible and embodied in the characters with whom the narrator interacts. Unlike the ship, whose closed world was conducive to autobiographical monologues, trains make stops that bring on new characters and let off old ones. Moreover, as the train moves through nations, verbal fantasies about selfhood are brought into tangible contact with the political reality.

After a brief layover in Paris, Yash takes a train to Lublin, Poland. Unfortunately, the train first passes through Hitler's Germany. The train ride, and an encounter with Nazi youth, mark out the vast difference between two common settings of Jewish travel: the train in Europe, the ship to the United States. In Yash's memories of his journey to the United States, everything was through the forward-looking, idealistic perspective of a young emigrant. Now that he is back in Europe, Jewish travel means facing terror. The ship was the vessel of redemption: the train the vessel of fear. No wonder that on the European train, among Jewish passengers, laughter and joy are wholly lacking. The train can no longer be re-created as a Jewish space, as it was in Abramovitsh and Sholem Aleichem. The force of history, in the form of the ascendancy of Hitler, has made this impossible.

In one of the most simple yet deep statements on Jewish travel, Glatstein writes: "Vuhin fort a yid? Keyn Poyln, keyn Rumenye. Vos? Keyn Tshekhoslovakav . . . keyn . . . keyn . . . keyn" (185). (Whither travels a Jew? To Poland, to Romania. What? To Czechoslavakia! To . . . to . . . to.)

He has come to realize that for Jewish travelers in a state of permanent exile, travel is not from a home in point A to a place in point B but a permanent state of passage through different locales. This statement matches the title of the book, *Ven Yash iz geforn* (When Yash went forth), in that his journey exemplifies the archetypal Jewish journey: ever moving while never truly arriving. Moreover, as Yash comes to learn during the course of his journey, when he is repeatedly forced to acknowledge widespread American anti-Semitism, even in the United States he has not fully arrived. (The second book, *Ven Yash iz gekumen,* will mark his arrival in Poland, but his mother is now dead, and all who are left are the Jews who have not been able to emigrate and are in a state of grotesque stagnation.)

On the train, Yash meets a German who is seemingly disturbed by the current situation in his country. However, their interaction is the opposite of what would happen on the ship. Whereas on the ship, one after another of the characters came to Yash, the man with the "por tayere oyern" (172) (golden ears), to pour out his life story, here on a train going through various nations the German instead states that (203) (we must not speak) of the current situation in Germany. The overabundance of free-flowing speech on the ship has been replaced on the train by a stark decree of silence. Restrictiveness has replaced freedom.

As the train moves through Switzerland, the German makes a fervent nationalistic statement that the land over which they are traveling once belonged to Germany (206). Yash cannot understand the German's obsession with land, stating: "Der yid in mir, der tsigayner in mir. Der velt-patriot, der avanturist, der internatsyanolist—ikh hob zikh aleyn genumen dreyen farn oyer un zikh zidlen mit dem gantsn voylbakantn antisemitishn leksikon, derfar, vos mir iz nisht bashert aza vareme batsiung tsu shtiker opgebisene landshtrekes, vos eyn land roybt baym andern—der yid in mir!" (206). (The Jew in me, the gypsy in me, the world patriot, the adventurer, the internationalist—I tweaked my own ear and berated myself, using the whole, well-worn anti-Semitic lexicon, and all because I was destined to feel the same warm feeling toward disparate stretches of land, which one country robs from another. And all because of the Jew in me!) For Glatstein the Jew embodies simultaneously the international ideal of brother- or sisterhood and the destruction of that ideal by his inescapable ethnicity in an anti-Semitic world. Where other people are tied to nations, Jews serve as permanent rebuttals of nationalism. At the same time, however, they yearn to feel the tie to the land that other people feel.

Glatstein is using the notion of the positive diaspora to challenge nationalistic fascism. Glatstein thus seeks to give the status

of Jews as "homeless" a positive spin by asserting that homelessness is a force of internationalism against fascistic nationalism.
This matches James Clifford's notion that exiled peoples can challenge nationalism and that the "nation-state, as common territory
and time, is traversed and, to varying degrees, subverted by diasporic attachments."[51] Glatstein's assertion, however, also serves
as a challenge to Jewish nationalism in the form of Zionism.[52]
Glatstein is using a prodiaspora perspective to assert the moral su-
premacy of diaspora Jews who are not foolishly tied to land. Intense nationalistic ties to territory are what have caused so many
of the modern horrors against Jews and other minority groups.
Glatstein is thus giving a warning to Zionists while using the diaspora as a moral rebuff to the nationalism sweeping Europe.

As the train moves into Germany, a group of Nazi youth enter
(208). All of Glatstein's previous attempts to reclaim and avow his
Jewishness are instantly obliterated as the Nazis make him too
fearful to assert his Jewishness. While desperate to scream out "I
am a Jew," he remains silent. Meanwhile, his German "friend"
greets the youth with a "Heil, Hitler." Later the German is pa-
thetically embarrassed about having "hidden" his true nature and
having pretended to be a Nazi sympathizer. However, the German did not have to say "Heil, Hitler" to the young, laughing
Nazi youth. For Glatstein, in contrast, the stakes are much higher.
Nationalistic fascism has completely curtailed his realm of choice.
He must not show who he really is. This reflects upon the theme
throughout the novel of the suppression of Jewish selfhood.

The encounter with the Nazi youths anticipates the crisis of
restrictions of Jews that will permeate the second novel, *Ven Yash
iz gekumen*. The trip to Lublin has decentered Yash from his role
as spectator into the role of participant in the multivoiced dialogue of the journey. He has moved from an outsider to an awareness of his positioning as the Other. Where in the United States
he had the option to hide his Jewishness in an attempt to assimilate, in Germany he has no real choice: He must hide who he is to
protect himself from physical harm.

The final passage of the book describes the train's arrival in Poland, during which Yash makes the first real friend of the journey

and finally has a conversation, rather than just listening and reporting. The interaction occurs with a young Pole who is also returning to his family.[53] Both instantly understand and recognize each other like real, rather than idealized, brothers. This moment marks the return home, not to a place but to a tie with others.

As the train pulls into the station, the narrative turns into a real-time countdown of the train's arrival. We never witness the reunion with the mother that has been the focal point of the book. The book as a whole matches the statement "Vu fort a yid? Keyn keyn" (Where travels a Jew? Toward, toward) by suggesting that a Jew is always in transit and never fully arrives. For the Jewish passenger there is no arrival home and the journey is everything, because anti-Semitism has marked every locale as a point on an endless journey. Even in the United States, where he thought he had finally arrived, during the trip Yash comes to understand how deeply anti-Semitism is a part of the American scene.

Glatstein's use of a dual motif of travel—the ship and the train—serves as a highly sophisticated means to take to task standard notions of "home," "travel," and "return." In the novel Glatstein uses the contrast between ship and train travel to render a Jewish image of homecoming in which *homecoming* means not a return to a homeland (because he perceives Jews to be free of nationalistic longings [206]) but to an acceptance of one's deep, inextricable, intercontinental Jewish self.

Conclusion

In both *Oyfn yam* and *Ven Yash iz geforn* immigration and the journey are extended into larger issues of Jewish diaspora and displacement. On the individual level the works show the extremely difficult transition of the Jewish emigrant between the childhood "home" (that is not a homeland) of Europe and the adult place of the United States. In *Ven Yash iz geforn* we see this most clearly through Glatstein's weaving of a memory of the initial journey into the more adult perspective of the return trip.

In both works the ocean is the setting in which to negotiate one's understanding of one's dual Euro-American selfhood as a preparation to step onto the "unrestful" shore, which will offer scant time (and none of the poetic space of the sea) in which to delve so deeply into these issues. The ocean as the zone of creation is thus the ideal space in which to delve into, and re-create, one's self. For the Jewish emigrants life matches the ocean realm, where they are in a state of permanent movement (matching Glatstein's "vu fort a yid"). On the ocean both Shapiro and Glatstein learn that to safely live on shore they must maintain spiritual ties to the Jewish memories of their childhood.

Both Shapiro and Glatstein make the ship, like the train, a new setting for characters to tell stories. The stories match the floating, unlanded reality of the ship, where selfhood is in transit and everyone is searching for his own "voice." The ship's journey reflects upon the narrator's search to be an authentic and integrated individual, artist, and Jew. The path of integration, like the path of the ship, begins in Europe and ends in the United States. To land upon the new shore is, however, never to really depart the ship but always to keep one foot set on the European shore of departure and the other in the flux of the ocean journey.

5

Conclusion

Yehuda Halevi wrote, "In the East is my heart, and I
    dwell at the end of the West."
That's Jewish travel, that's the Jewish game of hearts
    between east and west,
between self and heart, to and fro, to without fro, fro
    without to,
fugitive and vagabond without sin. An endless journey,
    like the trip
Freud the Jew took, wandering between body and
    mind, between
mind and mind, only to die between the two.
Oh, what a world this is, where the heart is in one
    place and the body
in another (almost like a heart torn from a body and
    transplanted).
I think about people who are named for a place where
    they have
never been
and will never be. Or about an artist who draws a man's
    face
from a photograph because the man is gone. Or about
    the migration
of Jews,
who do not follow summer and winter, life and death
as birds do, but instead obey the longings of the heart.
    That's why
they are so dead, and why they call their God *Makom*,
    "Place."
And now that they have returned to their place, the
    Lord has taken up

wandering to different places, and His name will no
    longer be Place
but Places, Lord of the Places.
Even the resurrection of the dead is a long journey.
What remains? The suitcases on top of the closet,
that's what remains.

                —Yehuda Amichai, "Jewish Travel"

At the end of this book it is fitting to close with the words of the Israeli poet Yehuda Amichai.[1] What I have quoted is the second stanza of his phenomenal poem, "Jewish Travel: Change Is God and Death Is His Prophet," in which Amichai reorients Jewish travel in a post-Holocaust, post-Zionist landscape where the binary of "real" Europe and "mythic" Eretz Yisrael shifts. Before the Holocaust, as I have traced in this book, "real" Europe often existed simultaneously with the imagined Eretz Yisrael of Jewish longing. After the Holocaust, as Amichai's poem documents, Europe becomes the mythic space, the landscape of remembrances peopled by the ghosts of the dead, whereas Israel becomes the "real" land of wars, schools, and living nationalism.

Nevertheless, the binary was beginning to break down before the Holocaust as Yiddish writers described the changes brought to Jewish life by envisioning modernization as a force of movement and change, a catalyst for the shift from the static premodern shtetl to the postshtetl world of restless individuals moving and moving yet never fully arriving. For them modernization often meant motion, ceaseless motion, versus the entrenched (perhaps too entrenched) stasis of the shtetl of their literary imaginings. The Yiddish writers embraced the promise of the modernist endeavor, as well as its stylistics, and used their prose to problematize the changes brought by modernization for better and worse.

The second-generation writers whom I discussed in this book, Der Nister, Bergelson, Glatstein, and Shapiro, did not even mention mythic Eretz Yisrael as an alternative, imagined place to the real here and now of life in Europe and the United States. The binary shifted for them from Europe—Eretz Yisrael to modern Europe versus the mythic idyllic shtetl. For the second-generation writers the shtetl was the myth that existed in the minds of the Jews as memories and as longings for a return to a world of cohesive meanings.

Literary high modernism has tended to create the binary with the center in London, New York, or Paris and the margin in Calcutta, Cape Town, or Shanghai. (However, Joyce made marginal Dublin into a central locale of high modernism.) In the center are the writers of literary high modernism—Pound, Woolf, and Joyce versus the writers at the margins, Bergelson and Der Nister. This binary has been breaking down in recent years, as critics have focused on the numerous circles of writers at the margins who took up the high modernist project in a way that reflected their unique locales as peoples disempowered by colonization, racism, and anti-Semitism. What I have sought to do here is break down that binary of center-margin by documenting how Yiddish writers, while located in sites that were marginal in relation to literary high modernism, reoriented the world map by making it a Jewish terrain in their stories. They used the tools of high modernism— a self-conscious relationship to genre, stream-of-consciousness prose, open endings—to appropriate the center as a Judaized landscape and to relegate to the margins those we tend to think of as occupying the center. Where, then, is the center if the Jewish authors wrote as though they were the center and their modernism was only a tool for representing the real central shifts in day-to-day life that resulted from urbanization and modernization?

In Yiddish literature of travel we see how these writers refused to be located in the space of the oppositional figure of the "otherness machine."[2] In their literature the road was not a Polish road but a Jewish one. Or, in Der Nister's quest stories, it was a road that was not nationalized but a space that was dehistoricized. In their literature these Yiddish authors rewrote the world and embedded modernization in motion as a means to work through the processes that it heralded. The motion could represent the forces of urban destruction in "Dray khupes"; the eternal corrosive, intransitive movement of "A mayse mit a lets"; the disruptive power of the train car; or the dislocation of the modern person in the ship tales.

Modernization also became located in discursive movement where the changes of the modern world were presented in the stylistics of prose. Adopting the perspective of Abramovitsh, who used discursive action as a counterpoint to physical action, as, for example, in *Kitser masoes Binyomin hashlishi,* where gossip travels while people stagnate, the second generation made discursive motion a locale of the modern. In the unstable text of Der Nister or the pessimistic viewpoint of Bergelson, second-generation writers showed the breakdown of the cohesive "traditional" world of the eighteenth- and nineteenth-century novel. In place of realistic prose, the narratives are overdetermined and explicitly mediated by the authorial hand. (*Ven Yash iz geforn* is an exception; much of the account has aspects of a travelogue, and the real world of fascist Europe dominates the account.) Thus to make sense of the modern meant to use some of its tools (modernist prose) and motifs (the train) to show what it had wrought. See, for example, the fractured, endlessly self-referential Der Nisterian narrative, where the modern is both the figure of "der nister aleyn" (Der Nister himself) as a catalyst of unstoppable movement (from thin flesh to obesity and back again) and the prose, which is constructed along rhizomes of endlessly self-referential narrative shoots. Another example is the destabilizing text of Abramovitsh's *Kitser masoes Binyomin hashlishi,* whose constant reference to the prototype, *Don Quixote,* establishes the strange terrain where a bumpkin becomes a great explorer rather than dying a repentant dreamer.

If modernization is motion, then to inhabit the realm of the modern is to be in motion, always moving, never "home"—like the immigrants in both ship stories who discover an "authentic self" that must never land but always have feet on two shores. To be modern is to move forward, but to long for the lost past. For the Jews displacement was born of the profound hardship of

forced upheaval. But from the displacement comes the notion
that we saw in both Shapiro and Glatstein, that in flux is truth.
The modern condition becomes that of the immigrant who is on
unstable footing and disconnected from the fixed world of the
premodern shtetl. The choices are either despair, as represented
by Yanko Ravitsh, the man who committed suicide, or a search to
find meaning in uncertainty. The place of meaning becomes the
difficult balance of one foot on the European shore, the other on
the restless ocean.

Writers such as James Joyce also made the Jew (Leopold
Bloom) into a representation of the modern condition of flux. For
Glatstein, in contrast, the Jewish experience of fracture was the
result of real political occurrences, and the Jew therefore could not
represent the universal modern condition. Glatstein was thus responding to the modern experience with the specificity of the
Jewish subject. Basic to the modernist endeavor is the desire to
express the individual experience in relation to the modern world.
Glatstein too sought to express it and to show the modern subject
as a real Jew who refuted tropal representations. In his stories the
landscape of modernist individuals broadened beyond the European or American to include the Jew.

The Jews were forced into a position at the margins, but, for
Glatstein at least, that location also gave Jews insight into the
dangers of nationalism. This is not, however, the notion of the
"positive diaspora," because for Glatstein, no diaspora locale is
positive—in the United States anti-Semitism was also entrenched and made Jews into Marranos. Rather, the displacement
teaches its own lesson to those who will listen—that nationalism,
communism, blind American patriotism, or Nazism is built upon
empowering the strong by disenfranchising the weak.

It seems to me that critics often see Jews as having "legs," not
"roots." If they are merely walking over the land, rather than
rooted in it, their placement must always, and necessarily, be in
relation to the lands that they traverse ("their" lands). The other
choice becomes Zionist nationalism, where "we" are at home on
our land. Yiddish literature of travel offers a third means of
understanding how Jews on the cusp of modernism envisioned

the world, beyond "Diaspora" and "Zionism." It is not, however, a multicultural vision of Jews in the diaspora embracing their status.

The third possibility, I would suggest, is what we see in the literature of travel: the use of literature to revise the world and to envision the "here and now" of eastern Europe as our here and now. But I want to reiterate that each of the writers had a different agenda in relationship to place and to the Jews. *Our* does not mean that the Jews were a single, positive, communal entity—we saw how Sholem Aleichem subverted the positive Jewish community in *Di ayznban geshikhtes*. Moreover, writers such as Bergelson and Der Nister probably would have rejected the idea that there was any stable cultural entity called "the Jewish community." And this is also not to say that these writers had a territorialist political agenda.

What I am saying is that in textual terms the land was a setting that represented not only the relationship of the Jews to the Christians but also how modernization was changing Jewish life in eastern Europe. In extratextual terms, when writers reenvisioned the world as Jewish (as in the quest tales), Jews wrote the world on equal terms with non-Jews. Yet this also suggests the disempowerment of the Jews, where writing is a political act, perhaps the only one that they felt that they had, of resisting their status, a way of creating a literary world in which they are in the center. The means of resistance were not generally head-on confrontations but the sophisticated narrative tools of irony, symbolism, and intertextualities. Although it uses many tools of high modernism, the literature became a way to resist the oppressive forces of modernization that pushed Jews even more to the side, the margin, than they had been in the premodern era. This we see in Glatstein's reckoning of the "new man" of the 1930s; he allows everyone to be re-created but the Jew, who is pushed ever more into the place of the Marrano.

Modernization was something that these writers sought to appropriate through the literary act and to express as a narrative force of unbridled motion, which could be challenged by literary means (such as using symbolic appropriations to turn train cars into carriages, or turn the emigrant voyage into a romantic quest of self-integration by embedding romantic themes and images throughout the narrative). Modernization was a problematic, intense force to reckon with because it could destabilize meaning. To write about modernization meant expressing its corrosive effects and making the modern landscape into narratives of motion, whether of traveling figures, traveling words, or traveling worlds.

Notes
Bibliography

Notes

1. Introduction

1. In *Russian Modernism: The Transfiguration of the Everyday* (Cambridge: Cambridge University Press, 1997), 16-18, Stephen C. Hutchings shows that the use of patently fictional narratives to comment on real life is basic to modern narrative, particularly to Russian modernism.

2. Dan Miron, *The Image of the Shtetl and Other Studies of Modern Jewish Literary Imagination* (Syracuse, N.Y.: Syracuse University Press, 2000), 32-48.

3. Amy C. Singleton, *No Place Like Home: The Literary Artist and Russia's Search for Cultural Identity* (Albany: State University of New York Press, 1997), 33.

4. Ibid., 32.

5. For a discussion of the *talush*, or "uprooted" man, see Nurit Govrin's *Alienation and Regeneration*, trans. John Glucker (Tel Aviv: MOD Books, 1989), 20-30.

6. I am using the term *Galut* to refer to the Jewish religious idea of exile, whereas I use *diaspora* as a general term for the displacement of people.

7. For a consideration of the biblical notion of dual locations, see Arnold Eisen's *Galut: Modern Jewish Reflections on Homelessness and Homecoming* (Bloomington: Indiana University Press, 1986). The translation is from Jewish Publication Society, *Tanakh: A New Translation of The Holy Scriptures According to the Traditional Hebrew Text* (New York: Jewish Publication Society, 1985), 320.

8. For an interesting consideration of the dual feelings of power and powerlessness caused by the Galut, see David Biale, *Power and Powerlessness in Jewish History* (New York: Schocken, 1986), 34-57.

9. W. D. Davies, *The Territorial Dimension of Judaism* (Berkeley: University of California Press, 1982), 33.

10. J. Hillis Miller, *Topographies* (Stanford: Stanford University Press, 1995), 3.

11. Franco Moretti, *Atlas of the European Novel* (New York: Verso, 1998), 3.

12. Wai Chee Dimock, "Literature for the Planet," *PMLA* 116, no. 1 (January 2001): 175.

13. Simon Schama, *Landscape and Memory* (New York: Alfred A. Knopf, 1995), 29, 36.

14. James Clifford, "Diasporas," *Cultural Anthropology* 9, no. 4 (1994): 318.

15. The Yiddish is from Sholem Abramovitsh, *Kitser masoes Binyomin hashlishi*, in *Ale verk fun Mendele Moycher-Sforim*, ed. N. Mayzl (Warsaw: Farlag Mendele, 1928), 9:10. The translation is from Sholem Abramovitsh, *The Brief Travels of Benjamin the Third*, trans. Ted Gorelick, in *Tales of Mendele the Book Peddler: Fishke the Lame and Benjamin the Third*, ed. Dan Miron and Ken Frieden (New York: Schocken, 1996), 307.

16. Clifford, "Diasporas," 307.

17. Daniel Boyarin and Jonathan Boyarin, "Diaspora: Generation and the Ground of Jewish Identity," *Critical Inquiry* 19, no. 4 (Summer 1993): 720.

18. See Miron's essay, "The Literary Image of the Shtetl," in *Image of the Shtetl*, 1–48.

19. David Biale, Michael Galchinsky, and Susannah Heschel, "Introduction: The Dialectic of Jewish Enlightenment," in *Insider/Outsider: American Jews and Multiculturalism* (Berkeley: University of California Press, 1998), 8.

20. Caren Kaplan, *Questions of Travel: Postmodern Discourses of Displacement* (Durham, N.C.: Duke University Press, 1996), 36.

21. Bryan Cheyette and Laura Marcus suggest that even the recent "reconstruction of modernity," and *both* the positive and negative reconsideration of the "efficacy of western modernity," have "continued to banish Jewish difference." See their "Introduction: Some Methodological Anxieties," to *Modernity, Culture, and "the Jew"* (Cambridge, U.K.: Polity Press, 1998), 2–3.

22. See, for instance, Zygmunt Bauman's *Modernity and the Holocaust* (Ithaca, N.Y.: Cornell University Press, 1989).

23. For an analysis of the relationship between "minority" and postmodern fragmentation, see Phillip Brian Harper's *Framing the Margins:*

The Social Logic of Postmodern Culture (New York: Oxford University Press, 1994).

24. Iain Chamber, *Migrancy, Culture, Identity* (London: Routledge, 1994), 27.

25. Susan Suleiman, "Introduction: On Signposts, Travelers, Outsiders, and Backward Glances," *Poetics Today* 17, no. 3 (Fall 1996): 286.

26. Julia Kristeva, *Strangers to Ourselves,* trans. Leon S. Roudiez (New York: Columbia University Press, 1991), 1.

27. Susan E. Shapiro, "Écriture judaïque": Where are the Jews in Western Discourse?" In *Displacements: Cultural Identities in Question,* ed. Angelika Bammer (Bloomington: Indiana University Press, 1994), 192.

28. Ibid., 192-93.

29. Edward Said, "Reflections on Exile," *Granta* 13 (1984): 159. He rewrote this article and covered some new territory in his more recent essay for *Harper's Magazine* entitled "The Mind of Winter: Reflections on Life in Exile," September 1984, pp. 49-55.

30. Said, "Reflections on Exile," 160.

31. The quotation is from Angelika Bammer's introduction to *Displacements: Cultural Identities in Question* (Bloomington: Indiana University Press, 1994), xiv.

32. And sometimes even critics who are attempting to resituate the field of travel studies slip into these types of presumptions. For instance, a work considered groundbreaking in the field of decentered travel studies is Mary B. Campbell's *The Witness and the Other World: Exotic European Travel Writing, 400-1600* (Ithaca, N.Y: Cornell University Press, 1988). However, her book opens with the following highly problematic statement: "Soon after the Fall, human beings took their first journey—in this case, into exile from Paradise. We are, all of us, a displaced people." Not only does it reflect her Judeo-Christian bias but it is another case of the dehistoricization of real exile by using a metaphoric exile to connote a universal human condition.

33. Dennis Porter, *Haunted Journeys: Desire and Transgression in European Travel Writing* (Princeton, N.J.: Princeton University Press, 1991), 20; James Duncan and David Ley, introduction to *Place/Culture/Representation,* ed. James Duncan and David Ley (London: Routledge, 1993), 2.

34. Michael Gluzman's essay, "Modernism and Exile: A View From the Margins," in *Insider/Outsider: American Jews and Multiculturalism,*

ed. David Biale, Michael Galchinsky, and Susan Heschel (Berkeley: University of California Press, 1998), 231.

35. S. Shapiro, "Écriture judaïque," 182.

36. Chana Kronfeld, *On the Margins of Modernism: Decentering Literary Dynamics* (Berkeley: University of California Press, 1996), 232.

37. R. Edelmann, "Ahasuerus, the Wandering Jew," in *The Wandering Jew: Essays in the Interpretation of a Christian Legend*, ed. Galit Hasan-Rokem and Alan Dundes (Bloomington: Indiana University Press, 1986), 3.

38. Hyam Maccoby, "The Wandering Jew as Sacred Executioner," in Hasan-Rokem and Dundes, *The Wandering Jew*, 237, 238–39.

39. Carol Boyce Davies, *Black Women, Writing and Identity: Migrations of the Subject* (New York: Routledge, 1994), 153. "Politics of location" is a term first used by North American feminists in the 1980s as "a method of interrogating and deconstructing the position, identity, and privilege of whiteness" (Caren Kaplan, "The Politics of Location as Transnational Feminist Critical Practice," in *Scattered Hegemonies: Postmodernity and Transnational Feminist Practices*, ed. Inderpal Grewal and Caren Kaplan [Minneapolis: University of Minnesota Press, 1994], 139). The paradigmatic work is Adrienne Rich's 1984 essay, "Notes Toward a Politics of Location," in *Blood, Bread, and Poetry: Selected Prose, 1979–1985* (New York: W. W. Norton, 1986). For further works on the politics of location, see bell hook's writings, in particular "Choosing the Margin as a Space of Radical Openness," in *Yearning: Race, Gender, and Cultural Politics* (Boston: South End Press, 1990), 145–53, and James Clifford, "Traveling Cultures," in *Cultural Studies*, ed. Lawrence Grossberg, Cary Nelson, and Paula Treichler (New York: Routledge, 1992), 96–116.

40. bell hooks, "Representing Whiteness in the Black Imagination," in *Cultural Studies*, ed. Lawrence Grossberg, Cary Nelson, and Paula Treichler (New York: Routledge, 1992), 344.

41. In Gluckel of Hameln, *The Memoirs of Gluckel of Hameln*, trans. Marvin Lowenthal (New York: Schocken, 1977), the accounts, begun in 1690 by a German Jewish widow, document the many hazards that travelers encounter: robbers, pirates, soldiers.

42. Clifford, "Traveling Cultures," 105, 106.

43. The central collection of Jewish travelogues before the nineteenth century remains Elkan Nathan Adler, ed., *Jewish Travellers: A Treasury of Travelogues from Nine Centuries* (New York: Hermon Press, 1966).

44. Michael Seidel, *Exile and the Narrative Imagination* (New Haven, Conn.: Yale University Press, 1986), 4.

45. Steven Hutchinson, *Cervantine Journeys* (Madison: University of Wisconsin Press, 1992), 157.

46. Although the author's name is Sholem Abramovitsh, Yiddish readers often but mistakenly refer to him as "Mendele Moycher Sforim," which was the full name of his narrator.

47. Dean MacCannell, *The Tourist: A New Theory of the Leisure Class* (New York: Schocken, 1976), 2–3.

48. See Miron, "Folklore and Antifolklore in the Yiddish Fiction of the Haskala," in *Image of the Shtetl,* 49–80.

49. Elia Levita, *Bovo d'Antona* (Isny: 1541), was the prototype for the popular Bovo-bukh. For the Mayse Bukh in Yiddish, see Jacob ben Avrom, *Mayse-bukh,* in *Musterverk fun der yidisher literatur,* vol. 38 (Buenos Aires: Literatur-gezelshaft baym YIVO, 1969). For an English translation see *Maaseh Book,* ed. and trans. Moses Gaster (Philadelphia: Jewish Publication Society, 1934). No one has made a thorough study of pre-nineteenth-century Yiddish literature of travel. However, David Roskies's essay, "The Genres of Yiddish Popular Literature, 1790–1860," *Working Papers in Yiddish and East European Jewish Studies* 8 (February 1975), does include an overview of both the premodern popular romance (9–13) and the traveler's tale (14). Roskies also cites a number of travelers' stories, thus showing their popularity with the Yiddish reading public.

50. I am aware of how problematic it is (for me in particular) that this book does not include any works by women writers and only one story ("Dray khupes") has central female characters. However, the genre of travel fiction tends to follow the "gendered topography" described by Georges Van Den Abbeele — travel literature often excludes women, leaves them at home, or makes them the exotic objects of desire for travelers to foreign countries (Van Den Abbeele, *Travel as Metaphor: From Montaigne to Rousseau* [Minneapolis: University of Minnesota Press, 1992], xxv).

A number of recent works have sought to analyze "gendered topographies" and consider the stories of women travelers, but the scope of this book unfortunately does not permit a thorough consideration of gendered space. I could find no appropriate works by women writers to include, and, overwhelmingly, in the works themselves women are absent figures (the notable exception is Abramovitsh's *Kitser masoes Binyomin hashlishi,* whose gender politics I do consider in some detail). I cannot state strongly enough that this analysis is at best exclusionary (because the literature was), and my analysis of Yiddish literature of the road is entirely from male perspectives. It is thus a totally one-sided analysis.

51. [Yoysef Vitlin] *Robinzon di geshikhte fun Alter Leb* (Vilnius: Mats, 1880). David Roskies points out that Vitlin's adaption was based on a German story for children. See Roskies, *A Bridge of Longing: The Lost Art of Yiddish Storytelling* (Cambridge, Mass.: Harvard University Press, 1995), 62. For a full analysis of the story see my article "The Jewish Robinson Crusoe," *Comparative Literature* 54, no. 3 (2002): 215–28.

52. For the Hebrew critical edition, see *Shivhei haBesht*, ed. Avraham Rubinstein (Jerusalem: Rubin Mass, 1991). For an English translation see *In Praise of the Baal-Shem Tov*, trans. and ed. Dan Ben-Amos and Jerome R. Mintz (New York: Schocken, 1984).

53. For the bilingual edition (English and Hebrew) of the tales of Nahman of Bratslav, see *Seyfer sippurey mayses* (Jerusalem: Keren hadpasah shel hasidei Braslav, 1979). For an English translation see *Nahman of Bratslav: The Tales*, trans. and ed. Arnold Band. (New York: Paulist Press, 1978).

54. Dan Miron, "Sholem Aleykhem: Person, Persona, Presence," in *Image of the Shtetl*, 154.

55. Ibid., 144–45.

56. Mikhail Krutikov, *Yiddish Fiction and the Crisis of Modernity, 1905–1914* (Stanford: Stanford University Press, 2001), discusses how this "crisis of modernity" influenced Yiddish discourse. He gives an excellent overview and analysis of this subject against the historical context. Krutikov persuasively argues that 1905 was the watershed year when "fictional time and space, as well as the construction of character, underwent radical transformation in the direction of more openness to, and integration into, external reality" (115).

2. The Road

1. Again I want to stress that the Jewish wandering of the Galut has no connection whatsoever with the Christian Wandering Jew.

2. For a thorough analysis of the role of Mendele in Sholem Abramovitsh's works, see Dan Miron's *A Traveler Disguised: The Rise of Modern Yiddish Fiction in the Nineteenth Century*, 2d ed. (Syracuse, N.Y.: Syracuse University Press), 131–248.

3. *Fishke der krumer* came out as a story in 1869, and Abramovitsh expanded it into a novella that was published in 1888. It may be found in the third volume of *Alez verk fun Mendele Moycher-Sforim*, ed. N. Mayzel

(Warsaw: Farlag Mendele, 1928). An excellent translation into English appears as *Fishke the lame*, trans. Hillel Hilken, in *Tales of Mendele the Book Peddler: Fishke the Lame and Benjamin the Third*, ed. Dan Miron and Ken Frieden (New York: Schocken, 1996), 3–298.

4. Abramovitsh, *Fishke der krumer,* 81; Abramovitsh, *Fishke the lame,* 150.

5. Dan Miron and Anita Norich, "The Politics of Benjamin III: Intellectual Significance and Its Formal Correlatives in Sh. Y. Abramovitsh's Masoes Binyomin Hashlishi," in *The Field of Yiddish: Studies in Language, Folklore, and Literature,* 4th coll., ed. Marvin Herzog, Barbara Kirshenblatt-Gimblett, Dan Miron, and Ruth Wisse (Philadelphia: Institute for the Study of Human Issues, 1980), 1–115.

6. Vladimir Propp describes a wondertale this way: "A wondertale begins with some harm or villainy done to someone (for example, abduction or banishment) or with a desire to have something (a king sends his son in quest of the fire bird), and develops through the hero's departure from home and encounters with the donor, who provides him with a magic agent that helps the hero find the object of the search. Further along, the tale includes combat with an adversary (the most important form is slaying a dragon), a return, and a pursuit. . . . Later he escapes, is subjected to a trial by difficult tasks, and becomes king and marries, either in his own kingdom or in that of his father-in-law" (Propp, *Theory and History of Folklore,* trans. Ariadna Y. Martin and Richard P. Martin, ed. Anatoly Liberman (Minneapolis: University of Minnesota Press, 1984), 5:102.

7. Kathryn Karczewska, *Prophecy and the Quest for the Holy Grail: Critiquing Knowledge in the Vulgate Cycle* (New York: Peter Lang, 1998), 35.

8. Tzvetan Todorov, *Introduction to Poetics,* trans. Richard Howard (Minneapolis: University of Minnesota Press, 1992), 51.

9. Wolfgang Iser, *The Fictive and the Imaginary: Charting Literary Anthropology* (Baltimore: John Hopkins University Press, 1993), 12–13.

10. Percy Adams, *Travel Literature and the Evolution of the Novel* (Lexington: University Press of Kentucky, 1983), 155.

11. Roskies, *Bridge of Longing,* 30.

12. Cathy Popkin, *The Pragmatics of Insignificance: Chekhov, Zoshchenko, Gogol* (Stanford: Stanford University Press, 1993), 175.

13. For the Yiddish original see Abramovitsh, *Kitser masoes Binyomin hashlishi,* in *Ale verk fun Mendele Moycher-Sforim,* 9:81. For the excellent English translation, see Abramovitsh, *The Brief Travels of Benjamin the Third,* in Miron and Frieden, *Tales of Mendele,* 301–91.

14. Stephen C. Hutchings writes that Don Quixote (the model for Benjamin) also oscillates between "daily life" and "art" by the "multilayered contrast between Quixote's conception of himself as knight errant (derived from readings of chivalric romances) and the mundane realities encountered during his quest" (Hutchings, *Russian Modernism*, 22).

15. Olga Litvak offers a compelling argument that Abramovitsh's portrayal of Benjamin's journey "signifies Abramovich's rejection of Haskalah historicism in favor of an ironic stance toward modernization" (223) and that within the story is an "ironic depiction of the maskil as a failed Nicholaevan soldier" (228). For her discussion of this see "The Literary Response to Conscription: Individuality and Authority in the Russian-Jewish Enlightenment" (Ph.D. diss., Columbia University, 1999), 222–30.

16. Delphine Bechtel points out in *Der Nister's Work, 1907–1929: A Study of a Yiddish Symbolist* (New York: Peter Lang, 1990) that Der Nister (and perhaps Peretz) may have been influenced by other Hasidic storytellers as well, most notably the Maggid of Dubno. See p. 123. An outstanding new work that analyzes literary motifs in Nahman of Bratslav's *Seyfer sippurey mayses* and includes thorough biographical information is Ora Wiskind-Elper's *Tradition and Fantasy in the Tales of Reb Nahman of Bratslav* (Albany: State University of New York Press, 1998). Roskies also has an excellent chapter on Nahman's stories that, in particular, places his writing within the broader tradition of Yiddish storytelling. See *Bridge of Longing*, pp. 20–55. Arnold Band provides a fine introduction to Nahman's tales, as well as biographical information, in *Nahman of Bratslav: The Tales* (New York: Paulist Press, 1978), 9–39.

17. Roskies, *Bridge of Longing*, 27.

18. As recounted in Band's introduction to *Nahman of Bratslav*, 32–33.

19. Wiskind-Elper, *Tradition and Fantasy*, 51–55. *Kunstmärchen* is "a tale embodying folk-motifs but written by sophisticated modern authors." See James Trainer, "The Märchen," in *The Romantic Period in Germany*, ed. Siegbert Prawer (London: Weidenfeld and Nicolson, 1970), 97.

20. Roskies, *Bridge of Longing*, 27.

21. For the essay that outlines Shlovsky's theory of making strange, see his "Art as Technique" in *Russian Formalist Criticism: Four Essays*, trans. Lee T. Lemon and Marion J. Reis (Lincoln: University of Nebraska Press, 1965), 3–57.

22. Eisen, *Galut,* 53.

23. Wiskind-Elper, *Tradition and Fantasy,* 53.

24. Ibid., 54.

25. Karczewska, *Prophecy and the Quest for the Holy Grail,* 37.

26. See Dan Ben-Amos, introduction to *Folklore Genres,* ed. Dan Ben-Amos (Austin: University of Texas Press, 1976), xxii.

27. The fairy tales of the Brothers Grimm were not specifically *Kunstmärchen* because they denied that they were in any way altering the tales and instead believed that they were reporting them verbatim (while later studies have shown that this was not the case). Yet for my analysis what is important is that neither the *Kunstmärchen* nor the Grimm tales were constructed on the religious matrix of the Christian quest but rather on pagan folk concepts—even if reconstituted somewhat by the Grimms and others.

28. Karczewska, *Prophecy and the Quest for the Holy Grail,* 36.

29. Nahman of Bratslav, *Nahman of Bratslav,* 84, 143.

30. Roskies, *Bridge of Longing,* 28, 25.

31. Nahman of Bratslav, "The Master of Prayer," in *Nahman of Bratslav,* 226.

32. Ibid., 136.

33. It is difficult to accurately define the relationship between *Don Quixote* and *The Travels of Benjamin the Third.* Literary critics have variously labeled *Travels* a parody, a satire, and a rewriting of *Don Quixote.* However, I believe that Ruth Wisse evokes the relationship most accurately when she writes that the novel *Don Quixote* is a "frame device" for *Travels.* Her term is thus inclusive of both the satiric and parodic uses that Nahman makes of *Don Quixote* in *Travels.* See Wisse, *The Schlemiel as Modern Hero* (Chicago: University of Chicago Press, 1971), 32.

For a full comparison of *Don Quixote* and *Kitser masoes Binyomin hashlishi,* see my article, "The Jewish Don Quixote," *Cervantes* 17, no. 2 (1997): 94–105.

34. For a cogent analysis of Don Quixote's difficulty in discerning fact from fiction, see Ulrich Wicks, "Metafiction in *Don Quixote:* What Is the Author up to?" in *Approaches to Teaching Cervantes' Don Quixote,* ed. Richard Bjornson (New York: Modern Language Association, 1984), 69–76.

35. See Miron and Norich's essay, "Politics of Benjamin III," 57.

36. For the finest analysis of Abramovitsh's use of Mendele as a narrative device, see Miron, *Traveler Disguised,* chaps. 4–7.

37. Y. Goldberg asserts that Abramovitsh revives the "veg roman," or road story, an eighteenth-century narrative style, because he believed that the Jews of the nineteenth century lived in an eighteenth-century reality. See Goldberg, "Der Vegroman in der intimer stil; vegn Fishke der krumer," in *Di yidish literatur in nayntsetn hundert: zamlung fun yidisher literatur forshung in kritik in ratn farband*, ed. Khone Shmeruk and Chava Turniansky (Jerusalem: Magnes Press, 1993), 564.

38. Miron and Norich, "Politics of Benjamin III," 12.

39. Robert Packard, *Refractions: Writers and Place* (New York: Carroll and Graff, 1990), 115.

40. For a collection of Jewish travelogues that includes excerpts about many Jewish explorers whom Benjamin the Third cites as inspiring him (Benjamin of Tudela, Eldad the Danite, Rabbi Samuel Ben Samson), see Adler, *Jewish Travellers*. For Jewish travelogues in Hebrew, see J. D. Eisenstein, ed., *Ozar Massaoth* (New York: J. D. Eisenstein, 1926).

41. Michael Nerlich, *Ideology of Adventure: Studies in Modern Consciousness, 1100–1750* (Minneapolis: University of Minnesota Press, 1987), 40.

42. Wisse believes that a construct of the "heroic" arises from situations in which "real action is impossible." She writes, "The schlemiel becomes a hero when real action is impossible and reaction remains the only way a man can define himself" (*Schlemiel as Modern Hero*, 39).

43. Only with the massive pogroms of the 1880s did many Jewish writers and intellectuals begin to focus on how anti-Semitism hindered Jewish modernization. For an analysis of how the pogroms affected Jewish literary life, see Benjamin Harshav, *The Meaning of Yiddish* (Los Angeles: University of California Press, 1990), 119–38.

44. Abramovitsh, *Kitser masoes Binyomin hashlishi*, 91–92; Abramovitsh, *Brief Travels of Benjamin the Third*, 370. Subsequent direct quotations from these works will be followed by page citations in text.

45. Hutchinson, *Cervantine Journeys*, 48.

46. Hutchings shows how Russian writers from Dostoyevsky to Gogol foregrounded gossip to challenge overaesthetized European literature (*Russian Modernism*, 59–61).

47. See, for example, Abramovitsh, "In Which Benjamin Causes a Political Upheaval," chap. 7 in the Yiddish original of *Kitser masoes Binyomin hashlishi* (59–64) and in Halkin's translation (344–48).

48. For a fine structural analysis of *Kitser masoes Binyomin hashlishi*, including a consideration of the ties between Mendele, the characters,

and the story's end, see Menachem Peri's "Ha'analogiya umekoma be-mivne haroman shel Mendele Mokher-Sfarim," *Hasifrut* 1, no. 1 (1968): 65–100.

49. I wish to thank to Jeremy Dauber for this insight.

50. In *Classic Yiddish Fiction: Abramovitsh, Sholem Aleichem, and Peretz* (Albany: State University of New York Press, 1995), Ken Frieden notes that "the very fact that Benjamin is 'the Third' suggests that he is intended as a parodic recycling of earlier heroes and anti-heroes" (82). Benjamin's title thus both places him in the proud line of Jewish explorers and subverts that heritage by being a "parodic recycling" of their achievements.

51. For an interesting discussion of why Abramovitsh never completed *Kitser masoes Binyomin hashlishi,* see Miron and Norich, "Politics of Benjamin III," 104–8.

52. Krutikov, *Yiddish Fiction,* 70.

53. For an excellent analysis of how the voices of Mendele and Benjamin vary, see Miron, *Traveler Disguised,* 223–29.

54. For a compelling discussion of Abramovitsh's philosophy of "spatial mobility," see Miron and Norich, "Politics of Benjamin III," 28–30.

55. As Miron notes, the pair's "departure from Tuneyadevke is a brilliant parody of the biblical story of the Israelites' hasty escape from their house of bondage as well as the miraculous crossing of the Red Sea" (*Image of the Shtetl,* 23).

56. Wisse attempts to turn this view on its head and give it a positive spin when she writes, "The Schlemiel becomes a hero when real action is impossible and reaction remains the only way a man can define himself" (*Schlemiel as Modern Hero,* 39).

57. Hutchinson, *Cervantine Journeys,* 156.

58. For a discussion of the tradition of passive men in Yiddish literature, see Janet Hadda's *Passionate Women, Passive Men: Suicide in Yiddish Literature* (Albany: State University of New York Press, 1988), 119–76. The stereotypes also make the work reminiscent of Voltaire's *Candide—* another comedy about a comically naive and optimistic traveler.

59. Miron and Norich, "Politics of Benjamin III," 61.

60. I do not think their relationship is meant to be read as actively and positively homosexual but instead reflects the unfortunate historical reality: Abramovitsh and the culture were profoundly uncomfortable with homosexuality, regarding it as something weak, effeminate, and comic.

61. See Litvak's discussion of this in "Literary Response to Conscription," 225.

62. Wisse, *Schlemiel as Modern Hero,* 38.

63. Miron and Norich, "Politics of Benjamin III," 104.

64. Litvak argues, in contrast, that "at his trial, Benjamin sees himself as an adult for the first time, a small man capable of moral courage, not a larger-than-life conquering hero like his ideal, Alexander the Great; 'divorced' from the state, Benjamin comes to terms with his status as a 'married man'" ("Literary Response to Conscription," 230).

65. Naomi Seidman has an interesting analysis of Abramovitsh's 1894 Hebrew story, "In the Days of Noise," which she interprets as a rewriting of *Kitser masoes Binyomin hashlishi* but with Mendele and Reb Leyb as the pilgrims to Eretz Yisrael. See Seidman, *A Marriage Made in Heaven: The Sexual Politics of Hebrew and Yiddish* (Berkeley: University of California Press, 1997), 53–57.

66. In a fascinating analysis Irene Tucker shows how Abramovitsh "turns the transparency and self-evidence of geographical placedness into a figure of speech" (287) in his writing in general and in *Benjamin the Third* specifically. See Tucker, "Speaking Worlds: S. Y. Abramovitsh and the Making of Hebrew Vernacular," in *A Probable State: The Novel, The Contract, and the Jews* (Chicago: University of Chicago Press, 2000), 183–290.

67. The passage is from the Yiddish original: Peretz, "Dray khupes: Tsvey royte—eyne a shvartse," in *Ale verk fun Y. L. Peretz (*New York: CYCO Bikher, 1947), 5:14. The English translation is from Peretz, "The Three Wedding Canopies," in *The Great Works of Jewish Fantasy and Occult,* ed. and trans. Joachim Neugroschel (New York: Overlook, 1987), 68. Subsequent direct quotations from these works will be followed by page citations in text.

68. Michael Riffaterre, *Fictional Truth* (Baltimore, Md.: John Hopkins University Press, 1990), 33.

69. Mikhail Bakhtin, *The Dialogic Imagination: Four Essays,* trans. Michael Holquist and Caryl Emerson, ed. Michael Holquist (Austin: University of Texas Press, 1981), 224–26.

70. Ibid., 234.

71. Wolfgang Mieder, *Tradition and Innovation in Folk Literature* (Hanover, N.H.: Press of New England, 1987), 2.

72. Roskies, *Bridge of Longing,* 127.

73. See Khone Shmeruk, "Der Nister's 'Under a Fence': Tribulations of a Soviet Yiddish Symbolist," in *The Field of Yiddish: Studies in Language, Folklore, and Literature,* 2d coll., ed. Uriel Weinriech (London: Mouton, 1965), 269, n.16.

74. For a discussion of literature in the Soviet Union during the 1920s, see Robert Maguire, *Red Virgin Soil: Soviet Literature in the 1920s*, 2d ed. (Ithaca, N.Y.: Cornell University Press, 1987). A good introduction to the 1920s by Robert Maguire appears in *Russian Literature of the 1920s: An Anthology*, ed. Carl R. Proffer, Ellendea Proffer, Ronald Meyer, and Mary Ann Szporluk (Dana Point, Calif.: Ardis, 1987), vii–xvii.

75. Shmeruk, "Der Nister's 'Under a Fence,'" 263.

76. I am taking the biographical information from several sources. The most extensive information in English appears in Leonard Wolf's introduction to his translation of Der Nister's *Di Mishpokhe Mashber*. See Der Nister, *The Family Mashber*, trans. Leonard Wolf (New York: Summit Books, 1987), 7–16. Roskies sprinkles biographical information throughout his compelling chapter on Der Nister in *Bridge of Longing*, 191–229. The most extensive biographical information in Yiddish, with a list of critical sources on Der Nister, appears in Khone Shmeruk, ed., *A shpigl oyf a shteyn* (Tel Aviv: Farlog Peretz, 1964), 737–41. The information is reprinted from "Der Nister" in Zalman Reyzen's five-volume *Di Leksikon fun der yidisher literatur* (New York: 1956–63).

Four stories by Der Nister are translated into English in *Yenne Velt: The Great Works of Jewish Fantasy and Occult*, trans. and ed. Joachim Neugroschel (New York: Pocket Books, 1976). Der Nister's phenomenal story, "Unter a ployt (revyu)," translated into English by Seymour Levitan as "Behind a Fence," appears in *A Treasury of Yiddish Stories*, ed. Irving Howe and Eliezer Greenberg (New York: Penguin, 1989), 574–96. Der Nister's works in Yiddish are extremely rare. The best collection appears in Shmeruk's *A shpigl oyf a shteyn*, 123–220.

77. Der Nister describes this pilgrimage in his essay "Peretz hot geredt un ikh hob gehert" (Peretz spoke and I heard) in *Der Nister: dertseylungen un esseyen*, ed. Nakhman Meisel (New York: YKUF, 1957), 279–89.

78. See, for instance, Roskies's anguished, but failed, attempt to understand why Der Nister returned, in *Bridge of Longing*, 217.

79. On the influence of the Yiddish chapbooks see Roskies, *Bridge of Longing*, 201, and Bechtel's *Der Nister's Work*, 127–29; on the influence of the Hasidic tales of Nahman of Bratslav, see Roskies, *Bridge of Longing*, 196; Bechtel, *Der Nister's Work*, 123–27, and Daniela Mantovan's "Der Nister and His Symbolist Short Stories (1913–1929): Patterns of Imagination" (Ph.D. diss., Columbia University, 1993), 85–90; on the influence of Peretz see Roskies, *Bridge of Longing*, 199, and Bechtel, *Der Nister's Work*, 27–32. Mantovan asserts that Andersen was one of Der

Nister's favorite writers (see "Der Nister and His Symbolist Short Stories," 108). On the influence of folk tales see Roskies, *Bridge of Longing*, 201–2; Bechtel, *Der Nister's Work*, 108–22; and Mantovan, "Der Nister and His Symbolist Short Stories," 108–13.

80. For instance, in *The Russian Symbolists: An Anthology of Critical and Theoretical Writings* (Ann Arbor, Mich.: Ardis, 1986) Ronald Peterson collects many central essays by leading figures in the movement, yet their discussions of what symbolism is demonstrate a remarkable lack of uniformity. Peterson's book is the best source for primary texts by leading symbolists that have been translated into English.

81. For a full study of Russian symbolism see Avril Pyman's *A History of Russian Symbolism* (Cambridge: Cambridge University Press, 1994). An excellent discussion of symbolism by Ewa M. Thompson appears in *Handbook of Russian Literature,* ed. Victor Terras (New Haven, Conn.: Yale University Press, 1985), 460–64. For an anthology of the main symbolist documents, see Peterson's *Russian Symbolists.*

82. The contradictory pulls of decadence and pessimism versus religion and aestheticism caused the movement to reach a crisis of doctrine in 1910 that began its demise. See Thompson, "Symbolism," 463.

83. See his letter to his brother, quoted in Shmeruk's "Der Nister's 'Under a Fence,'" 285.

84. See Thompson, "Symbolism," 461, and Pyman, *History of Russian Symbolism,* which have numerous sections about Nietzsche's influence.

85. For a discussion that considers the symbolist's attraction to mysticism, see George Ivask's "Russian Modernist Poets and the Mystic Sectarians," in *Russian Modernism: Culture and the Avant-Garde, 1900–1930,* ed. George Gibian and H. W. Tjalsma (Ithaca, N.Y.: Cornell University Press, 1976), 85–107.

86. Vyacheslav Ivanov, "The Precepts of Symbolism," in Peterson, *Russian Symbolists,* 147. Roskies has an interesting discussion of Der Nister as high priest in his chapter entitled "The Storyteller as High Priest: Der Nister" in *Bridge of Longing,* 191–229. For a discussion of what Der Nister learned from Nahman's stories, see Roskies, *Bridge of Longing,* 196. Der Nister revived his interest in Nahman of Bratslav in *Di Mishpokhe Mashber* when he made the Bratslaver sect of Hasidism a central force in the novel.

87. Thompson, "Symbolism," 460.

88. Miron, *Image of the Shtetl,* 72.

89. See Der Nister, "Peretz hot geredt un ikh hob gehert," 279–89. The reverential prose about Peretz in this essay reflects, I would suggest,

Der Nister's nostalgia in 1940 for the lost world of Yiddish writers, as much as it is a true picture of how he felt as a youth visiting the master. The essay shows Der Nister's painful longing for the Yiddish literary world that was being destroyed.

90. I owe great thanks to Mikhail Krutikov and his comments on Der Nister, which suggested this idea to me. Krutikov's ideas led me to rework this section.

91. Roskies, *Bridge of Longing*, 199.

92. Ibid.

93. Der Nister, "Tsum barg," in *Gedakht* (Berlin: Literareshter Farlag, 1922), 1:49–100. There is no translation of this story to English, so the translations are mine. I want to thank David Roskies for his patient, careful, and considerable assistance with my translations. I first read of the connection between Der Nister and Nietzsche in Bechtel's *Der Nister's Work*, 151–52. She points out that "the introductory chapters of Nietzsche's *Also sprach Zarathustra* were published for the first time in Yiddish in the *Yidisher almanakh*, 1, ed. Sh. Gorelik (Kiev: Kunstfarlag, 1909), a volume in which Der Nister published his 'Friling,' and consequently he could not have missed it" (151, n.14).

94. As quoted in Pyman, *History of Russian Symbolism*, 207. Two books that deal extensively with the influence of Nietzsche on Bely are Vladimir E. Alexandrov, *Andrei Bely: The Major Symbolist Fiction* (Cambridge, Mass.: Harvard University Press, 1985), and John E. Malmstad, ed., *Andrey Bely: Spirit of Symbolism* (Ithaca, N.Y.: Cornell University Press, 1987).

95. Friedrich Nietzsche, *Thus Spake Zarathustra*, trans. Thomas Common (New York: Macmillan, 1917), 25, 27.

96. Ibid., 161–62.

97. Robert A. Maguire and John Malmstad, "Petersburg," in Alexandrov, *Andrey Bely*, 102.

98. Jeremy Dauber suggested this idea.

99. Riffaterre, *Fictional Truth*, xv; Philip R. Wood, "The Transformation of the Quest from Modernity to Postmodernist and the Third Industrial Revolution," in *Literature and the Quest*, ed. Christine Arkinstall (Atlanta: Rodopi, 1993), 145.

100. Roskies discusses this shift in setting to the "noisy, smelly, venal and hazardous" in his analysis of "Unter a ployt," in *Bridge of Longing*, 225.

101. For considerations of Der Nister's later writings see Roskies, *Bridge of Longing*, 220–29; Bechtel, *Der Nister's Work*, 215–69; Shmeruk,

"Der Nister's 'Under a Fence'"; and Marc Caplan,"Performance Anxieties: Carnival Spaces and Assemblages in Der Nister's 'Under a Fence,'" *Prooftexts: A Journal of Jewish Literary History* 18, no. 1 (1998): 1–18.

102. "A mayse mit a lets, mit a moyz un mit dem Nister aleyn" appears in Der Nister's collection *Fun mayne giter* (Kharkov: Melukhe farlag fun der USSR, 1929), 43–80. The translations are mine as no one has published a translation of the story into English.

103. Roskies, *Bridge of Longing*, 222.

104. Bakhtin, *Dialogic Imagination*, 180.

105. Peter Brooks, *Body Work: Objects of Desire in Modern Narrative* (Cambridge, Mass.: Harvard University Press, 1993), 21.

106. Bakhtin, *Dialogic Imagination*, 177, 178.

107. Roskies, *Bridge of Longing*, 222.

108. Miron and Norich, "Politics of Benjamin III," 1–115.

109. Deborah A. Harter, *Bodies in Pieces: Fantastic Narrative and the Poetics of Fragment* (Stanford: Stanford University Press, 1996), 2.

110. Maguire, *Red Virgin Soil*, 101.

111. Irina Paperno, introduction to *Creating Life: The Aesthetic Utopia of Russian Modernism*, ed. Irina Paperno and Joan Delaney Grossman (Stanford: Stanford University Press, 1994), 3.

112. The centrality of corporeality in satiric works is part of a larger narrative structure in which the traditional hierarchy of people and things is flattened and new structures are established between disparate things. Bakhtin's description of the Rabelaisian chronotope is appropriate as well for Der Nister's grotesque corporeal stories, which have the same type of narrative destructuring portrayed through "series." In these works things are coupled and decoupled in often grotesque but wholly new ways: "The disunification of what had traditionally been linked, and the bringing-together of that which had traditionally been kept distant and disunified, is achieved in Rabelais via the construction of series [rjady] of the most varied types, which are at times parallel to each other and at times intersect each other. With the help of these series, Rabelais can both put together and take apart. The construction of series is a specific characteristic of Rabelais' artistic method. All these widely varied series can be reduced to the following basic groups: (1) series of the human body, in its anatomical and physiological aspects; (2) human clothing series; (3) food series; (4) drink and drunkenness series; (5) sexual series (copulation); (6) death series; (7) defecation series. Each of these seven series possesses its own specific logic, and each series has its own dominants. All these series intersect one another; by constructing

and intersecting them, Rabelais is able to put together or take apart anything he finds necessary" (Bakhtin, *Dialogic Imagination*, 170).

What Bakhtin is asserting is that in these stories meaning is imparted by the flattening of the traditional vertical hierarchy and the restructuring of the world along new corporeal series. Thematic meaning is located in the intersection of different narrative threads, rather than in a simple linear plot development.

113. Gabriele Schwab writes that "nonsense forms an alliance between dream and logic in order to challenge the boundaries of so-called ordinary language" (*The Mirror and the Killer-Queen* [Bloomington: Indiana University Press, 1996], 67).

114. Mikhail Krutikov suggested this to me.

115. This story appears in Nahman of Bratslav, *Nahman of Bratslav*, 143–61.

3. The Train

1. Der Nister wrote an interesting essay that begins by describing a train that is the compartment for a variety of Jews en route to the "Yiddish homeland" of Birobidzhan. He compares them with the Jews of Mendele's generation. See "Mit ibervanderer keyn Birobidzhan," in *Der Nister*, 257–78.

2. Jonathan Crary, *Techniques of the Observer: On Vision and Modernity in the Nineteenth Century* (Cambridge, Mass.: MIT Press, 1990), 10.

3. Elyokum Zunser, "Der ayznban," in *Elyokum Zunsers verk*, ed. Mordkhe Schaecter (New York: YIVO, 1964), 1:69–73.

4. See Richard Mowbray Haywood, *The Beginnings of Railway Development in Russia in the Reign of Nicholas I, 1835–1842* (Durham, N.C.: Duke University Press, 1969), and J. N. Westwood's *A History of Russian Railways* (London: Allen and Unwin, 1964).

5. Zunser, "Lid fun ayznban," in *Elyokum Zunsers verk*, 255–59. The translation to English is mine.

6. Nicholas Faith, *The World the Railways Made* (London: Bodley Head, 1990), 235.

7. Eric J. Hobsbawm, *Industry and Empire: The Making of Modern English Society, 1750 to the Present Day* (New York: Pantheon, 1968), 2:89.

8. See, for instance, Faith, *The World the Railways Made*, 272–73.

9. Stephen L. Baehr has written an excellent essay on the role of the train in late nineteenth-century Russian literature. See Baehr, "The Troika and the Train: Dialogues between Tradition and Technology in

Nineteenth-Century Russian Literature," in *Issues in Russian Literature before 1917: Selected Papers of the Third World Congress for Soviet and Eastern European Studies* (Columbus, Ohio: Slavica, 1989), 85-106.

10. Leo Tolstoy, *Anna Karenin*, trans. Rosemary Edmonds (London: Penguin, 1975), 510.

11. See David M. Bethea's discussion of the two views of the train in *The Shape of the Apocalypse in Modern Russian Fiction* (Princeton, N.J.: Princeton University Press, 1989), 59-74.

12. Baehr, "Troika and the Train," 88-89.

13. Faith, *The World the Railways Made*, 271-72.

14. Roger Green, *The Train* (Oxford: Oxford University Press, 1982), 6.

15. I am using "Shem un Yefes in a vogn" in my analysis, even though it was originally written in Hebrew, because Abramovitsh himself translated it into Yiddish in 1910 and meant for it to stand on its own as a Yiddish text. While for the most part Abramovitsh translated his story literally, he was selective in his use of the numerous intertextualities of the Hebrew original. The original Hebrew version is titled "Shem veyefet ba'agala," in *Kol kitvey Mendele Mokher-Sfarim* (Tel Aviv: Dvir, 1947), 399-405. For the Yiddish version see *Ale verk fun Mendele Moycher-Sforim* (Warsaw: Farlag Mendele, 1928), 13:3-36. For an excellent translation by Walter Lever into English from the Hebrew that includes full citations by David Roskies of the intertextual references, see "Shem and Japheth on the Train," in *The Literature of Destruction; Jewish Responses to Catastrophe*, ed. David G. Roskies (New York: Jewish Publication Society, 1989), 123-36.

16. As Miron points out in *A Traveler Disguised*, while it seems that in this story "Mendele finally breaks into full authorship," Miron prefers to label this story and other later ones as examples of "monologues in which Mendele narrates personal reminiscences to a present public. In them he stands near the footlights, halfway between the audience and the fictional action, exactly as he did before. It is only that what formerly constituted the curtain raiser now fills the entire show" (199-200). For a full consideration of Mendele's literary role, see pp. 130-249.

17. Kaplan, *Questions of Travel*, 27.

18. The biblical intertexts in the opening paragraph are much more pronounced in the Hebrew original than the Yiddish. For an excellent discussion of the intertexts in the Hebrew (some of which are found in the Yiddish), see Roskies's *Against the Apocalypse: Responses to Catastrophe*

in Modern Jewish Culture (Cambridge, Mass.: Harvard University Press, 1984), 70–72.

19. Abramovitsh, "Shem un Yefes in a vogn," 8. The translation is mine, although some subsequent translations come from Lever's translation, "Shem and Japheth on the Train." I use my own translations when I need literal ones or to stress the grammar and poetics or when there is a difference between the Hebrew and Yiddish. When I quote from Lever, the passage is followed by a page citation; when no page is noted, the translation is mine.

20. Faith, *The World the Railways Made*, 40; Crary, *Techniques of the Observer*, 11.

21. Sholem Aleichem uses the same common Yiddish phrase— "ayngeprest vi hering in a fas"—for describing train travel in the *Ayznban-geshikhtes* (143).

22. In *Literature of Destruction* (124), Roskies notes that this passage is a parody of Talmudic diction in Ketubbot 39b.

23. Wolfgang Schivelbusch, *The Railway Journey: The Industrialization of Time and Space in the Nineteenth Century* (Berkeley: University of California Press, 1986), 36.

24. Roskies pointed this out to me in a conversation in 1998.

25. Roskies, *Literature of Destruction*, 117.

26. Dan Miron traces the publication history of the stories in *Image of the Shtetl*, 256–334. For the Yiddish original of *Di ayznban-geshikhtes*, I am using *Ale verk fun Sholem-Aleykhem*, vol. 6 (New York: Folksfond, 1923). The English translation appears in *Tevye the Dairyman and The Railroad Stories*, trans. Hillel Halkin (New York: Schocken, 1987), 135–284. For a thorough discussion of the biographical background of *Di ayznban-geshikhtes*, see Miron, *Image of the Shtetl*, 256–64.

27. Roskies, *Bridge of Longing*, 177.

28. Schivelbusch, *Railway Journey*, 66–67.

29. Ibid.

30. Miron, *Image of the Shtetl*, 274, 275.

31. Schivelbusch, *Railway Journey*, 72.

32. Baehr discusses how in Russian literature as well the vocabulary of "machines like locomotives, steamships, sewing machines or steam engines became quite frequent" ("Troika and the Train," 85).

33. Roskies, *Against the Apocalypse*, 173.

34. For a thorough analysis of the role of non-Jews in the works of Sholem Aleichem, and how they reflected the real ethnic makeup of the

region, see Israel Bartal's "Dmut halo-yehudim v'chevratam be'yetzirat Shalom-Aleichem," *Hasifrut* 26 (1978): 39–71.

35. For the Yiddish original see *Arum vokzal,* in *Ale verk fun Dovid Bergelson* (Buenos Aires: ICUF, 1961), 1:15–91. For the English translation see *At the Depot,* in *A Shtetl and Other Yiddish Novellas,* trans. and ed. Ruth Wisse (New York: Behrman House, 1973), 81–139. For the most thorough analysis of Bergelson's first period of writings, including an excellent examination of *Arum vokzal,* see Abraham Novershtern's 1981 doctoral dissertation for Hebrew University, Jerusalem, "Aspektim mivniim baproza shel David Bergelson mereshitah ad 'midas ha-din.'" The English translation of the dissertation title is "Structural aspects of David Bergelson's prose from its beginnings until 'Mides-Hadin.'"

36. The biographical information on Bergelson is found in B. Tshubinski, "Dovid Bergelson," in *Leksikon fun der nayer yidisher literatur,* ed. Shmuel Niger and Jacob Shatzky (New York: Altveltlekhen Yidishn Kultur Kongres, 1956), 1:380–83.

37. Novershtern, "Aspektim," xiv. The Hebrew dissertation begins with a synopsis in English.

38. Faith, *The World the Railways Made,* 35–36.

39. As Novershtern shows in his dissertation (225–30), the opening also fluctuates between specific and general time, and specific and general descriptions, which together tend to blur the reality and support the impressionistic style that Bergelson is using.

40. The Marxist critic Yekhezkl Dobrushin sought to show that all the symbolism in *Arum vokzal* has a single meaning. He asserts that *Arum vokzal* is a total critique of the bourgeois and their immoral life following the failed 1905 revolution. See Dobrushin, *Dovid Bergelson* (Moscow: Emes, 1947), 31.

41. See Georges Van Den Abbeele's discussion of the conflation of commerce and travel in his book *Travel as Metaphor,* xvi.

42. Mikhail Krutikov, *Yiddish Fiction and the Crisis of Modernity, 1905–1914* (Stanford, Calif.: Stanford University Press, 2001), 39.

43. Wisse, introduction to *At the Depot,* 82.

44. Novershtern, "Aspektim," 223.

45. Dobrushin's Marxist reading of the ending is that it is totally ironic and that everything remains as hopeless as it was. I would, however, suggest that it is not so clearly black and white. Like much in *Arum vokzal,* the meaning seems to suggest one thing, but it is nevertheless left open. See Dobrushin, *Dovid Bergelson,* 59.

4. The Ship

1. See Sholem Aleichem, *Motl Peyse dem khazn's* in *Ale verk fun Sholem-Aleykhem* (New York: Folksfond, 1918–23), 18:12–56, for the ocean journey. The English translation is *Adventures of Mottel the Cantor's Son*, trans. Tamara Kahana (New York: Collier, 1953). See pp. 142–51 for the voyage.

2. For an analysis of Yiddish immigration novels with a cohesive topology of immigration as a break from the shtetl, see Krutikov, *Yiddish Fiction*, 191–261.

3. Roskies charts out the sea adventure in maskilic and popular Yiddish literature in "The Genres of Yiddish Popular Literature, 1790–1860," in *Working Papers in Yiddish and East European Jewish Studies* 8 (New York: YIVO, 1975), 18–22.

4. Nahman of Bratslav, *Nahman of Bratslav*, 167–87.

5. Roskies, *Against the Apocalypse*, 109–111.

6. Hutchinson, *Cervantine Journeys*, 159.

7. Robert Foulke, *The Sea Voyage Narrative* (New York: Twayne, 1997), 9, 10.

8. This passage is from Auden, *The Enchafèd Flood, or The Romantic Iconography of the Sea*, based on his 1949 lectures at the University of Virginia (New York: Vintage, 1967), 7. Of all the works I read on sea narratives, Auden's offered the deepest insights. Written in a stream-of-consciousness style, his poetic language traces the common motifs of the sea in literature. The work as a whole is remarkable both for its insight and beauty.

9. When Shapiro wrote *Oyfn yam* he was fluent enough in English to translate writers such as Dickens but nevertheless chose to continue composing in Yiddish (Curt Leviant, introduction to *The Jewish Government and Other Stories*, trans. and ed. Curt Leviant [New York: Twayne, 1971], ix–xvii). Glatstein was a leading political Yiddishist who throughout his career asserted the aesthetic and cultural importance of Jewish American authors' continuing to write in Yiddish. Late in his career Glatstein summed up his view of the mixed blessing of writing only in Yiddish in his poem "Di freyd fun yidishn vort" (The joy of the Yiddish word) from his 1961 book, *The Joy of the Yiddish Word*. He wrote:

> Oh, let me through to the joy of the Yiddish word.
> Give me whole, full days.
> Tie me to it, weave me in,

Strip me of all vanities.
Send crows to feed me, bestow crumbs on me,
A leaking roof and a hard bed.
But give me whole, full days,
Let me not forget for a moment
The Yiddish Word.

(From Benjamin Harshav and Barbara Harshav, eds., *American Yiddish Poetry: A Bilingual Anthology* [Berkeley: University of California Press, 1986], 364–65.)

10. Matthew Frye Jacobson, "'The Quintessence of the Jew': Polemics of Nationalism and Peoplehood in Turn-of-the-Century Yiddish Fiction," in *Multilingual America: Transnationalism, Ethnicity, and the Languages of American Literature,* ed. Werner Sollors (New York: New York University Press, 1998), 110.

11. On the struggles with parents, see, for example, Anzia Yezierska's 1925 *Bread Givers* (New York: Persea, 1999); Isidor Schneider's 1935 *From the Kingdom of Necessity* (New York: Penguin, 1935); and Meyer Levin's 1937 *The Old Bunch* (New York: Citadel, 1995).

On disillusionment see Abraham Cahan's 1917 *The Rise of David Levinsky* (New York: Penguin, 1993), and Samuel Ornitz's 1923 *Haunch, Paunch and Jowl: An Anonymous Autobiography* (New York: Pocket Books, 1968). Immigrant works that focus on intermarriage include the paradigmatically idealistic image of intermarriage in Israel Zangwill's 1908 play, *The Melting Pot* (New York: Macmillan, 1909). Novels that use intermarriage to highlight the problems of assimilation include Elias Tobenkin's 1916 *Witte Arrives* (New York: Gregg, 1968), Myron Brinig's *This Man Is My Brother* (New York: Farrar and Rinehart, 1932), and Nat J. Ferber's *One Happy Jew* (New York: Farrar and Rinehart, 1934). For a fine consideration of how marriage to a Christian woman became a means to mark out the hazards and triumphs of assimilation, see Frederick Cople Jahar's "The Quest for the Ultimate Shiksa," *American Quarterly* 35 (Winter 1983): 518–42.

12. David Martin Fine discusses this in his article, "In the Beginning: American-Jewish Fiction, 1880–1930," *Handbook of American-Jewish Literature,* ed. Lewis Fried (New York: Greenwood, 1998), 15–34, as well as in his book *The City, The Immigrant, and American Fiction, 1880–1920* (Metuchen, N.J.: Scarecrow, 1977), 102–20. For a brief consideration of how anti-immigrant sentiment influenced immigrant narratives in general, see Toby Rose and Kathryn Payant's introduction to *The Immigrant Experience in North American Literature: Carving out a*

Niche (Westport, Conn.: Greenwood, 1999), xiii–xxvii. For a discussion of the history of U.S. nativism, see Roger Daniels, *Coming to America: A History of Immigration and Ethnicity in American Life* (New York: HarperCollins, 1990), 265–84. For a collection of documents and essays on the anti-immigrant sentiment of the nativist years, see Jon Gjerde, ed., *Major Problems in American Immigration and Ethnic History* (Boston: Houghton Mifflin, 1998): 133–68.

13. Fine discusses this in "In the Beginning."

14. Ludwig Lewisohn, *The Island Within* (New York: Syracuse University Press, 1997); Michael Gold, *Jews Without Money* (New York: Carroll and Graf, 1996).

15. See Sam B. Girgus's *The New Covenant: Jewish Writers and the American Idea* (Chapel Hill: University of North Carolina Press, 1984), 67–71.

16. See, for instance, Allen Guttmann's thesis that Cahan's novel is a model of "regretful success," in *The Jewish Writer in America: Assimilation and the Crisis of Identity* (New York: Oxford University Press, 1971), 32–33, and Sanford Pinsker's analysis in *Jewish-American Fiction, 1917–1987* (New York: Twayne, 1992), 1–7. For an important essay focusing on Cahan's language struggles, see Aviva Taubenfeld's "Linguistic Borders and the Immigrant Author in Abraham Cahan's Yekl and Yankel der Yankee," in *Multilingual America: Transnationalism, Ethnicity, and the Languages of American Literature,* ed. Werner Sollors (New York: New York University Press, 1998), 144–65.

17. Current analysis of *Oyfn yam* includes Robert Harvey Wolf's Ph.D. dissertation for Columbia University, "A Yiddish Manichaean: The Dualistic Fiction of Lamed Shapiro," 1994. While I consider his analysis of *Oyfn yam* to be quite flawed, he does include a bibliography of Shapiro's works and criticism that may be useful for those interested in researching Shapiro. Wolf's analysis of *Oyfn yam* is found on pp. 67–80. Other brief considerations of *Oyfn yam* include Leviant's introduction to his collection of translations of Shapiro's stories, *Jewish Government,* xv, and V. Tsukerman's essay, "L. Shapiro," *Dos naye land* 1, no. 6 (Oct. 20, 1911): 19. For a fine consideration of Shapiro's popular pogrom stories of 1907–10, see Abraham Novershtern's "Di pogrom-tematik in di verk fun L. Shapiro," *Di Goldene Keyt* 106 (1981): 121–50.

18. Benjamin Harshav, *Language in Time of Revolution* (Berkeley: University of California Press, 1993), discusses the shift in Jewish literature after the pogroms of the 1880s and the move toward experimental modernist prose of the "second generation." See in particular pt. 1. For a

further, fine consideration of the second generation of writers, see Harshav's *Meaning of Yiddish*, 139–86.

19. Roskies composed a thorough biography of Shapiro's life in "L. Shapiro," in *Leksikon fun der nayer yidisher literatur*, ed. Berl Cohen, Ezriel Naks, and Eliyahu Shulman (New York: Congress for Jewish Culture, 1981), 533–36. Also see Leviant, introduction, ix–xvii. See Wolf's "Yiddish Manichaean," 67–80, for a bibliography of Shapiro's works and criticism.

20. Many of Shapiro's pogrom stories, including "The Kiss" and "The Cross," may be found in *The Jewish Government and Other Stories*. In "L. Shapiro" Tsukerman points out that Shapiro probably would have continued writing in the romantic vein of *Oyfn yam* but for the constant pogroms of the period, which forced him to focus on anti-Jewish violence (19). For an excellent analysis of Shapiro's pogrom stories, see Novershtern, "Di Pogrom-tematik," 121–50.

21. Paul Gifford, "Getting There or Not—The Fortunes of the Initiatic Journey and the Crisis of Culture," in *Literature and Quest*, ed. Christine Arkinstall (Atlanta: Rodopi, 1993), 18.

22. The ties between the pieces are so numerous that it is difficult to believe that Shapiro did not use Coleridge's poem as an inspiration for *Oyfn yam*. Similar motifs include the use of the iceberg to impart vast loneliness, the passing by of a ghostlike ship, and the massive female figure that rises from the ocean to confront the narrator.

23. Jonathan Raban, introduction to *The Oxford Book of the Sea* (Oxford: Oxford University Press, 1992), 15.

24. Auden, *Enchafèd Flood*, 11.

25. Keats, "On the Sea," 230.

26. Raban, *Oxford Book of the Sea*, 17.

27. Percy Bysshe Shelley, "A Vision of the Sea," in *John Keats and Percy Bysshe Shelley: Complete Poetical Works* (New York: Modern Library, 1932), 634, ll. 26–34.

28. Raban, *Oxford Book of the Sea*, 17.

29. Shapiro does not use the word *subconscious*, as Freud's notions were only then beginning to enter the general vocabulary. Instead, Shapiro uses words such as *unrest* and *lost* to impart similar ideas that were then making their way into modern art and literature.

30. Lamed Shapiro, *Oyfn yam*, in *Di yidishe melukhe un andere zakhn* (New York: Naytsayt, 1919), 193–229. There is no English translation, so the translations are mine.

31. Bert Bender, *Sea-Brothers: The Tradition of American Sea Fiction from Moby-Dick to the Present* (Philadelphia: University of Pennsylvania Press, 1988), 4.

32. Samuel Taylor Coleridge, *The Rime of the Ancient Mariner,* in *The Complete Poetical Works of Samuel Taylor Coleridge,* ed. Ernest Hartley Coleridge (Oxford: Clarendon Press, 1912), 1:188, ll. 55–62.

33. Bernard Blackstone, *The Lost Travelers: A Romantic Theme with Variations* (Westport, Conn.: Greenwood, 1983), 32.

34. For instance, Shapiro asserts that he will never forget the night he was standing on deck and was flooded with memories of the shtetl (198), and he later states that "all of life is nothing more than my father's long Jewish coat" (225).

35. Glatstein is sometimes translated into English as Glatshteyn.

36. Harshav and Harshav, *American Yiddish Poetry,* 36.

37. Harshav, *Meaning of Yiddish,* 175–86.

38. Glatstein's *Ven Yash iz geforn* was first published in book form in 1938. I am using the pagination from that edition, which was published in New York by *In Zikh,* the Yiddish journal that had serialized it before bringing it out as a book. The English translation, *Homeward Bound,* trans. Abraham Goldstein (New York: T. Yoseloff, 1969), leaves out large portions of the novel, including nearly all the sections that relate anti-Semitic encounters. Therefore, I am using my own translations to English, and all parenthetic page references in text are to the book published by *In Zikh.*

Jacob Glatstein (1896–1971) emigrated from Lublin to the United States in 1914 when he was eighteen. In 1921 he published his first book of verse and soon became a leading Yiddish modernist writer. Glatstein was also a prolific essayist and a reporter for a number of Yiddish papers. For a compelling discussion of how Glatstein challenged the doctrines of "international modernism" during the 1930s, see Ruth Wisse's essay, "Language as Fate: Reflections of Jewish Literature in America," in *Studies in Contemporary Jewry: An Annual* (New York: Oxford University Press, 1996), 12:137–43.

For the most thorough biographical information about Glatstein in English, see Janet Hadda's *Yankev Glatshteyn* (Boston: Twayne, 1980). Hadda's book also contains a good bibliography of his writings. For additional biographical information on Glatstein in English, see Harshav and Harshav, *American Yiddish Poetry,* 204–6. For biographical information in Yiddish see the Glatstein entry by D. Diamant in *Leksikon fun der nayer yidisher literature* (New York: Yidishn kultur kongres, 1958), 2:256–61. For a more recent important discussion of these novels, see Miron's epilogue to his translation of *Ven Yash iz geforn* into Hebrew, titled *Keshe Yash nasa* (Tel Aviv: Hakibbutz Hameuchad, 1994), 205–21.

For an excellent comprehensive collection of Glatstein's poetry translated into English, see Harshav and Harshav, *American Yiddish Poetry*, 208–385. Other translations include *The Penguin Book of Modern Yiddish Verse*, ed. Irving Howe, Ruth Wisse, and Khone Shmeruk (New York: Penguin, 1987), 425–77, and *Selected Poems of Yankev Glatstein*, trans. and ed. Richard Fein (New York: Jewish Publication Society, 1987).

For a consideration of the autobiographical aspects of *Ven Yash iz geforn* see Jan Schwarz's 1997 doctoral dissertation for Columbia University, "When the Lamp of Art Is Made to Shine through Life's Foolscap: A Study of the Yiddish Literary Autobiography," 162–223. Also see my article, "The Self as Marrano in Jacob Glatstein's Autobiographical Novels," *Prooftexts* 18, no. 2 (1998): 207–23.

39. For a compelling discussion of how Glatstein challenged the doctrines of "international modernism" during the 1930s, see Wisse, "Language as Fate," 137–43.

40. Glatstein, *Ven Yash iz gekumen* (New York: M. S. Sklarsky, 1940). The English translation, *Homecoming at Twilight*, trans. Norbert Guterman (New York: T. Yoseloff, 1962), does not do full justice to the Yiddish original.

41. For a consideration of Glatstein's use of a polyphonic narrative in the Yash novels, see my article "The Self as Marrano in Jacob Glatstein's Autobiographical Novel," *Prooftexts* 18 (1999): 207–23.

42. Glatstein's original introduction appeared in *In Zikh* 6 (October 1934): 179–80.

43. Another interesting comparison that Glatstein makes between the two works is that because Adamic was accompanied by his wife, he had a fail-safe method for inserting moments of dialogue into his descriptions. Glatstein, who was traveling alone, had to rely on sporadic conversation with strangers. It is interesting that Glatstein, who in his introduction casts himself in the role of journalist, does not even consider a monologic style of description. Mikhail Bakhtin states that Dostoyevsky also consistently reported in a polyphonic style. Bakhtin's argument for tying Dostoyevsky's work as a journalist to his use of a polyphonic style can thus be used for considering the tie between Glatstein's journalism and the polyphonic style. See Bakhtin, *Problems*

of Dostoevsky's Poetics, ed. and trans. Caryl Emerson (Minneapolis: University of Minnesota Press, 1994), 29–30.

44. Adamic's work, however, does not present only a rosy picture of life in Yugoslavia. Although his accounts of the Yugoslavian peasants are highly sentimental, he does explicitly show the brutal regime of the government. Yet his portrayals of the government serve throughout as a means to contrast how wonderful the United States is versus his old land, which is in the grips of a totalitarian regime.

45. *Marrano* (a word that originally had an extremely negative connotation) refers to the Jews of late fifteenth-century Spain who outwardly converted to Christianity but continued to secretly practice their Judaism. The term is also used for the descendants of converts living outside Spain.

46. Glatstein, 1955 interview by A. Tabatshnik, "A Conversation with Jacob Glatstein," trans. Joseph C. Landis, in *Yiddish* 1 (1973): 44–45.

47. This notion is always expressed in terms of men.

48. The main exception to the Gentiles' general disinterest in the rise of Hitler is a American-born doctor of German heritage who forcefully challenges the anti-Semitism of another U.S. passenger and argues passionately against anti-Semitism of all types. By so doing he causes the other passengers to share his anger at the anti-Semites. See p. 133.

49. For a consideration of the dual selfhood of U.S. Jews, and how their perceived ability to "hide" their Jewishness became an excuse for American anti-Semitism, see Daniel Itzkovitz, "Secret Temples," in *Jews and Other Differences: The New Jewish Cultural Studies,* ed. Jonathan Boyarin and Daniel Boyarin (Minneapolis: University of Minnesota Press, 1997), 176–202. Also, for an examination of how many American Jews have internalized the need to "hide" their Jewishness and the often extreme actions this may lead to, see Sander L. Gilman, "The Visibility of the Jew in the Diaspora: Body Imagery and Its Cultural Context" (B. G. Rudolph Lectures in Judaic Studies, May 1992, Syracuse University, Syracuse, N.Y.), 26–31.

50. One example of a perceived difference between Jews and blacks from the perspective of a black man was written originally in the late 1950s by Frantz Fanon: "All the same, the Jew can be unknown in his Jewishness. He is not wholly what he is. One hopes, one waits. His actions, his behavior are the final determinant. He is a white man, and, apart from some rather debatable characteristics he can sometimes go unnoticed. . . . The Jew is disliked from the moment he is tracked down. But in my case everything takes on a *new* guise. I am given no chance. I

am overdetermined from without. I am the slave not of the 'idea' that others have of me but of my own appearance.

"And already I am being dissected under white eyes, the only real eyes. I am *fixed*. Having adjusted their microtomes, they objectively cut away slices of my reality. I am laid bare. I feel, I see in those white faces that it is not a new man who has come in, but a new kind of man, a new genus. Why, it's a Negro!" (From the 1952 essay, "The Fact of Blackness," as reprinted in *The Post-Colonial Studies Reader*, ed. Bill Ashcroft, Gareth Griffiths, and Helen Tiffin; trans. Charles Lam [New York: Routledge, 1997], 325.)

51. Clifford, "Diasporas," 307.

52. Glatstein's challenge to Zionism is also manifested in a passage that describes Yash's learning of the death of the great Hebrew poet Bialik. In this section he recalls listening to Bialik castigate Yiddish in the name of the Zionist revival of Hebrew. The passage about Bialik's renunciation of Yiddish and the anger that this caused Glatstein is found on p. 190.

53. See Schwarz, "When the Lamp of Art," 178–79, for an analysis of Yash's encounter with the Pole.

4. Conclusion

1. Many thanks to Allison Schaecter for her suggestions on this chapter.

2. Sara Suleri, *Meatless Days* (Chicago: University of Chicago Press, 1989), 105.

Bibliography

Abramovitsh, Sholem. *The Brief Travels of Benjamin the Third*. Trans. Ted Gorelick. In *Tales of Mendele the Book Peddler: Fishke the Lame and Benjamin the Third*, 301–91. Ed. Dan Miron and Ken Frieden. New York: Schocken, 1996.

———. *Fishke der krumer*. In *Ale verk fun Mendele Moycher-Sforim*. Ed. N. Mayzel. Vol. 3. Warsaw: Farlag Mendele, 1928.

———. *Fishke the Lame*. Trans. Hillel Hilken. In *Tales of Mendele the Book Peddler: Fishke the Lame and Benjamin the Third*, 3–298. Ed. Dan Miron and Ken Frieden. New York: Schocken, 1996.

———. *Kitser masoes Binyomin hashlishi*. In *Ale verk fun Mendele-Moykher Sforim*, 9:3–118. Ed. N. Mayzl. Warsaw: Farlag Mendele, 1928.

———. "Shem and Japheth on the Train." Trans. Walter Lever. In Roskies, ed., *Literature of Destruction*, 123–36.

———. "Shem un Yefes in a vogn." In *Ale verk fun Mendele-Moykher Sforim*, 13:3–36. Ed. N. Mayzel. Warsaw: Farlag Mendele, 1928.

———. "Shem veyefet ba'agala," in *Kol kitvey Mendele Mokher-Sfarim*, 399–405. Tel Aviv: Dvir, 1947.

Adamic, Louis. *The Native's Return: An American Visits Yugoslavia and Discovers His Old Country*. New York: Harper, 1934.

Adams, Percy. *Travel Literature and the Evolution of the Novel*. Lexington: University Press of Kentucky, 1983.

Adler, Elkan Nathan, ed. *Jewish Travellers: A Treasury of Travelogues from Nine Centuries*. New York: Hermon Press, 1966.

Aksenfeld, Yisroel. *Dos shterntikhl*. Ed. M. Viner (Moscow, 1938).

———. "The Headband." In *The Shtetl*, 49–72. Trans and ed. Joachim Neugroschel. New York: Richard Marek, 1979.

Alexandrov, Vladimir E. *Andrei Bely: The Major Symbolist Fiction*. Cambridge, Mass.: Harvard University Press, 1985.

Amichai, Yehuda. "Jewish Travel: Change Is God and Death Is His Prophet." In *Open Closed Open: Poems*, 117–24. Trans. Chana Bloch and Chana Kronfeld. New York: Harcourt, 2000.

Appiah, Kwame Anthony. "Is the Post- in Postmodernism the Post- in Postcolonial?" *Critical Inquiry* 17, no. 2 (Winter 1991): 336–57.

Auden, W. H. *The Enchafèd Flood, or The Romantic Iconography of the Sea*. University of Virginia Lectures, 1949. New York: Vintage, 1967.

Baehr, Stephen L. "The Troika and the Train: Dialogues between Tradition and Technology in Nineteenth-Century Russian Literature." In *Issues in Russian Literature before 1917: Selected Papers of the Third World Congress for Soviet and Eastern European Studies*, 85–106. Columbus, Ohio: Slavica, 1989.

Bakhtin, Mikhail. *The Dialogic Imagination: Four Essays*. Trans. Michael Holquist and Caryl Emerson, ed. Michael Holquist. Austin: University of Texas Press, 1981.

———. *Problems of Dostoevsky's Poetics*. Trans. and ed. Caryl Emerson. Minneapolis: University of Minnesota Press, 1994.

Bammer, Angelika, ed. *Displacements: Cultural Identities in Question*. Bloomington: Indiana University Press, 1994.

Band, Arnold. "The Bratslav Theory of the Sacred Tale." In *Nahman of Bratslav: The Tales*, 28–39. Trans. Arnold Band. New York: Paulist Press, 1978.

Bartal, Israel. "Dmut halo-yehudim v'chevratam be'yetzirat Shalom-Aleichem." *Hasifrut* 26 (1978): 39–71.

Bauman, Zygmunt. "Assimilation into Exile: The Jew as a Polish Writer." *Poetics Today* 17, no. 4 (Winter 1996): 567–97.

———. *Modernity and the Holocaust*. Ithaca, N.Y.: Cornell University Press, 1989.

Bechtel, Delphine. *Der Nister's Work, 1907–1929: A Study of a Yiddish Symbolist*. New York: Peter Lang, 1990.

Ben-Amos, Dan, ed. *Folklore Genres*. Austin: University of Texas Press, 1976.

ben Avrom, Jacob. *Maaseh Book*. Ed. and trans. Moses Gaster. Philadelphia: Jewish Publication Society, 1934.

———. *Mayse-bukh*. In *Musterverk fun der yidisher literatur*. Vol. 38. Buenos Aires: Literature-gezelshaft baym YIVO, 1969.

Bender, Bert. *Sea-Brothers: The Tradition of American Sea Fiction from Moby-Dick to the Present*. Philadelphia: University of Pennsylvania Press, 1988.

Benét's Reader's Encyclopedia, 3d ed. New York: Harper and Row, 1987.

Bergelson, David. *Arum vokzal.* In *Ale verk fun Dovid Bergelson,* 1:15–91. Buenos Aires: ICUF, 1961.

———. *At the Depot.* In *A Shtetl and Other Yiddish Novellas,* 81–139. Trans and ed. Ruth Wisse. New York: Behrman House, 1973.

Bethea, David M. *The Shape of the Apocalypse in Modern Russian Fiction.* Princeton, N.J.: Princeton University Press, 1989.

Bhabha, Homi K. "Forward: Joking Aside: The Idea of a Self-Critical Community." In Cheyette and Marcus, *Modernity, Culture, and "the Jew,"* 15–20.

Biale, David. *Power and Powerlessness in Jewish History.* New York: Schocken, 1986.

Biale, David, Michael Galchinsky, and Susan Heschel, eds. *Insider/ Outsider: American Jews and Multiculturalism.* Berkeley: University of California Press, 1998.

Blackstone, Bernard. *The Lost Travelers: A Romantic Theme with Variations.* Westport, Conn.: Greenwood, 1983.

Blake, William. "To the Evening Star." In *The Portable Blake.* Ed. Alfred Kazin, 63. New York: Viking, 1967.

Blunt, Alison, and Gillian Rose, eds. *Writing Women and Space: Colonial and Postcolonial Geographies.* New York: Guilford, 1994.

Bokher, Elia. *Bove-bukh.* In *Musterverk fun der yidisher literatur.* Vol. 8. Buenos Aires: Literature-gezelshaft baym YIVO, 1962.

Boyarin, Daniel, and Jonathan Boyarin. "Diaspora: Generation and the Ground of Jewish Identity." *Critical Inquiry* 19, no. 4 (Summer 1993): 693–725.

———, eds. *Jews and Other Differences: The New Jewish Cultural Studies.* Minneapolis: University of Minnesota Press, 1997.

Brinig, Myron. *This Man Is My Brother.* New York: Farrar and Rinehart, 1932.

Brodsky, Joseph. "Nobel Prize Acceptance Speech—Stockholm, December 1987." Reprinted in *New York Review of Books,* January 1, 1988, p. 20.

Broe, Mary Lynn, and Angela Ingram, eds. *Women's Writing in Exile.* Chapel Hill: University of North Carolina Press, 1989.

Brooks, Peter. *Body Work: Objects of Desire in the Modern Narrative.* Cambridge, Mass.: Harvard University Press, 1993.

Cahan, Abraham. *The Rise of David Levinsky.* New York: Penguin, 1993.

Campbell, Mary B. *The Witness and the Other World: Exotic European Travel Writing, 400–1600.* Ithaca, N.Y.: Cornell University Press, 1988.

Caplan, Marc. "Performance Anxieties: Carnival Spaces and Assemblages in Der Nister's "Under a Fence." *Prooftexts: A Journal of Jewish Literary History* 18, no. 1 (1998): 1–18.

Cervantes, Miguel. *Don Quixote of La Mancha.* Trans. Walter Starkie. New York: Signet, 1979.

Chamber, Iain. *Migrancy, Culture, Identity.* London: Routledge, 1994.

Chekov, Anton. *The Cherry Orchard.* Trans. Ronald Hingley. In *Five Major Plays by Anton Chekhov,* 266–329. New York: Bantam, 1977.

Cheyette, Bryan, and Laura Marcus, eds. *Modernity, Culture, and "the Jew."* Cambridge, U.K.: Polity Press, 1998.

Clifford, James. "Diasporas." *Cultural Anthropology* 9, no. 4 (1994): 302–38.

———. "Notes on Theory and Travel." *Inscriptions* 5 (1989): 177–88.

———. "Traveling Cultures." In *Cultural Studies,* 96–112. Ed. Lawrence Grossberg, Cary Nelson, and Paula Treichler. New York: Routledge, 1992.

Coleridge, Samuel Taylor. *The Rime of the Ancient Mariner.* In *The Complete Poetical Works of Samuel Taylor Coleridge,* 1:185–200. Ed. Ernest Hartley Coleridge. Oxford: Clarendon, 1912.

———. "To the Evening Star." *The Poems of Samuel Taylor Coleridge.* Ed. Ernest Hartley Coleridge. New York: 1917. 17.

Crary, Jonathan. *Techniques of the Observer: On Vision and Modernity in the Nineteenth Century.* Cambridge, Massachusetts: MIT Press, 1990.

Daniels, Roger. *Coming to America: A History of Immigration and Ethnicity in American Life.* New York: Harper Collins, 1990.

Davies, Carol Boyce. *Black Women, Writing, and Identity: Migrations of the Subject.* New York: Routledge, 1994.

Davies, W. D. *The Territorial Dimension of Judaism.* Berkeley: Berkeley University Press, 1982.

Defoe, Daniel. *Robinson Crusoe.* New York: Signet, 1980.

Deleuze, Gilles, and Felix Guattari. "Rhizome Versus Trees." In *The Deleuze Reader,* 7–39. Ed. Constantin V. Boundas. New York: Columbia University Press, 1993.

Der Nister. "A mayse mit a lets, mit a moyz un mit dem Nister aleyn." In *Fun mayne giter,* 43–80. Kharkov: Melukhe-farlag fun der USSR, 1929.

———. "Behind a Fence." Trans. Seymour Levitan. *A Treasury of Yiddish Stories,* 574–96. Ed. Irving Howe and Eliezer Greenberg. New York: Penguin, 1989.

———. *Der Nister: dertseylungen un esseyen.* Ed. Nakhman Meisel. New York: YKUF, 1957.

———. *The Family Mashber.* Trans. Leonard Wolf. New York: Summit Books, 1987.

———. "Mit ibervanderer keyn Birobidzhan." *Der Nister: Dertseylungen un esseyen,* 257–78. New York: YKUF, 1957.

———. "Tsum barg." In *Gedakht,* 1:49–100. Berlin: Literarisher Farlag, 1922.

———. "Unter a ployt." In Shmeruk, *A shpigl oyf a shteyn,* 186–220.

———. *Yenne Velt: The Great Works of Jewish Fantasy and Occult.* Ed. and Trans. Joachim Neugroschel. New York: Pocket Books, 1976.

Diamant, D. "Jacob Glatshteyn." In *Leksikon fun der nayer yidisher literature,* 2:256–61. New York: Yidishn kultur kongres, 1958.

Dimock, Wai Chee. "Literature for the Planet," *PMLA* 116, no. 1 (January 2001): 173–88.

Dobrushin, Yekhezkl. *Dovid Bergelson.* Moscow: Emes, 1947.

Dostoyevsky, Fyodor. *Notes from the Underground.* Trans. Michael R. Katz. New York: W. W. Norton, 1989.

Duncan, James, and David Ley, eds. *Place/Culture/Representation.* London: Routledge, 1993.

Edelmann, R. "Ahasuerus, The Wandering Jew." In *The Wandering Jew: Essays in the Interpretation of a Christian Legend,* 1–11. Ed. Galit Hasan-Rokem and Alan Dundes. Bloomington: Indiana University Press, 1986.

Eisen, Arnold. *Galut: Modern Jewish Reflections on Homelessness and Homecoming.* Bloomington: Indiana University Press, 1986.

Eisenstein, J. D., ed. *Ozar massaoth.* New York: J. D. Eisenstein, 1926.

Erik, Max. "Vegn Sholem-Aleykhem's ksovim fun-a-komivoyazhor." In *Visnshaft un revolutsiye,* 3–4:161–72. Kiev: 1934.

Faith, Nicholas. *The World the Railways Made.* London: Bodley Head, 1990.

Fanon, Frantz. "The Fact of Blackness." Trans. Charles Lam. In *The Post-Colonial Studies Reader,* 323–27. Ed. Bill Ashcroft, Gareth Griffiths, Helen Tiffin. New York: Routledge, 1997.

Ferber, Nat J. *One Happy Jew.* New York: Farrar and Rinehart, 1934.

Fine, David Martin. *The City, The Immigrant and American Fiction, 1880–1920.* Metuchen, N.J.: Scarecrow Press, 1977.

———. "In the Beginning: American-Jewish Fiction, 1880–1930." *Handbook of American-Jewish Literature,* 15–34. Ed. Lewis Fried. New York: Greenwood, 1998.

Foulke, Robert. *The Sea Voyage Narrative*. New York: Twayne, 1997.

Frieden, Ken. *Classic Yiddish Fiction: Abramovitsh, Sholem Aleichem, and Peretz*. Albany: State University of New York Press, 1995.

Fussell, Paul, ed. *The Norton Book of Travel*. New York: W. W. Norton, 1987.

Galchinsky, Michael. "Scattered Seeds: A Dialogue of Diasporas." In Biale, Galchinsky, and Heschel, *Insider/Outsider*, 185–212.

Garrett, Leah. "The Jewish Don Quixote." *Cervantes* 17, no. 2 (1997): 94–105.

———. "The Jewish Robinson Crusoe." *Comparative Literature* 54, no. 3 (2002): 215–28.

———. "The Self as Marrano in Jacob Glatstein's Autobiographical Novels." *Prooftexts* 18 (1998): 207–23.

Gifford, Paul. "Getting There or Not—The Fortunes of the Initiatic Journey and the Crisis of Culture." In *Literature and Quest*, 17–27. Ed. Christine Arkinstall. Atlanta: Rodopi, 1993.

Gilman, Sander L. *Inscribing the Other*. Lincoln: University of Nebraska Press, 1991.

———. "The Visibility of the Jew in the Diaspora: Body Imagery and Its Cultural Context." B. G. Rudolph Lectures in Judaic Studies, May 1992, Syracuse University, Syracuse, N.Y.

Girgus, Sam B. *The New Covenant: Jewish Writers and the American Idea*. Chapel Hill: University of North Carolina Press, 1984.

Gjerde, Jon, ed. *Major Problems in American Immigration and Ethnic History*. Boston: Houghton Mifflin, 1998.

Glatstein, Jacob. *Homecoming at Twilight*. Trans. Norbert Guterman. New York: T. Yoseloff, 1962.

———. *Homeward Bound*. Trans. Abraham Goldstein. New York: T. Yoseloff, 1969.

———. *Keshe Yash nasa*. Trans. Dan Miron. Tel Aviv: Hakibbutz Hameuchad, 1994.

———. *Selected Poems of Yankev Glatstein*. Trans. and Ed. Richard Fein. New York: Jewish Publication Society, 1987.

———. *Vebahagiya yash*. Trans. S. Shenhud. Tel Aviv: Dvir, 1957.

———. *Ven Yash iz geforn*. New York: In Zikh, 1938.

———. *Ven Yash iz gekumen*. New York: M. S. Sklarsky, 1940.

Gleckner, Robert F., and Gerald E. Enscoe, eds. *Romanticism: Points of View*. Detroit: Wayne State University Press, 1975.

Gluckel of Hameln. *The Memoirs of Gluckel of Hameln*. Trans. Martin Lowenthal. New York: Schocken, 1977.

Gluzman, Michael. "Modernism and Exile: A View from the Margins." In Biale, Galchinsky, and Heschel, *Insider/Outsider*, 231–53.

Gold, Michael. *Jews without Money*. New York: Carroll and Graf, 1996.

Goldberg, Y. "Der vegroman in der intimer stil; vegn Fishke der krumer." In *Di Yidish Literatur in nayntsetn hundert: Zamlung fun yidisher literatur forshung in kritik in ratn farband*, 559–84. Ed. Khone Shmeruk and Chava Turniansky. Jerusalem: Magnes, 1993.

Govrin, Nurit. *Alienation and Regeneration*. Trans. John Glucker. Tel Aviv: MOD Books, 1989.

Green, Roger. *The Train*. Oxford: Oxford University Press, 1982.

Grewal, Inderpal. *Home and Harem: Imperialism, Nationalism, and the Culture of Travel*. Durham, N.C.: Duke University Press, 1990.

Grewal, Inderpal, and Caren Kaplan, eds. *Scattered Hegemonies: Postmodernity and Transnational Feminist Practices*. Minneapolis: University of Minnesota Press, 1994.

Guttmann, Allen. *The Jewish Writer in America: Assimilation and the Crisis of Identity*. New York: Oxford University Press, 1971.

Hadda, Janet. *Passionate Women, Passive Men: Suicide in Yiddish Literature*. Albany: State University of New York Press, 1988.

———. *Yankev Glatshteyn*. Boston: Twayne, 1980.

Harper, Phillip Brian. *Framing the Margins: The Social Logic of Postmodern Culture*. New York: Oxford University Press, 1994.

Harshav, Benjamin. *Language in Time of Revolution*. Berkeley: University of California Press, 1993.

———. *The Meaning of Yiddish*. Los Angeles: University of California Press, 1990.

Harshav, Benjamin, and Barbara Harshav, eds. *American Yiddish Poetry: A Bilingual Anthology*. Berkeley: University of California Press, 1986.

Harter, Deborah A. *Bodies in Pieces: Fantastic Narrative and the Poetics of Fragment*. Stanford, Calif.: Stanford University Press, 1996.

Hartman, Geoffrey. "Romanticism and Antiself-consciousness." In Gleckner and Enscoe, *Romanticism*, 231–53.

Haywood, Richard Mowbray. *Beginnings of Railway Development in Russia in the Reign of Nicholas I, 1835–1842*. Durham, N.C.: Duke University Press, 1969.

Hobsbawm, Eric. *Industry and Empire: The Making of Modern English Society, 1750 to the Present Day*. New York: Pantheon, 1968.

hooks, bell. "Representing Whiteness in the Black Imagination." In *Cultural Studies*, 338–46. Ed. Lawrence Grossberg, Cary Nelson, and Paula Treichler. New York: Routledge, 1992.

———. *Yearning: Race, Gender, and Cultural Politics.* Boston: South End Press, 1990.

Howe, Irving, Ruth Wisse, and Khone Shmeruk, eds. *The Penguin Book of Modern Yiddish Verse.* New York: Penguin, 1987.

Hume, Michael, ed. *Literature and Travel.* Atlanta: Rodopi, 1993.

Hutchings, Stephen C. *Russian Modernism: The Transfiguration of the Everyday.* Cambridge: Cambridge University Press, 1997.

Hutchinson, Steven. *Cervantine Journeys.* Wisconsin: University of Wisconsin Press, 1992.

In Praise of the Baal-Shem Tov. Trans. and ed. Dan Ben-Amos and Jerome R. Mintz. New York: Schocken, 1984.

Iser, Wolfgang. *The Act of Reading: A Theory of Aesthetic Response.* Baltimore, Md.: John Hopkins University Press, 1981.

———. *The Fictive and the Imaginary: Charting Literary Anthropology.* Baltimore, Md.: John Hopkins University Press, 1993.

Itzkovitz, Daniel. "Secret Temples." In Boyarin and Boyarin, *Jews and Other Differences,* 176–202.

Ivanov, Vyacheslav. "The Precepts of Symbolism." In Peterson, *Russian Symbolists,* 143–56.

Ivask, George. "Russian Modernist Poets and the Mystic Sectarians." *Russian Modernism: Culture and the Avant-Garde, 1900–1930,* 85–107. Ed. George Gibian and H. W. Tjalsma. Ithaca, N.Y.: Cornell University Press, 1976.

Jacobson, Matthew Frye. "'The Quintessence of the Jew': Polemics of Nationalism and Peoplehood in Turn-of-the-Century Yiddish Fiction." In *Multilingual America: Transnationalism, Ethnicity, and the Languages of American Literature,* 103–22. Ed. Werner Sollors. New York: New York University Press, 1998.

Jahar, Frederick Cople. "The Quest for the Ultimate Shiksa." *American Quarterly* 35 (Winter 1983): 518–42.

Jewish Publication Society, trans. *Tanakh: A New Translation of the Holy Scriptures According to the Traditional Hebrew Text.* Philadelphia: Jewish Publication Society, 1985.

Kaplan, Caren. "The Politics of Location as Transnational Feminist Critical Practice." In Kaplan and Grewal, *Scattered Hegemonies,* 137–52.

———. *Questions of Travel: Postmodern Discourses of Displacement.* Durham, N.C.: Duke University Press, 1996.

Karczewska, Kathryn. *Prophecy and the Quest for the Holy Grail: Critiquing Knowledge in the Vulgate Cycle.* New York, Peter Lang, 1998.

Keats, John. "On the Sea." In *John Keats and Percy Bysshe Shelley: Complete Poetical Works,* 230. New York: Modern Library, 1932.

Kipling, Rudyard. *Kim.* New York: Penguin, 1992.

Korn, Rokhl. "Fun yener zayt lid." In *The Penguin Book of Modern Yiddish Verse,* 525. Ed. Irving Howe, Ruth R. Wisse, and Khone Shmeruk, trans. Seymour Levithan. New York: Penguin, 1987.

Kristeva, Julia. *Strangers to Ourselves.* Trans. Leon S. Roudiez. New York: Columbia University Press, 1991.

Kronfeld, Chana. *On the Margins of Modernism: Decentering Literary Dynamics.* Berkeley: University of California Press, 1996.

Krutikov, Mikhail. *Yiddish Fiction and the Crisis of Modernity, 1905–1914.* Stanford, Calif.: Stanford University Press, 2001.

Kushner, Tony. *Angels in America, Part 1: Millennium Approaches.* New York: Theatre Communications Group, 1993.

Leviant, Curt, ed. and trans., Introduction to *The Jewish Government and Other Stories,* ix–xvii. New York: Twayne, 1971.

Levin, Meyer. *The Old Bunch.* New York: Citadel, 1995.

Lewisohn, Ludwig. *The Island Within.* New York: Syracuse University Press, 1997.

Litvak, Olga. "The Literary Response to Conscription: Individuality and Authority in the Russian-Jewish Enlightenment." Ph.D. diss., Columbia University, 1999.

MacCannel, Dean. *The Tourist: A New Theory of the Leisure Class.* New York: Schocken, 1976.

Maccoby, Hyam. "The Wandering Jew as Sacred Executioner." In *The Wandering Jew: Essays in the Interpretation of a Christian Legend,* 236–61. Ed. Galit Hasan-Rokem and Alan Dundes. Bloomington: Indiana University Press, 1986.

Maguire, Robert. Introduction to *Russian Literature of the 1920s: An Anthology,* vii–xvii. Ed. Carl R. Proffer, Ellendea Proffer, Ronald Meyer, and Mary Ann Szporluk. Dana Point, Calif.: Ardis, 1987.

———. *Red Virgin Soil: Soviet Literature in the 1920s.* 2d ed. Ithaca, N.Y.: Cornell University Press, 1987.

Maguire, Robert A., and John Malmstad. "Petersburg." In Malmstad, *Andrey Bely,* 96–144.

Malmstad, John E., ed. *Andrey Bely: Spirit of Symbolism.* Ithaca, N.Y.: Cornell University Press, 1987.

Manger, Itsik. "Ikh hob zikh yorn gevalgert." Trans. Leonard Wolf. In Howe, Wisse, and Shmeruk, *Penguin Book of Modern Yiddish Verse,* 591.

Mantovan, Daniela. "Der Nister and His Symbolist Short Stories (1913–1929): Patterns of Imagination." Ph.D. diss. Columbia University, 1993.

Massey, Doreen. *Space, Place, and Gender*. Minneapolis: University of Minnesota Press, 1994.

Metzer, Jacob. "Research Report No. 48: Railroad Development and Market Integration: The Case of Tsarist Russia." Hebrew University, Department of Economics, Jerusalem, June 1973.

Mieder, Wolfgang. *Tradition and Innovation in Folk Literature*. Hanover, N.H.: Press of New England, 1987.

Miller, J. Hillis. *Topographies*. Stanford, Calif.: Stanford University Press, 1995.

Mills, Sara. *Discourses of Difference: An Analysis of Women's Travel Writing and Colonialism*. New York: Routledge, 1991.

Miron, Dan. *A Traveler Disguised: The Rise of Modern Yiddish Fiction in the Nineteenth Century*. 2d ed. Syracuse, N.Y.: Syracuse University Press, 1996.

———. Epilogue to *Keshe Yash nasa* by Jacob Glatstein. Tel Aviv: Hakibbutz Hameuchad, 1994.

———. *The Image of the Shtetl and Other Studies of Modern Jewish Literary Imagination*. Syracuse, N.Y.: Syracuse University Press, 2000.

———. "Mas'a be'eizor hadimdumim." Afterword to *Sippurei rakevet*, 227–300. Trans. Dan Miron. Tel Aviv: Dvir, 1989.

Miron, Dan, and Anita Norich. "The Politics of Benjamin III: Intellectual Significance and Its Formal Correlatives in Sh. Y. Abramovitsh's *Masoes Binyomin Hashlishi*." In *The Field of Yiddish: Studies in Language, Folklore, and Literature*, 1–115. Ed. Marvin Herzog, Barbara Kirshenblatt-Gimblett, Dan Miron, and Ruth Wisse. Philadelphia: Institute for the Study of Human Issues, 1980.

Moretti, Franco. *Atlas of the European Novel*. New York: Verso, 1998.

Nahman of Bratslav. *Nahman of Bratslav: The Tales*. Trans. and ed. Arnold Band. New York: Paulist Press, 1978.

———. *Seyfer sippurey mayses*. Jerusalem: Keren hadpasah shel hasidei Braslav, 1979.

Nerlich, Michael. *Ideology of Adventure: Studies in Modern Consciousness, 1100–1750*. Minnesota: University of Minnesota Press, 1987.

Neubauer, John. "Bakhtin versus Lukacs: Inscriptions of Homelessness in Theories of the Novel." *Poetics Today* 17, no. 4 (Winter 1996): 531–46.

Nietzsche, Friedrich. *Thus Spake Zarathustra*. Trans. Thomas Common. New York: Macmillan, 1917.

Novershtern, Abraham. "Aspektim mivniim baproze shel David Bergelson mereshitah ad 'midas ha-din,'" Ph.D. diss., Hebrew University, 1981.

———. "Di pogram-tematik in di verk fun L. Shapiro." *Di Goldene Keyt* 106 (1981): 121–50.

[Ornitz, Samuel.] *Haunch, Paunch and Jowl: An Anonymous Autobiography.* New York: Pocket Books, 1968.

Packard, Robert. *Refractions: Writers and Place.* New York: Carroll and Graff, 1990.

Paperno, Irina. Introduction to *Creating Life: The Aesthetic Utopia of Russian Modernism,* 1–11. Ed. Irina Paperno and Joan Delaney Grossman. Stanford, Calif.: Stanford University Press, 1994.

Pavel, Thomas. "Exile as Romance and Tragedy." *Poetics Today* 17, no. 3 (Fall 1996): 305–15.

Peretz, I. L. "Dray khupes: Tsvey royte—eyne a shvartse." In *Ale verk fun Y. L. Peretz,* 5:14–72. New York: CYCO Bikher, 1947.

———. "The Three Wedding Canopies." In *The Great Works of Jewish Fantasy and Occult,* 60–104. Trans. and ed. Joachim Neugroschel New York: Overlook, 1987.

Peri, Menachem. "Ha'analogiya umekoma bemivne haroman shel Mendele Mokher-Sfarim." *Hasifrut* 1, no. 1 (1968): 65–100.

Peterson, Ronald, ed. and trans. *The Russian Symbolists: An Anthology of Critical and Theoretical Writings.* Ann Arbor, Mich.: Ardis, 1986.

Pinsker, Sanford. *Jewish-American Fiction, 1917–1987.* New York: Twayne, 1992.

Popkin, Cathy. *The Pragmatics of Insignificance: Chekhov, Zoshchenko, Gogol.* Stanford, Calif.: Stanford University Press, 1993.

Porter, Dennis. *Haunted Journeys: Desire and Transgression in European Travel Writing.* Princeton, N.J.: Princeton University Press, 1991.

Prawer, Siegbert, ed. *The Romantic Period in Germany.* London: Weidenfeld and Nicolson, 1970.

Propp, Vladimir. *Theory and History of Folklore.* Trans. Ariadna Y. Martin and Richard P. Martin, ed. Anatoly Liberman. Minneapolis: University of Minnesota Press, 1984.

Pyman, Avril. *A History of Russian Symbolism.* Cambridge: Cambridge University Press, 1994.

Raban, Jonathan, ed. *The Oxford Book of the Sea.* Oxford: Oxford University Press, 1992.

Rabelais, François. *Gargantua and Pantagruel.* Trans. Burton Raffel. New York: Norton, 1991.

Rabinovitsh, Sholem. [Sholem Aleichem]. *Adventures of Mottel the Cantor's Son.* Trans. Tamara Kahana. New York: Collier, 1953.

——. *Di ayznban-geshikhtes.* In *Ale verk fun Sholem-Aleykhem.* Vol. 6. New York: Folksfond, 1923.

——. *Motl Peyse dem khazn's.* In *Ale verk fun Sholem-Aleykhem.* Vol. 18. New York: Folksfond Edition, 1918-23.

——. *The Railroad Stories.* Trans. Hillel Halkin. In *Tevye the Dairyman and the Railroad Stories,* 135-284. New York: Schocken, 1987.

Rich, Adrienne. *Blood, Bread, and Poetry: Selected Prose, 1979-1985.* New York: W. W. Norton, 1986.

Riffaterre, Michael. *Fictional Truth.* Baltimore, Md.: John Hopkins University Press, 1990.

Rose, Toby, and Kathryn Payant, eds. Introduction to *The Immigrant Experience in North American Literature: Carving out a Niche,* xiii-xxvii. Westport, Conn.: Greenwood, 1999.

Roskies, David G. *A Bridge of Longing: The Lost Art of Yiddish Storytelling.* Cambridge, Mass.: Harvard University Press, 1995.

——. *Against the Apocalypse: Responses to Catastrophe in Modern Jewish Culture.* Cambridge, Mass.: Harvard University Press, 1984.

——. "The Genres of Yiddish Popular Literature, 1790-1860." *Working Papers in Yiddish and East European Jewish Studies* 8 (February 1975).

——. "L. Shapiro." In *Leksikon fun der nayer yidisher literatur,* 533-36. Ed. Berl Cohen, Ezriel Naks, and Eliyahu Shulman. New York: Congress for Jewish Culture, 1981.

——, ed. *The Literature of Destruction: Jewish Responses to Catastrophe.* New York: Jewish Publication Society, 1988.

Said, Edward. "The Mind in Winter: Reflections on Life in Exile." *Harper's Magazine,* September 1984, pp. 49-55.

——. "Reflections on Exile." *Granta* 13 (1984): 159-72.

Schama, Simon. *Landscape and Memory.* New York: Alfred A. Knopf, 1995.

Schivelbusch, Wolfgang. *The Railway Journey: The Industrialization of Time and Space in the Nineteenth Century.* Berkeley: University of California Press, 1986.

Schneider, Isidor. *From the Kingdom of Necessity.* New York: Penguin, 1935.

Schwab, Gabriele. *The Mirror and the Killer-Queen.* Bloomington: Indiana University Press, 1996.

Schwarz, Jan. "When the Lamp of Art Is Made to Shine through Life's

Foolscap: A Study of the Yiddish Literary Autobiography." Ph.D. diss., Columbia University, 1997.

Seidel, Michael. *Exile and the Narrative Imagination*. New Haven, Conn.: Yale University Press, 1986.

Seidman, Naomi. *A Marriage Made in Heaven: The Sexual Politics of Hebrew and Yiddish*. Berkeley: University of California Press, 1997.

Shapiro, Lamed. "Di yidishe melukhe." In *Di yidishe melukhe un andere zakhn*, 7–63. New York: Naytsayt, 1919.

———. "The Jewish Government." In Leviant, *Jewish Government and Other Stories*, 1–42.

———. *Oyfn yam*. In *Di yidishe melukhe un andere zakhn*, 193–229. New York: Naytsayt, 1919.

Shapiro, Susan. "Écriture judaïque: Where are the Jews in Western Discourse?" In Bammer, *Displacements*, 182–203.

Shelley, Percy. "A Vision of the Sea." In *John Keats and Percy Bysshe Shelley: Complete Poetical Works*, 634. New York: Modern Library, 1932.

Shivhei haBesht. Ed. Avraham Rubinstein. Jerusalem: Rubin Mass, 1991.

Shlovsky, Victor. "Art as Technique." In *Russian Formalist Criticism: Four Essays*, 3–57. Trans. Lee T. Lemon and Marion J. Reis. Lincoln: University of Nebraska Press, 1965.

Shmeruk, Khone. "Der Nister's 'Under a Fence': Tribulations of a Soviet Yiddish Symbolist." In *The Field of Yiddish: Studies in Language, Folklore, and Literature*, 263–87. Ed. Uriel Weinreich. London: Mouton, 1965.

———, ed. *A shpigl oyf a shteyn*. Tel Aviv: Farlog Peretz, 1964.

Singer, Isaac Bashevis. "Oyf a fur." *Forverts*, November 24, 1969, p. 2, and November 25, 1969, pp. 2 and 5.

———. "Oyf an alter shif." *Zamlbikher* 1 (May 1936): 214–31.

Singleton, Amy C. *No Place Like Home: The Literary Artist and Russia's Search for Cultural Identity*. Albany: State University of New York Press, 1997.

Sprinker, Michael, ed. *Edward Said: A Critical Reader*. Cambridge, Mass.: Blackwell, 1992.

Stevenson, Robert Louis. *Kidnapped*. New York: Penguin, 1995.

Suleiman, Susan. "Introduction: On Signposts, Travelers, Outsiders, and Backward Glances." *Poetics Today* 17, no. 3 (Fall 1996): 283–87.

Suleri, Susan. *Meatless Days*. Chicago: University of Chicago Press, 1989.

Tabatshnik, A. "A Conversation with Jacob Glatstein." Trans. Joseph H. Landis. *Yiddish* 1 (1973): 40–53.

Taubenfeld, Aviva. "Linguistic Borders and the Immigrant Author in Abraham Cahan's 'Yekl and Yankel der Yankee.'" In *Multilingual America: Transnationalism, Ethnicity, and the Languages of American Literature*, 144–65. Ed. Werner Sollors. New York: New York University Press, 1998.

Thompson, Ewa M. "Symbolism." In *Handbook of Russian Literature*, 460–64. Ed. Victor Terras. New Haven, Conn.: Yale University Press, 1985.

Tobenkin, Elia. *Witte Arrives*. New York: Gregg, 1968.

Todorov, Tzvetan. *Introduction to Poetics*. Trans. Richard Howard. Minneapolis: University of Minnesota Press, 1992.

Tolstoy, Leo. *Anna Karenin*. Trans. Rosemary Edmonds. London: Penguin, 1975.

Trainer, James. "The Märchen." In Prawer, *Romantic Period in Germany*. 97–120.

Tshubinski, B. "Dovid Bergelson." In *Leksikon fun der nayer yidisher literatur*, 1:380–83. Ed. Shmuel Niger and Jacob Shatski. New York: Alveltlekher Yidisher Kultur Kongres, 1956.

Tsukerman, V. "L. Shapiro." *Dos naye land* 1, no. 6 (October 20, 1911): 17–19.

Tucker, Irene. *A Probable State: The Novel, The Contract, and the Jews*. Chicago: University of Chicago Press, 2000.

Van Den Abbeele, Georges. *Travel as Metaphor: From Montaigne to Rousseau*. Minneapolis: University of Minnesota Press, 1992.

Vitlin, Yoysef. *Robinzon di geshikhte fun Alter Leb*. Vilnius, Lithuania: Mats, 1880.

Voltaire. *Candide, or Optimism*. Trans. John Butt. New York: Penguin, 1986.

Wellek, Rene. "The Concept of Romanticism in Literary History." In Gleckner and Enscoe, *Romanticism*, 181–207.

Westwood, J. N. *A History of Russian Railways*. London: Allen and Unwin, 1964.

Wicks, Ulrich. "Metafiction in *Don Quixote:* What Is the Author up to?" In *Approaches to Teaching Cervantes' Don Quixote*, 69–76. Ed. Richard Bjornson. New York: Modern Language Association, 1984.

Wiskind-Elper, Ora. *Tradition and Fantasy in the Tales of Reb Nahman of Bratslav*. Albany: State University of New York Press, 1998.

Wisse, Ruth. "Language as Fate: Reflections on Jewish Literature in America." In *Literary Strategies: Jewish Texts and Contexts*, ed. Ezra Mendelsohn, 12:129–47. New York: Oxford University Press, 1996.

———. *The Schlemiel as Modern Hero*. Chicago: University of Chicago Press, 1971.

———, ed. *A Shtetl and Other Yiddish Novellas*. New York: Behrman House, 1973.

Wolf, Leonard. Introduction to Der Nister, *The Family Mashber*, 7–26. Trans. Leonard Wolf New York: Summit Books, 1987.

Wolf, Robert Harvey. "A Yiddish Manichaean: The Dualistic Fiction of Lamed Shapiro." Ph.D. diss., Columbia University, 1994.

Wood, Philip R. "The Transformation of the Quest from Modernity to Postmodernism and the Third Industrial Revolution." In *Literature and the Quest*, 145–55. Ed. Christine Arkinstall. Atlanta: Rodopi, 1993.

Wordsworth, William. "Composed by the Sea-Side, near Calais, August, 1802." *The Poems*, 1:576. Ed. John O. Hayden. New York: Penguin, 1990.

Yezierska, Anzia. *Bread Givers*. New York: Persea, 1999.

Zangwill, Israel. *The Melting Pot*. New York: Macmillan, 1909.

Zunser, Elyokum. "Der Ayznban." In *Elyokum Zunsers verk*, 1:69–72. Ed. Mordkhe Schaecter. New York: YIVO, 1964.

———. "Lid fun ayznban." In *Elyokum Zunsers Verk*, 1:255–59. Ed. Mordkhe Schaecter. New York: YIVO, 1964.

Index

"A Vision of the Sea" (Shelley), 132
Abramovitsh, Sholem Yankev (Mendele the Bookseller), 130, 153, 161;
Fishke der krumer (Fishke the lame), 28–30, 47; *Kitser masoes Binyomin hashlishi* (The brief travels of Benjamin the Third), 10, 17, 29, 30, 32, 33, 34, 38–56, 57, 58, 61, 62, 65–66, 83, 84, 87, 88, 106, 169, 183n. 33; road stories of, 28–29; "Shem un Yefes in a vogn" (Shem and Jefes on a train), 19, 91, 93, 95, 96–105, 121, 122, 192n. 15; writings of, 23
Adamic, Louis, 147–48, 157, 200nn. 43, 44
Adventure tales, 18, 29, 39
African Americans: black woman traveler, 16; differences between Jews and, 159, 201n. 50
Ahasuerus, 15
Aksenfeld, Yisroel, *Dos shterntikhl* (The headband), 21–22, 87
"Alien" and "native," differences between, 11–12
American Jews, 156–57, 158, 159
Americanization, process of, 124, 128–30
Amichai, Yehuda, 167
Andersen, Hans Christian, 68
Anna Karenina (Tolstoy), 94
Anti-Semitism, 45, 54, 109, 110–11, 112, 127, 149, 151, 156–59, 161, 162, 164, 170
Arthurian romances, 36, 37
Atlas of the European Novel (Moretti), 8
Auden, W. H., 126, 127
Austen, Jane, 8, 115

Ba'al Shem Tov, Israel (the Besht). *See* Besht, the
Badkhn, the. *See* Zunser, Elyokum
Bakhtin, Mikhail, 57–58, 190n. 112
Balzac, Honoré de, 84
Barter system, 107
Bely, Andrei, 73, 75
Benegeli, Cide Hamete, 40, 49
Benjamin of Tudela, 17
Bergelson, David, 24, 67, 167–69, 171; *Arum vokzal* (At the depot), 25, 91, 95, 113–21, 122
Besht, the (Israel Ba'al Shem Tov), 22
Blackstone, Bernard, 142
Bohemianism, 160
Border state, the quest and interpretation of the, 72
Bourgeois travel, 97, 99, 107
Bovo d'Antona (Levita), 20–21
Boyarin, Daniel, 12, 15
Boyarin, Jonathan, 12, 15
British railroad, 3, 90–91, 93–94
Brodsky, Joseph, 3
Bunyan, John, 36